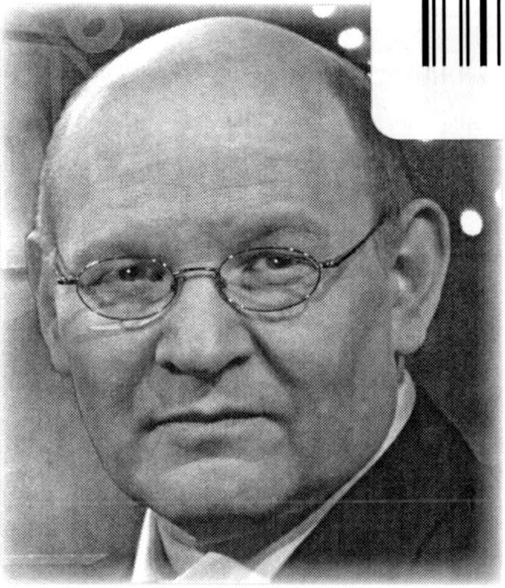

Coren is host of the nightly Michael Coren Show on CTS television. The station is on basic cable in Ontario and Alberta and available on satellite and digital throughout Canada. He also co-hosts *Two Bald Guys With Strong Opinions* every weekday with former Liberal Party President Stephen LeDrew on CFRB 1010 radio. Michael is a weekly columnist, published every Saturday, with the Toronto, Ottawa, Calgary, Edmonton and Winnipeg *Sun* and *The London Free Press*. He is also a columnist for *Women's Post* and *The Interim* and a regular contributor to *The National Post* and *Catholic Insight*. He is the best-selling author of twelve books, including biographies of G.K. Chesterton, H.G. Wells, Arthur Conan Doyle, J.R.R. Tolkien and C.S. Lewis. He has contributed to the *Dictionary of National Biography* and several other anthologies. He is published in many countries and in more than a dozen languages. He has received several honorary doctorates and awards for his writing. In 2005 he won The Ed Murrow Award for Radio Broadcasting, in 2006 The RTNDA Radio Broadcasting Award and in 2007 the Communicator Award in Hollywood for his television show. A highly popular and entertaining public speaker, Coren can be contacted for appearances at www.michaelcoren.com

"Michael Coren has a rare gift: he's a brilliant intellectual, but with a double dose of humour and common sense. His columns often make you mad and make you smile at the same time and they are a must-read road map for anyone looking to make sense of current events. He's not afraid to be politically incorrect, and he'll often surprise you with his fresh take on age-old debates."
~ Ezra Levant

"I have always enjoyed enthusiastic and intelligent exchanges and explorations with Michael Coren both on air and in print."
~ NDP Leader Jack Layton

"This book of columns and essays is reminiscent of Michael's daily TV talk show and it is a compelling, controversial read. While I often don't agree with his opinions, I respect Michael's ability to expose all sides of the issues facing us today and his ability to speak about those issues with wit and elequence."
~ Sid Ryan

"Fearless. Unpredictable. Funny. Never boring. There's nobody and nothing like Michael Coren in journalism anywhere!"
~ David Frum

"Coren's use of language is sophisticated and lucid ... skilful and sensitively written. It will enrage his detractors and appeal to Coren's many fans."
~ *Ottawa Citizen*

"Coren is, quite simply, one of the most delightful prose stylists in Canadian journalism today."
~ *Calgary Herald*

"Coren writes with enormous charm."
~ Humphrey Carpenter, *Sunday Times*

Freedom Press
12 - 111 Fourth Ave. Suite 185
St. Catharines, ON L2S 3P5

ISBN 978-0-9812767-2-4

Cover Design by Michael Moon
Book Design by David Bolton

FREEDOM PRESS
CANADA INC.

As I See It

Michael Coren

FREEDOM PRESS
CANADA INC.

To Joe Nadler.

Contents

INTRODUCTION

THIS COLLECTION IS ASSEMBLED FROM VARIOUS COLUMNS, ARTICLES AND REVIEWS FROM THE *NATIONAL POST*, THE *SUN* CHAIN OF NEWSPAPERS, THE *GLOBE & MAIL* AND ELSEWHERE, MAINLY BETWEEN 2005 AND 2009. WHILE THEY ARE LOOSELY ASSEMBLED UNDER CHAPTER AND THEME HEADINGS, I HAVE MADE NO ATTEMPT TO EDIT THEM WITH THE BENEFIT OF HINDSIGHT OR TO AVOID CERTAIN REPETITIONS OF PHRASE OR STYLE. THIS WOULD BE UNFAIR BECAUSE A COLUMNIST'S WORK SHOULD STAND ON ITS OWN MERITS OR LACK OF THEM AND TO ADAPT OPINIONS OR STYLE AT A LATER DATE SEEMS RATHER EXPLOITATIVE AND MISLEADING. THESE ARE MY OPINIONS OF NUMEROUS SUBJECTS, ISSUES, DEBATES AND PEOPLE. THE WORLD, AS IT WERE, AS I SEE IT.

I have written extensively in recent years on the Middle East, on faith and religion, on life and sexuality, on literature and on politics so these form the chapters. I am speaking to different audiences in different newspapers but my intention is always to deliver my point in a balanced, intelligent and compelling manner. Whether I fail or succeed, of course, is up to the reader.

Over the past five years when a column or article appears I have received an average of 100 e-mails and letters – in addition to those I am sent due to my television and radio show. I reply to many but ignore some. It shows, of course, the influence of contemporary journalism and I hope that this book can be a pleasant reminder to the tens of thousands of people who have been so directly supportive and a shock to those who have tried to silence or abuse me. I'm almost as grateful to the latter as I am to the former.

I'm most thankful to the many people who have helped me so much in recent years, and I am terribly sorry to those I fail to mention by name. Forgive me. In particular I owe much to Dave Wilson, Dorie Cowling, Mike Zwiep, John Turley-Ewart, Marnie Soupcoff, Jonathan Kay, Lorrie Goldstein, Rob Granatstein, Tristan Emmanuel, David Frum, Steve Kowch, Paul Tuns and most of all to my wife Bernadette and my children Daniel, Lucy, Oliver and Elizabeth. All of these columns, however, are my own responsibility and do not necessarily reflect the views and opinions of those I have thanked.

Toronto, March 2009

MC

Faith & Religion

Jesus

In the final analysis it comes down to faith. Christianity that is. But as we prepare to celebrate the birthday of Christ Jesus we might just remember that intellectual giants such as, for example, Thomas Aquinas and John Henry Newman, make a compelling argument for the intellectual vacuity of lack of belief. Or that it's difficult to read, say, C.S. Lewis or Dostoyevsky, and not to be challenged into something a little deeper than a smug secular piety.

In other words, in addition to belief there is intellect. Problem is, we live in an increasingly numb and dumb culture where the dictatorship of feelings has replaced the delicacy of analysis. A grimy coalition of sound-bite arguments and pop philosophy is sweeping the field.

Thus the extraordinary success of a book such as *The Da Vinci Code*. This novel has been bought hook, line and movie rights by credulous readers who are no longer capable of distinguishing fact from fiction. It is no more based in truth than is a comic book, but legions of people assume it says something profound and original about "the real Jesus."

The list goes on. Television documentaries boasting new evidence that disproves Christianity, best selling books claiming to refute Christ and disguising ancient myths as modern theories, fatuous feature films, downright lies and hysteria in the mass media.

So we should establish a few basic facts. Most significant, perhaps, is that almost every discovery in Biblical archeology in recent years appears to prove The Bible right, even to the point of surprising serious and orthodox Christian and Jewish scholars. It's been oddly pathetic observing liberal panic as another dig in The Middle East puts flesh to the bones of Scripture.

As for Jesus Himself, there are some absolute truths here. Jewish records refer to Jesus of Nazareth, and did so even before Christ's own followers had written about Him. Obviously these Jewish sages did not believe that Jesus was the Messiah, but they refer to him quite clearly as the son of Mary, the alleged father being a man we know little about.

Then we have Josephus, a Jewish general who betrayed his people and became a friend of the Romans and, indeed, a Roman himself. His writings are vital for any understanding of the Jews in the first century, but his writings must be placed in context.

Josephus mentions Jesus, the Jesus, in his writings. It is almost certain that later writers, Christian enthusiasts, revised his words to make them seem more pro-Christian. Hence in some obviously edited versions of his work Josephus, a Jewish man, suddenly sounds like a Christian. He was not and these expansions of his references to Jesus are to be dismissed.

The point, however, is that it is the revisions and not the original statements that should be expunged from the debate. Josephus knew of Jesus because no observer of the time could not know of Him. Josephus refers to His ministry and followers. Some people have, as it were, tried to throw out the baby with the bath water. Resulting in their entire argument becoming rather wet.

Then we have the Roman historian Tacitus. He discusses the great fire in Rome, how Nero was thought responsible and how the emperor blamed the Christians, named after Christus, who was crucified by "one of our governors, Pontius Pilate."

The Roman biographer Seutonius also refers to Jesus and a riot across the Tiber by supporters and foes of Christianity. Pliny the younger, Governor of Asia Minor, also speaks of Christ and Christians. Then there is the Gospel evidence for Jesus. Written by supporters of course. But the more we learn about the Gospels the earlier we can place them and the more authentic they are shown to be.

New research and the latest discoveries tell us so very much. The remarkable *Ryland Papyrus* on the Nile includes parts of John's Gospel. Serious scholars now agree that the Gospels were completed well before 100 AD. That is, while some who were present during Christ's life still lived. More than this, while multitudes were alive whose parents told them stories of personal witness and experience.

In fact no Biblical expert worth the name doubts that Jesus lived, that He claimed to be The Messiah and that many who knew Him believed that claim. The idea that He was just a great moral teacher or that we can believe some but not all what He taught is, frankly, absurd. He claimed to be the Son of God. If He wasn't, He was lying or insane. Liars are not to be believed and madmen are not to be followed even in part.

But should we believe? Consider the first generation martyrs. People die for the wrong reasons, but they assume them to be the right reasons. If their faith in any idea or any person can be broken, they are no longer willing to make the ultimate sacrifice. Yet men and woman who knew Jesus, lived with Him, saw Him die and saw Him rise again. They then went to their death with a smile.

Important this. The followers of Christ were in chaos when they saw Him crucified. It was the resurrection, an event He had promised, which thrust them into belief and, frequently, a martyr's death. There is no explanation for the documented martyrdom of those who knew Jesus other than that they knew, without doubt, that He was the Messiah and that He had been raised from the dead.

They were not few in number and they were not slow of wit. Intelligent, street-wise people. Dockworkers, fisherman, former terrorists and prostitutes, collaborating bureaucrats and brilliant teachers. All and every. They knew.

It is why I shall bow my head and bend my knee this Christmas as I sing, speak and pray my love for Jesus and thank God for the birth of God's son. It is my salvation. It is everybody's salvation. If, of course, we are willing to think about it. Merry Christmas.

MC

My Faith

I SUPPOSE IT'S THE GREATEST JOKE OF ALL. DELICIOUSLY IRONIC AS WELL. MY CHRISTIAN FAITH HAS BEEN PROFOUNDLY ENCOURAGED BY THOSE MOST EAGER TO SMOTHER IT. PUT SIMPLY, I WAS HELPED ALONG THE ROAD FROM INDIFFERENCE TO BELIEF BY THE BANALITY OF ATHEISM. SINCE REACHING THE AGE OF REASON I'VE HAD THE USUAL OLD REGULARS THROWN AT ME. WHY DO BAD THINGS HAPPEN TO GOOD PEOPLE, WHY DOESN'T HE MAKE HIMSELF MORE OBVIOUS, WHY IS EVIL COMMITTED IN THE NAME OF RELIGION? THROW IN THE INQUISITION, THE CRUSADES AND SOME LIES ABOUT PAPAL CULPABILITY DURING THE HOLOCAUST AND YOU HAVE THE STANDARD GOD-HATING MANIFESTO.

The more I dealt with all this the more I realized that the very belief being attacked was absolutely and abundantly true. More than this, the reason it was under attack in the first place was precisely because it was true.

The tiniest seeds of my Christianity were planted, I think, much earlier and by an Oxford professor who happened to be one of the finest children's writers of all time. I was six-years-old when C.S. Lewis's *The Lion, The Witch and the Wardrobe* was read to be me by Miss Power – I assume I was also in love with her and yes, my wife does know – at Redbridge School in Essex, England. Part of Lewis's gift is that he strokes rather than grabs. As a child from a working-class, secular, part Jewish family I had no idea then that Lewis was writing and I was hearing about Christ.

Leave the beauty and the story to stew for a few years, expose the child to the natural law certainties given by God that permeate the human condition and then send him out into a series of great universities where atheism is as predicable as self-indulgent moans about tuition fees. To quote the philosopher Pat Benatar, 'hit me with your best shot.' So they did.

If God were good He would make Himself obvious.

Not really. God makes himself just sufficiently evident to allow us freedom. If He were easy to find, we'd all believe and thus have no real choice. If He was almost impossible to find it would be cruel and unfair. He chooses the middle path. He's there if we seek to look but not so if we don't care. He's the great lover, not the satanic rapist. He desperately wants us to love Him and return to Him but we have to make that decision ourselves.

Yes, but even people who believe in Him often suffer. And look at all the pain in the world.

Bad things happen to good people because, well, bad things happen to good people. The teachings of Christ do not guarantee a good life but a perfect eternity. These seventy or eighty years on Earth are merely time spent in the land of shadows and, anyway, human suffering is more an indictment of humans than of God. Also, if life has no ultimate meaning and people are often absolute swine, why does any of this matter in the first place?

But Christians are sometimes hypocrites and awful things have been done in the name of Christianity.

Yes, yes, yes! Christians can occasionally not live up to the teachings of Christ. Whoopee. People failing as Christians is not the same as Christianity being untrue, any more than people voting for a poor government is the same as democracy being a failure. As for crimes in the name of Christ – of course. Crimes in the name of atheism, freedom, love, Canada, everything. It's human nature. Which is precisely why the supernatural is so important. In fact Christ Himself tells us that His name will be exploited.

You're weak, God is a crutch invented by scared and threatened people and the more we know the less we believe.

Could be. Sure, God could be an invention. Then again, absence of God could be an invention. By scared and threatened people who are too weak to follow His laws and are terrified of judgement. Be careful with the notion that knowledge means wisdom. 1930's Germany was one of the most educated and sophisticated cultures in human history. There are twits who do not believe, geniuses who do, and vice versa. It signifies nothing.

9

It was popular among rationalist thinkers in the late nineteenth-century to assume that advances in textual analysis, archaeological discovery and scientific breakthrough would disprove the Bible. Not quite. Virtually every time we find out something new in these fields it supports rather than challenges Scripture.

What became apparent to me was that the opposition to faith was as unappealing and bland as faith was appealing and thrilling. I read, prayed and thought myself into faith more than twenty years ago. It was gradual but inevitable. Miracles occurred but they need not have. I do not need a miracle to remind me that water quenches my thirst. Christ was there in my life, with me and in me and around me. Atheists showed me the way. God bless the little devils.

Then, just recently, the tarnished old arguments from the flimsy and trendy were re-published in expensive paperback editions by the likes of Christopher Hitchens and Richard Dawkins and we were all supposed to run away and hide. So I read them. Then began to laugh. It's the emperor and his new clothes. Naked, quite naked.

Nothing new here. Nothing clever or challenging either. Busting with errors, hysterical, clumsy, nasty and obviously incredibly frightened. Suddenly I realise what's going on. It's that God again, helping to strengthen my faith. "The best they can do", He's saying, "is blast you with the same old nonsense they threw at you when you first thought of coming my way."

Clever old God. Must remember to thank Him next time on my knees and receiving the flesh and blood of his Son and my saviour. Thanks for the non-believers, the God-haters, the atheists and all of their kind. Yes, the greatest joke of all.

MC

11

Christmas

TONIGHT I WILL FALL TO MY KNEES AT CHURCH AND THANK GOD FOR THE BIRTH OF HIS SON. WHY? THE NUMEROUS AND COMPELLING ARGUMENTS FOR THE TRUTH OF CHRISTIANITY, THE EVIDENCE OF THE EARLY CHURCH, THE EYE-WITNESS ACCOUNTS FROM NEUTRAL OR EVEN HOSTILE SOURCES, THE INDISPUTABLE LOGIC OFFERED BY AN AQUINAS OR A NEWMAN, THE EVEN-INCREASING TANGIBLE PROOF FROM ARCHAEOLOGICAL DIGS AND THE SIMPLE EVAPORATION OF LIBERAL AND SECULAR OBJECTIONS THAT WERE ONCE TAKEN SERIOUSLY.

But there is something else, something the educated and worldly are not supposed to embrace or even mention. Prayer and miracles. Oh well, the educated and worldly are allowed to be absurd and ridiculous at Christmas. Just as the Christmas when I prayed that my sister would come back into my life.

Stephanie is six years older than me and lives in Britain. We both loved our parents but a series of arguments and feuds drove a knife into the family and Stephanie distanced herself off from us. No blame, just a stew of reasons that seem wildly inconsequential with the clarity of hindsight.

I had tried to make contact with her but didn't even know her married name and in which town she lived. As for prayer, I was frightened that the answer might not be the one I desired. As Christmas approached, however, I did humble myself and ask God for my sister to become part of my life once again.

A week later the telephone rang. My mother was calling from England and she seemed excited, even frightened. "Mike" she said. "You're not going to believe this. I've got a letter here from Stephanie." A long pause. "She says she wants to make up, to meet." Another pause, and now tears. "I'm frightened of starting all the pain again."

My sister had not spoken to my parents in fifteen years. Suddenly I prayed for a resolution. My mother received a letter from my sister three days later, meaning that Stephanie almost certainly wrote it the same day that I asked for help.

There was a phone number on the letter. It was Christmas Eve but I called. Again, a time to be absurd and ridiculous. A man answers. "Is Steph there?" I asked. He wanted to know who it was. I told him. I then heard him tell Stephanie and heard her saying my name over and over again, as though if she stopped I would no longer be there. She was crying, almost hysterically.

She came to the phone and in between gulps for air she asked me why I hadn't made contact earlier. I told her I didn't know how to find her. Why, I responded, didn't she contact me? Because, she explained, she kept hearing that we all hated her. When I asked her who said this she couldn't remember.

I then asked why she had decided to break the silence. "Because I heard that dad was very ill and I just couldn't have lived with myself if I hadn't spoken to him before he died." At this point I choked a little. "But Steph, he's fine. He's not ill at all."

We chatted, we laughed, we cried. Then I told her that I must explain something that was very important, something that had changed my life forever. I told her that on a specific date some years ago I became a Christian. She didn't answer at first. She seemed shocked, perhaps angry. Then she asked me to repeat the date. "Mike", she said, her voice shaking. "Oh Mike, on that date in that year so did I. So did I!"

Christmas Eve more than a decade ago. Just a story that will be explained away by all those brilliant men and women who know that Christianity is for fools, that science and progress make us happy and content and religion is mere fantasy. But tonight I will, as I say, fall to my knees and thank God for the birth of His Son. So will my sister. So will myriad believers throughout the world. We will glory in being absurd and ridiculous. Thank God for that. Thank God.

MC

13

Holy Sepulcher

In Israel as in all countries that contain archeological sites of deep spiritual and religious significance there tend to be three levels of authenticity and holiness. First, those that are almost certainly not genuine but are soaked in prayer through centuries of devotion. Second, those that may or may not be the real thing but inspire believers. Third, those that are certainly or almost certainly the original places of world-changing events. The Church of the Holy Sepulchre in Jerusalem is regarded by virtually every serious archeologist and historian as the spot where Jesus Christ was crucified and buried and where, according to Christians, the resurrection took place.

So it's particularly tragic, and deeply ironic, that monks from various Orthodox factions have made coming to blows over who owns the place something of a, forgive me, dirty habit. More than this, they do the actual physical fighting just yards away from where the Prince of Peace forgave the world and in front of Israeli Jewish cops who have to get in the middle of the robed rowdies and try to make them behave like Christians.

The most recent incident was just two weeks ago, when the police arrested two clergymen who were punching and kicking each other as part of a brawl between the Armenian and Greek Orthodox contingents in the church. The Armenians had been taking part in an annual procession that commemorates the finding of the true cross seventeen centuries ago. The Greeks, however, insisted on their right to station one of their monks inside the Edicule, the small enclosure built over the likely location of the tomb of Jesus. The Armenians allegedly took umbrage at this and instead of turning the other cheek kicked, literally, a Greek cleric in the middle of one of his.

"We were keeping resistance so that the procession could not pass through and establish a right that they don't have," explained a Greek Orthodox monk, his left eye bleeding after his glasses had been smashed in a fight with an Armenian. "He attacked me from behind", he continued, implying that there was something particularly unholy about a sucker punch. The Armenian stealth monk was unavailable for comment.

In 2004 during another Orthodox festival a door to the Roman Catholic chapel was left open, almost certainly by mistake. This was regarded as being disrespectful and a fight ensued. Earlier this year on Palm Sunday another brawl began when a Greek monk was thrown out of the church by clergy from a rival group and when the Israeli police arrived they too were attacked, in a rare case of Christian unity, by everybody present.

It's all extraordinarily bizarre and grotesque but not quite beyond comprehension. Ancient, dark and layered in shrines and compartments, this is nothing like a conventional church and more a building constructed piecemeal over what was originally an outdoor execution site and a tomb built into a cave. Western pilgrims tend to be shocked if not dejected by the overwhelming gaudiness, the sheer confusion of the place and often clumsy juxtaposition of the profoundly holy and jarringly superstitious and small-minded.

But this is still the centre of Christianity, surviving in the middle of a world dominated by Islam for more than a thousand years. That it exists at all is a miracle; that it is a magnet for dispute is the sadly inevitable within that supernatural. As ugly as certain aspects of the church's culture can be, this remains an epicenter of the magnificent. Attend a dawn Mass on the very spot where Christ was placed after His death, with the first light of Jerusalem's sun sliding through the massive doors of the groaning building and the chants of the devout and gentle all around, and grace still breaks through the clouds of fleshy brokenness that characterize contemporary Jerusalem.

Six separate and disputing denominations control the church, however, and their internecine disputes can be absurd to the point of surreal hilarity. A ladder that was put over an entrance in the 19th century has yet to be moved because the sects cannot agree who has the authority to touch it. Some of the sects are aggressively ethnic in their foundation and are still fighting battles that have more to do with atavistic geopolitical claims and grievances than with the teachings of Christ. As for the Protestants – not one of the six who control the church's *Status Quo* – many of them prefer to think of what is known as The Garden Tomb in another part of the city as the authentic place of the crucifixion. It isn't, but it looks like it should be. And what is significant of course is that Jesus is not in either of these spots any longer.

So it's fallible, challenging, sometimes nauseating and, as with this latest incident, deeply embarrassing and shameful. People claiming to be Christian acting in a non-Christian manner in the name of Christ. Nothing new there. Christ Himself said it would happen and gave no guarantees that it wouldn't occur in the least appropriate of places. It proves nothing. I prefer to recall one of my many visits to this conduit to the holy, during the height of the bloody and costly Hezbollah war, when I sat with a Franciscan priest in the Church of the Holy Sepulchre and asked him to hear my confession. The two of us communicated in shattered English, French and Hebrew. His smile, God's forgiveness and the shadows of Jesus, triumphed over even a left hook from an angry Greek monk. There is beauty beyond compare here, if we are able and prepared to look between and beyond the human chaos.

MC

17

The Tomb

IT IS, I SUPPOSE, A GREAT CANADIAN MOMENT. PRODUCER JAMES CAMERON AND DIRECTOR SIMCHA JACOBOVICI ANNOUNCING TO THE WORLD THAT THEY HAVE FOUND THE TOMB OF JESUS, HIS WIFE, HIS CHILD AND ASSORTED FRIENDS AND RELATIVES. MOST OF THE JESUS FAMILY IN FACT. ALL HIDDEN AWAY IN A TOMB IN JERUSALEM.

Or not hidden away. Because the outlandish claim made by the two filmmakers in a new documentary and book is based on ten ossuaries, or small stone boxes for skeletal remains, that were discovered in a 2000-year-old tomb in 1980 and have since been stored by the Israel Antiquities Association. As such they have been scrutinized by some of the finest experts in the world.

The pair claim that because the names Yeshua bar Yosef (Jesus, son of Joseph), Maria (Mary) Mariamene e Mara (possibly Mary Magdalene), Judah son of Jesus and others are inscribed on six of the ossuaries the tomb in which they were sealed must have been the final resting place of Christ. More than this, because the DNA of Jesus and Mary in question reveals that they were not related, they have to have been married. So the child in the tomb is, yes, their son.

The chances of this all being a coincidence, the men say, are so remote as to be almost impossible. As for 2000-year-old DNA being unreliable and the preposterous notion that two people not linked by blood are necessarily married, we have yet to hear a convincing answer.

It is, as they say, difficult to know where to begin. To put this nonsense in the context of serious archeology and scholarship, this is akin to the current conspiracies announcing that 9/11 was an inside job perpetrated by the CIA and the Mossad. Or to paraphrase the great British writer G.K. Chesterton, when people stop believing in the truth they don't believe in something else, they believe in anything else.

Especially, of course, when it means a lucrative film and book contract and endless publicity. And James Cameron, the producer of *The Terminator*, *Aliens*, *Rambo* and *Titanic*, knows all about publicity. He doesn't, however, know very much about archeology and, as he himself said, "I'm not a theologist." Theologist! Who is James, who is?

The names Jesus and Mary were the most common amongst the Jews of first-century Palestine. There are, for example, at least two other well-known tombs of the period that contain ossuaries bearing the names Jesus, son of Joseph. There is even serious doubt as to whether the name Jesus is on these new caskets. Stephen Pfann from the University of the Holy Land in Jerusalem thinks the word is more likely Hanun, particularly as Semitic text of the era is extremely difficult to translate accurately.

Nor is he a lone intellectual voice refusing to take these "revelations" seriously. In fact there are few if any serious academics who give any credence at all to the claims. Professor Amos Kloner from Israel's Bar-Ilan University was the archeologist who first discovered the tomb. He argues that the ossuaries are irrelevant to Christian history.

Biblical anthropologist Joe Zias says the claims are "dishonest" and have "nothing whatsoever to do with Jesus. He was known as Jesus of Nazareth, not Jesus of Jerusalem, and if the family was wealthy enough to afford a tomb, which they probably weren't, it would have been in Nazareth, not here in Jerusalem."

Then we have to consider simple logic and apply it to known history. The Jewish and Roman authorities were obsessed with finding the body of Jesus. The early church was enormously threatening to them and if they could prove Christianity to be a lie – and if Christ was not resurrected and did not ascend into heaven the faith is certainly false – the Church would fold into just another local Jewish cult.

So Roman and Jewish soldiers and officials searched small and relatively lightly populated Jerusalem incessantly. They knew the city intimately but found no tomb. Yet according to a Canadian filmmaker it was there all the while, obvious to everyone and in full public display. With all due respect, reality simply cries out to be heard.

There are Christian, non-Christian and anti-Christian archeologists who have been working in Jerusalem and the rest of Israel for most of their lives. They are fluent in ancient languages and ancient history and have expanded our knowledge of the Bible and the life of Christ in ways thought impossible just half-a-century ago.

But they do not make pop documentaries and do not hold sensationalist press conferences. It was, of course, James Cameron who announced at the Oscars in 1998 that he was, "King of the world." Sorry Jimmy. My money is still on Jesus Christ.

MC

21

Da Vinci

THE BOOK, THE MOVIE AND NOW THE BOARD GAME. YES, THE *DA VINCI CODE* BOARD GAME IS CURRENTLY AVAILABLE AND WILL PROBABLY PROVIDE THE GULLIBLE WITH HOURS OF HARMLESS FUN. ROLL A DOUBLE SIX, PROCEED FIVE SQUARES AND THEN BEAT ONESELF WITH A WHIP WHILST MURDERING A NUN. AND ALL THE WHILE AUTHOR DAN BROWN BECOMES WEALTHIER AND CHRISTIANS DO A PRETTY GOOD JOB OF TURNING THE OTHER CHEEK.

The Islamic world went into mass revolt over a bunch of largely innocuous cartoons. Roman Catholics, the main victims of Brown's book, have merely gone to Mass. Brown makes repugnant and completely baseless attacks on Christianity in general but it is Catholicism with which he seems particularly angry.

Which places him firmly in the center of secularism's current obsession. The fetish of hatred against the single institution that stands firm against relativism, moral decay and self-indulgence. The Roman Catholic Church. As an institution it represents a mirror held up to the absurdities of western liberalism, and western liberalism despises the reflection.

Combine anti-Catholicism with a few beautiful heroes, mad monks, facile plots and the now obligatory conspiracy theory and the pages turn as fast as the figures on a certain author's bank account. A silly novel, however, is merely that. It is when Dan Brown claims to be writing of fact, as he does at some length in the book, that we have a duty to correct him.

He claims that Jesus was regarded even by His followers as merely a great moral teacher or at best a prophet. They never thought of Him as a Messianic figure, he continues, and the earliest written documents substantiate this. It was only at the Council of Nicaea in 325AD that Jesus was said to be divine.

Not quite. Jesus is called "God" seven times in the New Testament and is referred to as divine on dozens of occasions. He was crucified not for being a prophet or an ethicist, or for that matter a champion of social justice, but for claiming to be the Son of God. The early martyrs died because of this belief alone.

There are numerous letters from pagan and thus objective writers from the first and second century, long before Nicaea, describing how Christians believe Jesus to be divine; including one written to the Emperor Marcus Aurelius, who died in AD180. All the Council of Nicaea did was to affirm that Jesus was the Son of God as a self-evident truth.

Brown then says that *The Dead Sea Scrolls* are the earliest Christian writings in existence and that The Gnostic Gospels frequently mention Mary Magdalene and her marriage to Jesus.

This really is a howler. *The Dead Sea Scrolls* are Jewish writings and have no direct connection with Christianity at all. As for those much-discussed Gnostic Gospels, they at no time mention Jesus being married to Mary. But then Dan Brown probably doesn't expect his readers to actually read the Gnostic Gospels.

If they did they would be extremely disappointed. They are often misogynistic, frequently contradictory and tend to be self-serving and achingly dull. They were rejected by the Church because they were written relatively late and are wholly unreliable. It was not a case of Christianity trying to hide some greater truth but of Christianity only adopting books that were, well, Christian.

If Brown doesn't think much of the Church, he doesn't like Constantine very much at all. Except when he thinks him a virtual god. "The Bible, as we know it today, was collated by the pagan Roman Emperor Constantine." Who knew? Certainly not Constantine. Because the Old Testament existed even before the birth of Jesus, and the New Testament began to take shape at the end of the first century. The compilation was not finalized until the end of the fourth century.

Constantine, however, died in 337 AD. In other words, there is no way that he could have compiled The Bible. What he certainly did do was to commission Eusebius, the genius Bishop of Carthage, to make fifty copies of the Bible that already existed so that more people could read it. No serious historian has ever claimed otherwise or written anything to support Brown's thesis. Proving that Dan Brown is no historian.

Fine, argue his advocates, he doesn't claim to be. True, but he does claim that distinction for others. "The royal bloodline of Jesus Christ has been chronicled in exhaustive detail by scores of historians". The historians he lists are Margaret Starbird, Richard Leigh, Henry Lincoln, Clive Prince, Lynn Picknett and Michael Baigent. Problem. Just like Dan Brown these aren't historians either. Baigent has a basic degree in psychology and is working on an MA in mysticism and Picknett and Prince are best known for their work on the occult and UFOs. Phone home ET, and tell us about Jesus and his family who all live in France.

Brown is often at his most fatuous when he tries to be at his most clever. He writes that *YHWH*, the Jewish sacred name for God, is based on the word Jehovah. And Jehovah, he says, is a combination of the masculine Jah and the feminine Havah, signifying Eve. Thus God gave us feminism, Jesus was a pioneer of progressive gender politics and the Church has hidden all of this to preserve male power and exclude women, particularly Mary Magdalene, from their rightful place in society and culture.

Dan, you've got your politics and your semantics rather confused. *YHWH* doesn't come from Jehovah but Jehovah from *YHWH*. The word was used thousands of years before Jehovah came into existence, as late as the sixteenth-century.

He goes on to say that The Priory of Sion was founded in early medieval Europe. Untrue. It was registered with the French government in a dusty office in 1956. His central bad guy is an Opus Dei monk. Hardly. Opus Dei is an overwhelmingly lay organization and they have no monks. He states that five million women were killed by the Church as witches. Actually between 30,000 and 100,000 people, men and women, were executed for various crimes, including witchcraft. He refers to the Pope in the Vatican long before the Pope lived in the Vatican. And so on and so on and so on.

Even Tom Hanks, the star of the film, admits that there is a great deal of "hooey" in the movie and that people shouldn't take it all seriously. But Tom, would you act in a movie denying the Holocaust or questioning the obscenity of the African slave trade and then justify your work because it is only entertainment? The question is rhetorical, the answer illuminating.

The Da Vinci Code insists that evil men and women have for 2000 years been telling a grotesque lie and that they still torture and kill to maintain their power. Those people apparently include me, my wife, our children and our family and friends. Hundreds of millions of others too. What evil swine we must be. Make sure the popcorn has extra butter and hooray for Hollywood and publishing.

MC

Opus Dei

AN ELECTION CONDUCTED THROUGH THE PRISM OF SENSATIONALIST FICTION OR, TO PUT IT ANOTHER WAY, THE DICTATORSHIP OF THE NOVEL. IN THIS CASE A BAD NOVEL. DAN BROWN'S *THE DA VINCI CODE* HAS LARGELY BEEN FORGOTTEN BUT ITS GROTESQUE CARICATURE OF CATHOLIC ORGANISATION OPUS DEI HAS LEFT A CLOUD OF ABSURD MISUNDERSTANDING AROUND THIS GROUP WHOSE MAIN CRIME APPEARS TO BE ORTHODOXY. FOR DAN BROWN OPUS DEI, THE WORK OF GOD, SIGNIFIED CRAZED ALBINO ASSASSINS RUNNING AROUND FRANCE, SECRET PLOTS, DARK INTRIGUE AND SELF-FLAGELLATION. IN FACT IT'S MORE CHARITY MISSIONS IN SLUMS, SCHOOLS, RELIGIOUS RETREATS FOR BUSY PEOPLE AND WORK FOR THE POOR.

But Dan Brown is evidently big in Quebec and, much to the chagrin of the Bloc, so might be the Conservatives. So Gilles Duceppe announced that the Tory candidate in Saint-Hubert-Saint-Bruno, Nicole Charbonneau Barron, was an Opus Dei member. Then Raymond Gravel, a Catholic priest and outgoing Bloc MP, opined that, "Social conservatives such as members of Opus Dei may be running for office in order to change policies concerning abortion and same-sex marriage."

Earth to dotty separatist: it's not Opus Dei but the Roman Catholic Church that teaches that life begins at conception and that marriage can only be between a man and a woman. You might know that if you weren't suspended from all priestly duties because of your statements and behavior. Indeed it is entirely likely that in a less liberal place than Quebec in the 1980s this former prostitute who worked in Montreal's Gay leather bars would never have been ordained in the first place.

The more important point is that this is a game of gutter politics being played by frightened politicians. Opus Dei is entirely faithful to Catholic teaching, so if anyone objects to its people standing for office they should really say what they mean – that genuine Catholics are not welcome. That, however, might be too much even for the most ardent followers of the new religion of state secularism.

Opus Dei was founded by Spanish priest Josemaria Escriva in 1928, as a largely lay organization of Roman Catholics with the purpose of sanctifying ordinary work. The holy is within everyday people doing everyday things, wrote the founder, but they need guidance. It is now an international group with houses and followers throughout the world. It has more than 80,000 members, 1,800 of them priests. In Canada there are around 500 members, but the number of followers is dozens of times larger. It is also a Personal Prelature of the Pope, which means it has clout.

It's also traditional. The sacraments, the Rosary, the adoration of the Virgin Mary and the saints, strict moral discipline. What would have been considered average Catholicism just a few years ago, before "Catholics" such as Duceppe and Gravel came to prominence. It is relatively strong throughout Canada, and is growing particularly fast in Toronto, with a high school and a male and a female hall of residence to cater for university students. Actual membership is not easy and most of its adherents simply go along for evenings of "recollection."Others, however, commit themselves to celibacy and devote a certain part of their income to Opus Dei.

There have been rumours of extreme right-wing sympathies but this is largely nonsense. Because of the Spanish history of the organization, it is strong in Latin America and of course in Spain itself. Some members have supported juntas in Latin America, but they have also faced deportation, torture and murder because of their stand for social justice. Opus Dei obviously stands for Church authority and hierarchy and so has sometimes been in conflict with the Liberation Theology of certain Marxist Latin American priests. But then so did Pope John Paul the Great and now Pope Benedict, men who have shown quite extraordinary sympathy towards the victims of fascism and offered contrition for any Church failings in this regard.

No albino killers, no former sex-trade workers and not even any leaders of the Bloc Quebecois. Which rather disqualifies it from what many see as the Canadian body politic – one which is clad in fetish leather. It's not the work of God that's odd but political liars who start false fires.

MC

Church and State

Every few years or so political and social liberalism presents the culture with another empty mantra, intended to dismiss opponents and ridicule their arguments. Not long ago we had the racism fetish. Conservatives were racist and their policies based on racism.

Remove racist and insert sexist, homophobic or fascist. Or just punch a Tory in the face and say that he offended you.

The reaction to political correctness made all that seem rather stale. So the left moved on. To the grand rallying cry of the need to separate church and state. We hear it all the time, repeatedly used to support radical views and silence opposition.

Thing is, the entire concept is nonsensical in contemporary Canada. Worse than that, it's American. Yes, the country the liberals love to hate developed the notion of separating the state from the church. And it did so not to support the state but to protect the church.

The United States was founded by people who were overwhelmingly evangelical Christian, and who had suffered directly or through their forefathers from state persecution. A major aspect of this persecution had been the Church of England, the established church that had made life so very difficult for non-conformist Protestants and Roman Catholics.

In fact the entire separation idea was based on allowing religious influence by excluding one specific church denomination from dominating an entire culture. It was never supposed to protect the state from religion, in particular Christianity, because the founders of the United States did not believe that any such protection was necessary.

On the contrary, they saw religious faith as being an essential safeguard of the power and influence of the state. How correct they were. The leaders of the campaign against slavery were Christians and the people who forced President Lincoln's hand both before and during the Civil War were motivated by their Christian zeal.

A century later it was the church, organized and militant but non-violent, that under the guidance of Martin Luther King and a host of Christian leaders, thrust the civil rights movement into the consciousness of the American people. The government, the courts and the media merely followed the lead of the church.

When people today claim that they do not want church interference into their lives or the life of the state, however, all they really mean is that they do not want to listen to anyone who disagrees with them. Moaning on about church and state separation makes them feel as if their arguments carry some intellectual weight.

What is selfish is made to sound grand. What is merely political is made to sound philosophical. They would rather indulge their own complacency than allow people of faith to hold up a mirror and reflect the increasing moral flabbiness of the secular world.

That is particularly sad in this country, and startlingly ironic. The very people who obsess about the separation of church and state tend to worship at the altar of Canadian nationalism, public broadcasting and education and, most of all, socialized medicine.

The latter, of course, owes an incalculable debt to the great Tommy Douglas. Who was an ordained Baptist minister and evangelical Christian, motivated in his politics and campaigns by his faith and the need to inject church teachings into the Canadian state.

So if we use the logic of the contemporary liberal, Tommy Douglas should have shut up and minded his own business. As should, to name just a few, William Wilberforce when he worked to end slavery in the British empire, Lord Shaftsbury when he led the struggle against child labour and the Catholic monk Titus Brandsma who gave his life to rescue Jews in occupied Holland.

Frankly, I doubt if much of this will make any difference to some of the fiercest critics of the church today. Hey, just punch a priest in the face and say he offended you.

Religion

THE KNIGHTS OF COLUMBUS ORGANIZATION IS HARDLY A NEST OF BUZZING POLITICAL ACTIVISM. IN FACT MORAL CONSERVATIVES OFTEN CRITICIZE THE GROUP FOR NOT DOING ENOUGH TO SPEAK OUT ON ISSUES OF LIFE AND SEXUALITY. THEY ARE A ROMAN CATHOLIC FRATERNITY, FOUNDED IN THE NINETEENTH-CENTURY PRINCIPALLY TO HELP IMPOVERISHED WIDOWS OF CATHOLIC MEN, OFTEN IMMIGRANTS, WHO LOST THEIR LIVES OR WERE CRIPPLED WHILE WORKING IN APPALLING CONDITIONS.

Today they spend their time raising money for the poor and marginalized. They form an important part of a massive Christian charity network, without which the social services of this country would collapse almost overnight. Working in soup kitchens and financing drop-in centers was the central work of the Knights in Port Coquitlam, B.C. Until, that is, they found themselves accused of being un-Canadian bigots.

In 2003 they discovered that their hall had been rented by a lesbian couple to celebrate their wedding. But as Catholics the Knights followed Catholic teaching and the Church opposes same-sex marriage. They offered to find another hall for the couple, pay for its rental and also for new invitations to be printed. Sorry for the bother and all that and I'm sure you understand.

Not quite. The couple in question decided to take their oppressors to the provincial Human Rights Commission, who ruled last year that the women should be compensated for "undue hardship". Representatives of the complainants said that the punishment was too mild and that they intended to appeal the ruling.

Which only goes to prove that those silly old Neanderthals who oppose Gay marriage are being fanatical when they say that their rights are being questioned. No need for a Defence of Religion Act when religion is already protected under the Charter. Problem is, any claim that religion is already thus defended under the Charter or any other existing Canadian legislation is simply ill informed or blatantly dishonest.

Scott Brockie, a printer in Ontario, found this to his cost when he refused to accept work from a Gay organization. As a Christian, he said, he could not reconcile his faith with the contents of the material he was being asked to reproduce. He had Gay clients. It was the nature of the work and not the sexuality of the customer that gave him pause.

There were any number of other printers who were only too happy to take the contract and Mr. Brockie said he would fully understand if a Gay man refused to print material from a Christian organization opposed to homosexuality. No matter. He was fined $5000 by a Human Rights Commission and had to pay $40,000 in legal costs.

The fact is that no priest, rabbi or imam is going to be forced at bayonet-point to perform a Gay wedding. That, however, has never really been the issue. As one of the leaders of the Gay community said to me on television, "We'd never demand that someone conduct a ceremony, but if they oppose the law I do think we should question their charitable status."

The campaign to challenge the tax exemption of faith groups is already underway. It may fail but it will cost a huge amount of money for religious groups to defend their position. Money that would otherwise be directed towards charity. All people of faith are requesting, in a Defence of Religion Act or something similar, is a shadow of the protection for their beliefs that Canadian homosexuals currently enjoy for their lifestyle.

At heart it's about pluralism and co-existence, two virtues that are repeatedly trumpeted by many of the very people who, paradoxically, seem so opposed to any formal protection of religion. Gay men and women will always be able to find a minister to marry them and a hall in which to celebrate. The sensible, moderate and multicultural balance to this is legislation allowing serious Christians, orthodox Jews, practicing Muslims and many others the right to place a civil and civilized wall around their theology and property so as to preserve their heartfelt beliefs.

Let's be candid here. This debate hasn't concerned toleration of homosexuality for years. The Gay community has won countless legal and political battles and, whether they admit it or not, has embraced a messy triumphalism. It's not about tolerance but about affirmation; the expected and assumed affirmation of a lifestyle. Putting aside the perennial victim status that some religious people appear to relish, there is a justified fear that in the areas of education, expression and even basic practice the very faiths that built this country are under direct attack.

If Canadian values are to mean anything more than sound-bite morality, we have to give dignity and security to those whose religion demands dissent. The same religious imperative that obliged dissent from Martin Luther King when he opposed racism and William Wilberforce when he fought slavery. The same dissent that led the Roman Catholic Church to stand up to the multinational drug companies and forced them to make dozens of anti-AIDS drugs generic and thus affordable in Africa.

That action has saved countless thousands of lives. One of the largest donors to the Vatican is, by the way, the Knights of Columbus. The irony is almost overwhelming but the solution is extremely simple, will hurt nobody and is fair, just and, well, Canadian.

Mass Appeal

IT'S SELDOM THE CASE THAT CHRISTIAN LITURGY MAKES THE FRONT PAGES OF THE INTERNATIONAL PRESS. BUT THE IDEA OF POPE BENEDICT XVI ALLOWING THE MASS TO BE SAID MORE FREELY IN LATIN PROVOKED ALL SORTS OF INTEREST LAST WEEK. INCLUDING THE FANTASY THAT CATHOLICS WOULD NOW PRAY FOR THE CONVERSION OF, "THE PERFIDIOUS JEWS." A GROTESQUELY ABSURD SUGGESTION THAT RAISES SOME FUNDAMENTAL QUESTIONS ABOUT THE RESPONSIBILITY AND CREDIBILITY OF CERTAIN MEDIA COMMENTATORS.

When the Papal statement was actually issued over the weekend all it said was that, "In parishes where there is a stable group of faithful who adhere to the earlier liturgical tradition, the pastor should willingly accept their request to celebrate the Mass according to the rite of the *Roman Missal* published in 1962."

No nasty comments about the Jewish people, no heretics burning in the town square. In fact the announcement stresses that there are certain areas where the public liturgy has to follow the more modern form, including when it speaks of the Jews. The Good Friday service did once use the word perfidious, an ugly translation from "perfideles" or half-believer. In earlier times the congregation prayed first for the "*fideles*", meaning believers or church, then for the Jewish people and then for the "infidels" or unbelievers. Pope John XXIII removed the deeply troubling word more than forty years ago.

Roman Catholics do, however, still pray for the Jews at Easter. "Let us pray for the Jewish people, the first to hear the word of God, that they may continue to grow in the love of His name and in faithfulness to His covenant. Almighty and eternal God, long ago you gave your promise to Abraham and his posterity. Listen to your Church as we pray that the people you first made your own may arrive at the fullness of redemption."

It's vital to stress that this will not change. Some critics, naturally, will always be offended by any sense of a hierarchy of belief and any call for conversion. Yet an exclusive truth cannot, obviously, co-exist with another exclusive truth. Otherwise that truth would not be exclusive. If there is a God, there is not an absence of God. If water is wet, it is not dry.

Any serious Catholic believes that happiness and eternal life are to be found within the Catholic Church. To refuse to pray that other people will find their way into such a place would be positively selfish and cruel.

The problem is that in this intellectually dumb and morally numb age we like our truths, well, less truthful. "Might be" or "could be" or, usually, "anything you want it to be". Never "you should be".

The Pope has spoken extensively about this relativism, as he did when he was Cardinal Ratzinger. As Cardinal he also wrote at length about the central importance of the Hebrew Scriptures, the place of the Jews in the plan of salvation and the evils of anti-Semitism.

The latest announcement is far less about ecumenism than about restoring the tradition of the Church and allowing greater freedom of worship. For some time individual priests have only been allowed to say the Latin Mass if they had special permission from their bishop. Pope Benedict has now allowed priests and parishes to employ Latin or the vernacular, leaving the decision up to them.

In the paradoxical mindset of the contemporary liberal, any act that fails to impose what is perceived as being progressive is by its nature reactionary. As perverse as the argument that the truly tolerant must refuse to tolerate the intolerant. As such, be prepared for screams of anguish from the perennially offended. Frankly, it hardly matters.

Obviously the Vatican hopes that this move will bring back some of the hundreds of thousands of conservative Catholics who have joined quasi-Catholic groups outside of the Church in the past thirty years. Some of them left for obscure or sinister reasons but many will doubtless return. Yet this is nothing more than a welcome consequence of a far more profound reform.

The Second Vatican Council or Vatican II was intended to be an organic progression of 2000 years of Church tradition and teaching. Windows were supposed to be opened but an assortment of 1960s academics and left-wing priests preferred to smash them. Continuation became breach and a legion of abuses were allowed and even encouraged.

This latest pronouncement will enable the new and old order of the Mass to co-exist and learn from one another, as was the reasoning of Vatican II. It is abundantly encouraging, long overdue and, yes, perfidious to those Catholics who despise everything they are supposed to revere.

MC

37

Excommunication

According to various headlines across the world, the Pope has "welcomed back into the Church a Holocaust denying Bishop" and "Ripped to shreds Catholic-Jewish relations for a generation." Which says a great deal more about media inaccuracy and hysteria than it does about what has just happened within the Roman Catholic Church. What Pope Benedict actually did this weekend was to lift the excommunication of four bishops who were illicitly consecrated by the late Archbishop Marcel Lefebvre in 1988. Among them was Richard Williamson, an execrable individual who is indeed an unrepentant Holocaust denier and anti-Semite. But the original excommunication had nothing to do with these bishops' views and neither does the removal of the excommunication. Indeed, a major obstacle to this welcome and sensible move was the reputation of Williamson, who hates the Vatican as much if not more than he dislikes Jews. He also, by the way, believes that *The Sound of Music* is a pornographic movie and that no self-respecting person should ever watch it. So as repulsive as he may be, the man is also a buffoon.

The history of the issue dates back to Vatican II in the early 1960s. The council's recommendations were relatively mild but they were almost immediately purposely misinterpreted and abused so as to remove Latin from the Mass, ignore Papal teachings and attempt to transform the historic Church into a stew of ecumenical and subjective ideologies. This concerted liberal campaign did enormous damage but a new generation of Catholics who rejected 1960s and 70s relativism and embraced a resurgent orthodoxy, empowered by Popes John Paul II and Benedict XVI, have now won the day. During the darkest times, however, up to a million traditional Catholics left the Church to worship with The Society of St. Pius X, founded by the French Archbishop Lefebvre.

The vast majority of those who joined were merely conservative Catholics who were understandably disturbed by many of the excesses performed, incorrectly, in the name of Vatican II. Others, though, and many within the leadership, embraced a much more reactionary agenda. Some spoke fondly of collaborationist Vichy France, supported the French National Front and not only rejected the Second Vatican Council but denied that the Church had the authority to call it. Which was, of course, a paradoxically Protestant approach. Most infamous of all these leaders was and is Richard Williamson, who recently gave an interview on Swedish TV in which he claimed that there were no Nazi gas chambers and that the "so-called Holocaust" was a myth.

It's partly to isolate this invincibly smug wing nut and his followers, a small minority within the Society of St. Pius X organisation, that the Pope has expunged the excommunication. Because the main reason behind the action is the hope that hundreds of thousands of devout Catholics will return to the mainstream Church. Whether this will happen is open to question but it's likely that if it does Williamson, who would not be accepted as a Bishop within the Church, would leave and form yet another sect. Yet to concentrate on this man is not only an absurd digression from the real debate but also plays directly into his hands by giving him and his rancid ideas a profile they simply do not deserve. He is, as it were, a legend in his own lunchtime.

Numerous European Cardinals and Archbishops, including in France and Germany, have publicly welcomed the Papal announcement while simultaneously re-stating the self-evident fact that the Holocaust happened, that it was devilish, that Jesus, Mary and the Holy Family were Jewish and that to be anti-Semitic is to be anti-Christian. It's not clear what else they can say or do. There are numerous Catholics who have dreadful beliefs but they cannot be excommunicated merely for being wrong or bad. There are legions of alleged Catholics, even priests, who have taught fundamentally anti-Catholic beliefs and not been excommunicated; and just this week, for example, a number of senior American politicians who still claim to be part of the Church publicly encouraged eugenics and the killing of unborn children.

It's a complex and often disturbing dynamic. Washed far clearer by the tears of Pope John Paul the Great when he openly wept inside the great synagogue in Rome and spoke of the pain and suffering of the Jewish people and how a new bond of love and common fate had developed. All of his magnificent gestures towards the Jews were shared and supported by Pope Benedict, then Cardinal Ratzinger. That journey of testament to testament continues to this day, and to let it be halted by a lone, despised hater would be a terrible sin. Let him scream away at the songs of Julie Andrews while the real world, and the real Church, moves forward.

41

Excommunication Revisited

THE PHENOMENON IN NORTHERN IRELAND, GLASGOW AND EVEN PARTS OF NORTH AMERICA KNOWN AS THE "KICK THE POPE" BAND IS NOT WHAT IT WAS. IN YEARS PAST THESE GROUPS OF ANTI-CATHOLIC BIGOTS WOULD PLAY THEIR FIFES, BANG THEIR DRUMS AND RECITE UGLY SECTARIAN SONGS UNTIL THEY COULD SING NO MORE. IS THE DECLINE A SIGN THAT ANTI-CATHOLICISM IS DIMINISHING? NOT AT ALL. IT'S JUST THAT NOW IT WEARS A LIBERAL CAP RATHER THAN AN ORANGE SASH.

In late January Pope Benedict made the courageous decision to lift the excommunication of four bishops who were illicitly consecrated in 1988 by Archbishop Marcel Lefebvre , founder of the traditionalist Society of St. Pius X. One of these men, however, was a conspiracy theorist named Richard Williamson who questioned the truth about 911, denied the Holocaust and thought that *The Sound of Music* was a porn movie. In other words, he's a repugnant lunatic. But it takes more than repugnance and lunacy to earn excommunication or to have it lifted. It was not his views but the fact that he was illegally named a bishop that led to his being excommunicated and it is not his views that have led to the removal of the same. An excommunicated person can no longer receive the sacraments. No more and no less. Cannot, for example, receive communion, be married by the Church or go to confession and be absolved of sin.

In fact Williamson is largely irrelevant in all of this. There are up to a million supporters of the Society of St. Pius X and Pope Benedict wants to bring them back into the mainstream of the Roman Catholic Church. It's part of a grander campaign to deal with a legion of abuses that have crept into the Church since the mid-1960s when extremists tried to exploit the reforms of The Second Vatican Council. Which is why so many of those zealots are now using the Williamson affair to attack the Papacy and are spreading so many distortions and half-truths about a man who, as the guiding theologian behind Pope

John Paul II, did so much to revolutionize the relationship between the Catholic Church and the Jewish people.

To fail to understand these points is to misunderstand what we have seen in the past two weeks. Most of the attacks from inside the Church and from alleged Catholics have had nothing to do with the understandable sensitivities of the Jewish community but with a deeper attack on a Pope who is despised by those who desire a weak and modernist Church that has about as much to do with genuine Catholicism as Richard Williamson has to do with official Church teaching on the Holocaust. While Jewish groups are suspicious, they need to be aware that some of the harshest condemnations of what Pope Benedict has done are coming from a left that is usually first in criticising Israel. Indeed the latest trend from such people is to tie in the removal of the excommunication with Benedict's speech in Regensburg in 2006 in which he briefly and in passing repeated a medieval and entirely sensible question about the nature of Islam. As such he was one of the few world leaders willing to challenge an ideology that is far more dangerous to Jews and pluralism than is some isolated nutcase who denies the Holocaust.

The reporting of this issue has been positively scandalous. Extended articles have been written without one supporter of the Pope being quoted but several opponents of the man given numerous paragraphs. This is partly because many journalists simply do not understand Church law and politics but there is often sheer malice involved. That the Pope was unaware of Williamson's views on the Holocaust, for example, has been interpreted to prove that he is out of touch. What actually happened was that the surprisingly small Papal department dealing with this issue concentrated on the leader of the Society of St. Pius X and not Williamson. It's worth noting that even with an enormous staff, President Obama suffered three major vetting scandals in as many weeks.

While not its specific purpose, the Papal initiative has led to Williamson being reprimanded by the Society of St. Pius X and told never again to write or speak about politics and history. The Vatican made it clear in an official statement that Williamson must "distance himself in an absolutely unequivocal and public manner from his positions regarding the Shoah" and Pope Benedict has yet again declared that the Holocaust was, without question, a unique and historic evil. Something it is his responsibility as Pope to do.

But he is, yes, the Pope. His role as the direct descendant of St. Peter is not to manage an international public relations corporation but to lead the church of Jesus Christ. There are some Catholics who seem more concerned with mass popularity than with the integrity and mission of the Church. Pope Benedict upsets people when he questions the Iraq war, calls for the forgiving of Third World debt, opposes the death penalty and lambastes western materialism. These are as Papal as declaring that truth is at its most complete within Catholicism and stressing the need for unity in the Church. How tragic if we become distracted by one troubled man who, more than most, is in need of the sacraments. Particularly that of Confession.

MC

The Hands

ALBRECHT DURER WAS BORN IN THE LATE FIFTEENTH-CENTURY IN A SMALL MINING VILLAGE NEAR NUREMBERG IN GERMANY. ONE OF EIGHTEEN CHILDREN, HE SAW HIS FATHER WORK EIGHTEEN HOUR DAYS SIMPLY TO PUT BREAD ON THE TABLE. YET FOR ALL THIS, ALBRECHT AND HIS BROTHER ALBERT SHARED A DREAM. THEY WANTED TO GO TO ART SCHOOL.

It was obvious to the boys that they would never be able to afford such an education. An idea. One of them would work in the mines and pay for the other to go to college. When the student returned, he in turn would become a miner and pay for his brother to have an education.

They tossed a coin and Albrecht won. Off he went to the city, while his brother started long and dangerous work deep under the ground. For four years one brother studied painting, drawing and sketching, while the other dug and clawed at the very earth.

When Albrecht returned to the village the local people held a feast to celebrate. The young artist thanked everybody, drank their good health and then made a speech of thanks to his brother. And now, he said, it is your turn to go to college and mine to work in your place. "Pursue your dream and I will take care of you."

There was a pause, a prolonged silence. Albert looked thoughtful, even in pain. Suddenly he began to cry. The tears poured down his lined, hardened face and this tough, strong man seem to become a delicate child.

"No, brother, I cannot go. Look at what four years in the mines have done to my hands! The bones in every finger have been smashed at least once, and lately I have been suffering from arthritis so badly that I cannot even hold a glass, much mess less make delicate lines on canvas with a brush. No brother, for me it is too late."

Albrecht began to cry as well. He ran to his brother and embraced him. Two men weeping, for one another and for the agony and unfairness of life. All around them the people of the village lowered their eyes in respect and began to pray.

To pray. Which is what the Durer brothers also did. And as Albrecht saw his brother in prayer he realized why he had been sent to art college and what he now had to do. He sat down to immortalize those broken yet perfect hands of his brother, to capture their praying beauty forever.

Five hundred years later we regard Durer as one of the finest artists of the Renaissance and a true genius. There are some critics who doubt the authenticity of the story of the artist's brother, but even these cynics cannot deny that *The Praying Hands* has been seen by millions and will continue to inspire until the end of time.

Inspiration. It comes to many, including a man called John Newton, who lived in Britain in the eighteenth-century. Newton was a slaver. In other words, he commanded a ship that kidnapped men, women and children from Africa and sold them into a life of living hell known as slavery.

It was easy to find crews for such vessels, as money was good and the sailors were allowed to rape the women. If Africans died on the journey, no matter. Just throw them over board. They could always be replaced and were not as important as, for example, cattle or pigs.

But then Newton was struck down. Not physically but emotionally. He came to believe in Jesus Christ and to place his hands together in prayer, just like Albert Durer so many years earlier. Newton transformed his ways, embraced truth and light and wrote a certain hymn.

"Amazing grace! How sweet the sound That saved a wretch like me! I once was lost, but now am found; Was blind, but now I see."

The *Praying Hands* and *Amazing Grace*. There for us always. So is He. Christ Jesus. Once, always and for ever. He was born for us, died for us, rose again for us and will return for us.

As we celebrate His birthday we ought to remember the essence of the season. As did the Durer brothers, John Newton and all those who knew and know glory through the love of Christ. Merry Christmas.

MC

Mel Gibson

As a Roman Catholic with three Jewish grandparents I'm far more annoyed with Hollywood than I am with Mel Gibson. The reason? Gibson was drunk when he made his obnoxious comments about Jews and has since apologized. Most celebrities are sober when they make bigoted remarks about Christians and never make even an attempt at contrition.

Unlike Gibson's splenetic critics I have no window into the man's soul. They say that his eloquent and thorough confession within hours of the now infamous incident was insincere. Actually, we don't know. What we do know is that he is a conservative Catholic and that he dared to make *The Passion of the Christ*. Which means, if we are to be candid, as much to his liberal enemies in Hollywood as to his Christian friends outside of it.

How different from the case of the radical Democrat American politician Jesse Jackson, who in 1984 referred to Jews as "Hymies" and to New York City as "Hymietown". He denied the comments until forced into a corner and then asked for forgiveness because the words did not come from "my heart." The "apology" was accepted and Jackson moved on.

Yet often there is no need to apologize at all, especially if it's Christians rather than Jews who are the target. Last year *Comedy Central* hired comedian Dennis Leary to host something called "Merry F#%$in' Christmas", in which Leary said, "Listen, Christmas is built on a line of bullshit. Do I believe there was a baby Jesus? You bet your ass I do. But I believe that nine months before he was born someone sure as shit banged the hell out of his mom."

Not only did Leary not apologize but was soon given a lucrative contract to provide voice-overs for a series of children's movies for all the family.

The writers of *South Park* got into trouble when one of their episodes was taken off the air because of its attack on Scientology. Yet there was no censorship for their show entitled *Red Hot Catholic Love*, where it is announced by various cardinals that pedophilia is part of Vatican teaching. Or for the episode in which a statue of the Virgin Mary is shown with blood pouring from her rectum.

No apologies either from magicians and entertainers Penn and Teller after their reference to "Mother F#%$ing Teresa" on their HBO special. Goodness me, for Christians it has become routine. Expect to be insulted, abused and lied about in movies and on television.

Madonna knows this, and knows she'll always get away with it. She began her career with a sexualized mockery of the Virgin Mary and now she takes that career into middle age with a performance on a life-size crucifix, playing at being the Christ figure dressed in black leather in front of a cheering and lusting crowd. She does not do this *in spite* of whom she might offend but precisely *because* of whom she will offend. We can be as sure of that as we are that she would never behave in a similar way towards Islam.

She is, however, less direct than playwright Tony Kushner, who co-wrote Stephen Spielberg's *Munich*. Writing in *The Nation*, he called Pope John Paul II "a homicidal liar" who "endorses murder." Kushner usually writes fiction of course. But on PBS's allegedly objective *Newshour With Jim Lehrer* a case was made for mandatory DNA testing for those considered most likely to indulge in criminal behavior: The list was, "teenagers, homeless people, Catholic priests."

Closer to home the CBC's Michael Enright told an interviewer back in 1997 that the Roman Catholic Church was the greatest criminal organization in the world outside of the Mafia. An apology? Please, he was only expressing his opinion. His career blossomed.

Beyond the obvious double standard of some religions being fair game and others not, there is the question of why liberal artists can say extreme and vile things about the Jewish state, and yet escape the criticism thrown at Gibson, who has never uttered a word of judgment against Israel. After all, anti-Semitic comments may be unacceptable but the killing of Jews by Arab terrorists is surely worse.

Director Michael Moore explained the origins of Arab anti-Semitism thus: "Maybe it was when the Palestinian child looked up in the air and saw an American Apache helicopter firing a missile into his baby sister's bedroom just before she was blown into a hundred bits." And, "It's all part of the same ball of wax, right? The oil companies, Israel, Halliburton." Yet Moore remains a lion of the left and a prized guest in Hollywood, baseball cap included.

Gibson, however, wears a crucifix rather than a cap and his crime seems to be much more than his ugly, drunken words. There are times to apologize and there are times to shake one's head in despair.

~MC~

Atheism

MY GOLLY IT'S FUNNY WHEN LIBERAL-MINDED PEOPLE BECOME TERRIBLY SELF-RIGHTEOUS AND BEMOAN THE LACK OF FREE SPEECH IN CANADA. FUNNY BECAUSE LIBERAL-MINDED PEOPLE TEND TO BE THE MOST AGGRESSIVE AND INTOLERANT OF CENSORS. IN CANADA WE REGULARLY HAVE HUMAN RIGHTS COMMISSIONS CLOSING DOWN WEBSITES AND CONDEMNING AND FINING WRITERS, AND THE CRTC TELLING BROADCASTERS WHAT THEY ARE ALLOWED TO SAY

Mostly from one side of course. Almost without exception leftist opinions are permitted or even encouraged while conservatives are scrutinized or even gagged. Which leads to the positively hilarious scene of those same alleged liberals condemning a Roman Catholic school board which last week chose to remove Philip Pullman's book *The Golden Compass* from its library shelves.

Pullman is a talented author whose most famous book has been made into a soon to be released movie. The book has been in Catholic school libraries for some time but the publicity around the movie and the author has alerted people to the author's deeply held beliefs.

He is a militant and committed atheist. He was described by *The New Yorker* as one of Britain's most outspoken atheists and has openly admitted that, "I'm trying to undermine the basis of Christian belief". Which is fair enough of course. Go for it baby. You're part of a banal fashion trend and there is a lot of money to be made in the God-hating business.

The Golden Compass is the first, and least offensive, of a trilogy entitled *His Dark Materials*. It explains that the forces of evil are attempting to control the world and that those forces are, yes, eerily reminiscent of the Catholic Church. The symbolism and language is quite clear and Pullman has never denied it.

Again, this is absolutely acceptable in a free society. But it is also acceptable for a Catholic school to decide that a Catholic library for Catholic children should not promote an anti-Catholic book. If, for example, a Jewish school for children under the age of twelve refused to stock an anti-Semitic book we would, surely, consider the decision to be logical, correct and obvious.

That the book had been in some of these Catholic school libraries for several years is irrelevant. Overworked school librarians have little time and opportunity to know about all of the books they order and this one had been well reviewed. On a more sinister level, there are legions of ostensibly Catholic teachers at Catholic schools who are anything but Roman Catholic.

Contrary to popular cliché, nobody is trying to ban the book. Pullman's works are readily available in bookstores in every town. This is merely about Catholic schools trying to gently preserve their Catholic identity, which is supposed to be what multiculturalism is all about. And multiculturalism is a good thing. I know this because the left tells me so.

The left also says that people should have more power. So when parents successfully urge school trustees to remove an insulting book, this must be another good thing. Apparently not. All parents are equal but some are more equal than others.

Consistency, however, is not the overriding flavour in this stew. This has never been about liberty or literature but always about anti-Catholicism and the chattering classes imposing their manners and values on others. Dark materials apparently go a great deal further than Philip Pullman.

~MC~

The Middle East

The Crusades

ALMOST EVERY TIME A FANATIC SPEAKS IN THE NAME OF MUSLIM FUNDAMENTALISM WE HEAR REFERENCES TO CRUSADERS. IT'S SUPPOSED TO DESCRIBE THE WESTERN POWERS BUT IT'S APPALLINGLY INACCURATE ON A NUMBER OF LEVELS. BUT WE SHOULDN'T BE SURPRISED THAT SOME IN THE ISLAMIC WORLD DO NOT UNDERSTAND THE CRUSADES, IN THAT SO MANY PEOPLE IN THE WEST HAVE NO IDEA EITHER.

There is nothing easier and more productive to attack in these addled times than an enterprise with its origins in Europe or Christendom, particularly if the alleged victims are members of another religion or ethnicity. President Bush was obliged to expunge the word "crusade" from a speech about the war in Iraq and it is a standard insult in Arab rhetoric to call opponents "Crusaders" and to allege that The Crusades themselves have never actually ended.

Odd really, in that it was the Muslims themselves who started these wars in the first place. The Crusades were almost entirely defensive in nature, an attempt to gain back Christian lands that had been conquered by Islamic armies, often with the utmost brutality. Far from the multi-cultural liberals depicted by contemporary history, many of the leaders of the Islamic empire were grotesquely violent, profoundly intolerant and had entered the region without any moral right or cause.

Palestine, Syria and Egypt were at one point almost entirely Christian and represented the very epicenter of Christian thought and energy. By the eighth century Muslim armies has conquered North Africa and most of Spain and were determined to move into other Christian territory.

It is essential to remember that Roman Catholic Spain was invaded by foreign, Islamic soldiers and occupied for generations. It was only armed resistance by the Christian knights and people of the region that led to the country being liberated. Odd how this is not used as some historical stick with which to beat Islam, whilst Islam so frequently pours guilt over the west by referring to the Crusades.

In the eleventh century the Seljuk Turks declared war on Asia Minor, modern Turkey, an area that had then been Christian for a thousand years. This was a prolonged and deliberate world war, started by a loose coalition of Islamic nations and directed against the Byzantine Empire.

It was only after such systematic provocation that in 1095 Pope Urban II called for Europe to take back these Christian lands, mainly because of the screams for help from the eastern emperor in Constantinople. What followed was a number of attempts over more than a century, some successful and some ludicrous, to win back large chunks of the Middle East for Christianity. To restore the region to what it had been before Islamic expansion.

The last Crusaders were defeated and expelled by 1291, but in their time in the region they had experienced success as well as defeat. Jerusalem was captured, a Christian kingdom was established, new orders of Christian knights had been developed. There had been horror and heroism, grace and grime.

Our sound-bite culture, however, is allergic to nuance. Far easier and more politically convenient to depict Christians as festering warlords and Muslims as perennial victims. The problem is that life, history, religion and reality is a little more complex than that.

When Islamic armies initially invaded Christian lands they did allow Christianity and Judaism to be practiced, and respected some if not all of the holy places of these faiths. Having said this, no new churches were to be built, the public display of Christian symbols was banned and Christians had to pay tolls to enter churches and holy sites. Non-Muslims were second-class citizens and were frequently treated appallingly. Massacres and horrors, though not official state policy, were all too common.

The Seljuk Turks were particularly oppressive and far more extreme than their Muslim predecessors. They killed unarmed pilgrims, forbade Christian services and destroyed churches. Moreover, there is no serious doubt that Islam's intention was to move further west and take all of Europe. In the late fifteenth and early sixteenth-century Muslim troops forced Rome to be evacuated and also besieged Vienna. Hardly a war of resistance against an alien aggressor.

Nor were the men who took to the Crusades the impoverished thugs we have been led to believe. New research shows them to have generally been wealthy and to have left land and power behind in Europe. Many if not most were also devoutly religious and saw their duty as a pilgrimage. Holy people, however, sometimes commit unholy acts.

Some Crusaders certainly attacked and murdered Jews in Europe on the way to Palestine, even though their actions were repeatedly and strongly condemned by the Pope and the Roman Catholic Church. St. Bernard made a personal journey to Germany to prevent these anti-Semitic spasms.

Once in Palestine, Lebanon and Syria the battles themselves were conducted like any other military confrontation of the era. That is, with terrible loss of life, enormous suffering but far generally less mass cruelty and sadism than routinely employed by the atheistic military forces of Hitler, Stalin and their friends. Indeed the crass statement that "more people have died because of religion than anything else" is bizarre. The officially Godless regimes of the twentieth-century alone destroyed that vacuous claim.

The Crusaders were beyond control and merciless when they took Jerusalem in 1099. No quarter was given and innocent people were slaughtered. Very similar to what happened when cities fell all over the world, and very similar to what occurred when Muslims broke through in any number of places after prolonged and painful sieges.

It does not forgive such actions but it should give a context. Unless we place these events in their correct historical and psychological setting we merely play politics and exploit history. It may be emotionally comfortable for secular zealots and Muslim fundamentalist alike to assume the Crusaders to have been robotic and amoral killers, but it is a rape of truth.

Once under Christian control, Jerusalem and the greater Christian kingdom always had a Muslim majority and Muslims were allowed to practice their faith. Nor were there any major attempts to convert them to Christianity. Apart from one brief, non-violent and largely unsuccessful campaign by the Franciscans, Muslims were seldom the targets of proselytizing.

The region returned to Muslim rule and eventually to the Ottoman Turks, who united large parts of the Islamic world and were the most thorough imperialists of the Middle East. It's significant that when critics speak of colonization they forget that there was never really any genuinely European Christian empire in the region. After hundreds of years of Turkish control the western powers did conquer the Middle East for a brief period but this was geopolitical imperative rather than religious empire.

Today the Christians of what was once the hub of Christianity and the place of its birth are declining in number and are often persecuted. In Egypt the Christian community is marginalized and frightened, with murder and discrimination achingly common. In Israel and Palestine there is confusion and ambivalence, with towns such as Nazareth and Bethlehem hemorrhaging young Christian men and women.

On an international level Christianity is the most persecuted faith in the world and there are more martyrs for Christ now, as we speak, than ever before. Yet still the secular world insists on assuming that so much that was and is Christian has to be caricatured.

The Crusades should not have happened. Nor should the Islamic wars of conquest that did so much harm to Christians and Christianity and which provoked and produced the Crusades. A crucial difference, surely, is that Christian leaders and even Pope John Paul II have apologized for the wrongs done so many years ago, whilst others are still distorting the facts and abusing the results for their own baleful ends.

MC

The Pope and Islam

It was said after The Holocaust, by those who believed in freedom, decency and tolerance that, "We are all Jews now." After the events of the past week it is now time for those who still believe in these virtues, irrespective of religion or race, to stand up and proudly announce, "We are all Catholics now."

Yes, we are all Catholics now. Catholic like the Holy Father, who spoke scholarly and moderate words about Islam, dialogue and the error of spreading religion by force. Words for which there was never any need to apologize. Nor did he.

Pope Benedict merely said that he was sorry for any offense and pain that his comments may have caused. We must now wait for someone to apologize for the churches that were firebombed in Palestine shortly after the Pope's speech and for Somali religious leader Abubukar Hassan Malin who urged Muslims to "hunt down" Benedict and kill him "on the spot."

Apologize for the abusive and threatening demonstrations, including calls for the Pope to be executed, that British Muslims organized outside Westminster Cathedral in London last Sunday, as families with children made their way to Mass.

Apologize for the Shura Council in Iraq, an umbrella of several Sunni groups, which stated after the Pope's comments that, "We will break up the cross, spill the liquor and impose the head tax, then the only thing acceptable is a conversion or the sword."

Apologize for the Muslims' attacks on Catholic priests in Turkey in the past year, including the murder of Fr. Andrea Santoro. Apologize for those Muslim leaders who compared the Pope to Hitler and promised to kill him.

Apologize for the massive persecution of Christians in Egypt, including kidnappings, rape, murder and beatings. Apologize for the churches in Pakistan and Iraq that have burnt to the ground, for the beheading of Christian schoolgirls in Indonesia and for the arrests of Muslims who wish to convert to Christianity.

Apologize for the sermons in Mosques that compare Jews to monkeys and pigs and call for the Jewish people to be slaughtered. Apologize for those Muslim countries that make television dramas claiming Jews kill gentile babies so as to drink their blood.

Apologize for those Muslim leaders who declare that Spain and Portugal have to be "retaken" by Islam. Apologize for the invasion on the Christian heartlands of North Africa and the Middle East hundreds of years ago, just as Pope John Paul apologized for crimes committed during The Crusades, the European response to this expansion.

Apologize for the murder of three of the translators of Salman Rushdie's *The Satanic Verses*, for the murder of Dutch film director Theo Van Gogh and for the murder of Daniel Pearl.

Let me make it extremely clear that I do not blame all Muslims for what is done by some of their co-religionists in the name of Islam. But when Muslim country after Muslim country and Muslim mob after Muslim mob behave thus a certain pattern does seem to emerge.

I hope and pray that this violence and extremism does not represent authentic Islam and that there is room for genuine dialogue. But, frankly, I am not optimistic. As India's Cardinal Toppo commented after Pope Benedict's statement and the Muslim reaction, we must respond with "courage and prayer because truth needs no other defence."

Quite so. Once again, we are all Catholics now.

MC

Mr. El Masry

I SUPPOSE I OUGHT TO OFFER MY OPINION, PARTICULARLY AS IT WAS ON *THE MICHAEL COREN SHOW* ON CTS TELEVISION THAT THE ACCUSING ORGANIZATION'S LEADER MADE HIS INFAMOUS REMARKS. I REFER TO THE NOW WELL-PUBLICIZED HUMAN RIGHTS COMMISSION CASES BROUGHT BY THE CANADIAN ISLAMIC CONGRESS AGAINST JOURNALIST MARK STEYN AND *MACLEAN'S*.

The magazine printed extracts from *America Alone*, the latest book by the immensely talented Steyn. In it he gives population growth figures, indicating that Islam may well become the dominant faith in Europe. He also quotes assorted Islamic leaders who triumphantly predict Muslim rule.

There was plenty of disagreement and *Maclean's* printed numerous critical letters. But this was insufficient for the CIC, who complained to several Human Rights Commissions. The fact that this complaint is even being heard is a disgrace to Canada, but the story becomes almost surreal when we remember that the President of the CIC is Dr. Mohamad Elmasry.

On my show three years ago he said that all Israelis were legitimate targets for Palestinian suicide bombers. "They are part of the Israeli army, even if they have civilian clothes." I asked him to clarify or even withdraw his statement. He merely repeated it. Any Israeli over the age of 18, man or woman, is a valid target.

I made sure that my guest had plenty of time to reconsider and even carried the discussion over a commercial break into another segment. The second Muslim guest, a lawyer, was obviously stunned by the remarks and disassociated himself from the statements.

Within 24 hours the story had made an editorial in a Canadian national newspaper, within a week it had been covered in almost every newspaper in the country as well as the international press. Television and radio pounced on the issue as well.

Muslim and Arab organisations expressed disgust at the remarks and called for Elmasry to resign, the university where he worked condemned the comments, Jewish leaders were outraged and government security officials in Ottawa requested tapes of the show.

The Canadian Islamic Congress issued a flimsy press release describing the comments as being "regrettable and misunderstood." I can only judge by what he said, repeatedly, as he sat only feet away from me. It was abundantly clear. No "misunderstood" comments but a systematic analysis of who is an acceptable victim in Israel. In fact, he gave a long preamble where he compared such attacks to those of the French Resistance against the Nazis during The Second World War.

There are more than a million Israeli Muslim and Christian Arabs. There are legions of Israelis who do not serve in the armed forces or serve in non-military posts, who oppose government policy and the occupation, who are physically or mentally disabled, who are elderly grandparents.

All, however, are apparently valid targets in some blood-lust chamber of horrors. Grotesque and gruesome. But illegal? Not at all. Not according to me and not according to Canada's various human rights commissions, who did not hear any case against Elmasry.

The appropriate response to the man's violent fantasy was obvious. I chose not to invite him back as a guest. And if I had done so, your response should have been to change the channel. The same applies to Mark Steyn and *Maclean's*. If you don't like it, don't read it. Even if you are under the age of 18!

Christians in Egypt

THIS WEEK I WAS SUPPOSED TO INTERVIEW FATHER ZAKARIA BOUTROS ON MY TELEVISION SHOW. IT WOULD HAVE BEEN THE SECOND TIME I HAD SPOKEN TO THIS GENTLE, THOUGHTFUL MAN, ONE OF THE LEADING FIGURES OF THE EGYPTIAN COPTIC CHRISTIAN COMMUNITY AND NOW OBLIGED TO LIVE IN EXILE IN THE UNITED STATES AFTER TWICE BEING ARRESTED IN HIS HOMELAND. BUT ON THIS OCCASION THE INTERVIEW WAS SUDDENLY CANCELLED. A $60 MILLION BOUNTY HAD JUST BEEN PUT ON HIS HEAD BY MUSLIM EXTREMISTS IN IRAN AND SAUDI ARABIA, AL QAEDA WERE THOUGHT TO BE INTENT ON FULFILLING THE *FATWA*, AND IT WAS CONSIDERED TOO DANGEROUS TO ALLOW HIM TO TRAVEL TO CANADA. IN THAT THE UNITED STATES GOVERNMENT BOUNTY ON OSAMA BIN LADEN IS A MERE $25 MILLION, IT RATHER PUTS THE CASE OF THIS DISARMINGLY GENTLE AND JOVIAL PRIEST INTO PROPORTION.

Because while he is anonymous to most North Americans, Boutros is famous or notorious throughout North Africa, the Middle East and Central Asia, where his daily television broadcasts attract enormous audiences and his website millions of hits. His style is uncompromising. Speaking in Egyptian-accented Arabic and fluent in Islamic scholarship and the various sub-cultures of the Muslim world, he carefully unwraps the layers of the Koran and the life and teachings of Mohammad and presents his viewers with a virtually unprecedented critique of their faith. It's the combination of accessibility and originality that makes him so threatening to militant Islam.

"We know people are leaving Islam because of what I say and they know people are leaving Islam because of what I say" he explains. A long pause, then: "People in the west simply don't understand the significance of this in a world that has not and probably will not embrace pluralism. The Islamic response is not to argue with me but to try to kill me."

Nor is this just the sordid reaction of wealthy fanatics and terror mobs. Last month the Iranian parliament voted on a draft bill, the *Islamic Penal Code*, whereby any woman who left Islam would be punished with life in prison and any man with execution. 196 parliamentarians supported the bill, seven opposed it. The world's reaction, including the United Nations, to this contravention of myriad international laws has been screamingly silent.

Iran is in fact merely attempting to institutionalize what is already reality in Egypt, Pakistan, Sudan, Saudi Arabia and the Gulf states. Even in areas of the Islamic world such as Palestine and Iraq, where Christianity has traditionally been tolerated, conversion is still seen as socially and morally criminal.

Egypt is a particularly acute and troubling case because of the size of the Christian minority, the horror of their treatment and the systematic and cynical denial by the Egyptian government and their puppets and fellow travelers abroad. There are between eight and ten million Christians in Egypt, around 10% of the population, and for the last 30 years in particular they have faced organized discrimination in the law, education, employment and housing and as a consequence leave Egypt in disproportionately large numbers.

Beyond this now regular, degrading oppression there are numerous cases of grotesque violence. In January 2000, for example, in El-Kosheh, Upper Egypt, 21 Christians were killed in rioting by local Muslims, aided by the police. When authorities eventually reacted, they arrested more than a thousand local Christians, many of whom were tortured. There are numerous cases of Coptic girls being kidnapped by Muslim gangs and then being forcibly converted and married to Muslim men. If they flee these marriages and try to return to Christianity they are killed as apostates.

Church desecration is common, as are public burnings of Bibles and Christian literature. There are also documented cases of Christians being ritually crucified, the rape of Christian girls and the prolonged beating of children, some of them babies. These are not isolated incidents condemned by the state, but part of a reoccurring pattern often ignored and, in some regions, actively encouraged by police and militia. Egyptian apologists will point to certain Christians in positions of influence or, more frequently, argue that these accusations are propaganda lies told by Christians and Jews in North America and Europe.

They are not. Spend time with an Egyptian Christian living in forced exile and the stories and the pain tumble forth as the toxins of dark experience flow from their memory. Or speak to Fr. Zakaria Boutros, if he is allowed to travel and manages to survive the multi-million dollar bounty on his head.

Gaza

SO WE HAD IT AGAIN. THE WORLD PUTTING ON ITS SELF-RIGHTEOUS COAT SO THAT IT COULD HIDE ITS NAKED HYPOCRISY. ISRAEL BAD, VIOLENT AND STRONG, PALESTINIANS GOOD, PEACEFUL AND WEAK. INSTANT DEMONSTRATIONS OUTSIDE ISRAELI EMBASSIES AND CONSULATES WHEN 300 ARE KILLED IN RESPONSE TO YEARS OF HAMAS TERROR, YET NOT EVEN A HANDFUL OF PROTESTORS OUTSIDE OFFICES BELONGING TO SUDAN, SYRIA OR IRAN, WHERE HUNDREDS OF THOUSANDS HAVE BEEN SLAUGHTERED.

Of course the innocent died last week, but in the pursuit of the guilty. As opposed to Hamas and its campaign to mass murder only the innocent. Ask why both Egypt and the Palestinian Authority in the West Bank did so very little to counter Israel's actions and, according to many, may have given tacit or even active approval to the campaign. Because unlike Marxist Mary in Toronto and Jew-hating Jack in Montreal, they know the reality of the situation.

Israel leaves Gaza and prays that peace will be established, even though legions of Israelis predicted it would not happen. Hamas launches its missiles into Israeli schools, homes and hospitals within hours. Supporters of the Palestinians argue that, hey, very few Israelis are being killed so there shouldn't be any complaints. Finally, and after a patience never shown by a European and certainly an Arab nation, Israel responded. One of the reasons it took so long to do so is that it was gathering intelligence so as to harm as few civilians as possible.

So why the lack of balance, the animosity towards Israel and the downright lies in the international media? Any journalist who has worked in Israel and its neighbors in the past twenty years knows certain facts that are seldom if ever reported to the public. Such as, for example, the endearing hotel habits of the PLO. Reporters would stay at an especially grand venue just outside the walls of the Old City of Jerusalem. When they came to pay their bill they would be told that they had been guests of free Palestine but they would be given a receipt anyway, just in case they might want to claim something on their expense account.

Hardly unique or world shattering but fairly typical of the double-dealing that goes on in this part of the world. Until the mid 1970s Israel was a media darling, an embattled and attractive Jewish state struggling for its life as a bulwark of liberal democracy and even socialism. The left liked it, and if the left liked it we can be sure that journalists liked it.

In spite of what pop historians tell us, until the Yom Kippur War of 1973 Israel had by no means been the firmest ally of the United States. Washington ended the Suez war in 1956, much to the chagrin of Israel, by threatening a full-scale attack on British currency. In 1967 Israel flew French warplanes and drove British tanks. And France and Britain are, naturally, so much more sophisticated and worldly than the United States. So, in media terms, for Israel read America and for America read all that is wrong and bad with the world. Anti-Semitism is involved of course but this is a difficult one. Not every critic of Israel is anti-Semitic but every anti-Semite is a critic of Israel.

It doesn't help that western journalists contemptuously refer to Israeli soldiers as, "Shlomo." It means Solomon but is, believe me, spoken with an attempt at derisory generalization rather than admiration for wisdom. Yet in some ways the Israelis deserve it. They are so unutterably dreadful at the propaganda game. One constant is the Jewish perception of death compared to that of so many Arab Muslims. We are inundated with obscenely intimate images of dead Palestinian children in Gaza and people with open wounds and ripped limbs. Israel also has its smashed and shattered but will not allow photographers to play the vulture. Israeli officials keep journalists away from their dead and dying, Arab officials tend to lead them, often literally, by the hand to the killing fields.

Never was this more acute than with the case of Samir Kuntar, the Hezbullah "militant" on top of Hassan Nasrallah's "must free" list of Israeli prisoners. In 1979 he and his gang broke into the home of the Haran family in northern Israel. They took Danny Haran and his four-year-old son Anat to the beach and bashed the little boy's brains out on the rocks while his father watched. They then shot the man to death. Smadar Haran, the mother, hid in a loft with the couple's two-year-old daughter. But in holding her mouth over terrified little Yael's mouth in an attempt to save her, Smadar tragically smothered her daughter to death.

No photos were given to the press and this incident is never mentioned when prisoner exchange deals are discussed. This monster is now a celebrated guest of the Lebanese government and revered throughout Gaza as a hero of the resistance. This will not be explained as we are told by journalists based in the Middle East how Israel refuses to compromise. When reading and listening to them, however, remember that hardly any of them, and in particular the BBC, have yet to apologize for describing the battle of Jenin in 2002 as "an unprecedented Israeli massacre". It was widely implied, even stated, that there were several hundreds if not thousands of dead Palestinian civilians.

It was soon revealed that only 56 Palestinians had been killed, most of them heavily armed. Israel had lost 23 soldiers, mainly because they had cleared the town house by house rather than by bombardment in an attempt to save innocent Palestinian lives.

Something similar occurred just in Gaza. The numbers are seldom reliable and it is staggering how quickly dead Hamas soldiers and policemen are stripped of their uniforms and transformed into social workers and poets. Detailed analyses of European media in particular from the past seven days have shown that Israeli spokespeople were given a fraction of time given to Palestinian representatives. And in countries such as Spain and Britain the contempt for the Israeli position was almost palpable. I saw the cynicism of the Arab combatants and the fellow traveling credulity of western reporters first-hand during the Hezbollah war in 2006 when the same bodies would appear again and again in different poses in different photos.

The nuances of journalistic language say a great deal. Reporters referred last week to "American made" helicopters and F16s. Actually the modifications made to these machines by the Israelis are enormous, but surely their place of origin is largely irrelevant. The same reporters do not refer to "Israeli made" tanks, as the Merkavas certainly are, or to the "Israeli made" machine guns, pistols and assault rifles. It is yet another way of making Israel appear the bully.

It isn't. It's an imperfect and besieged nation that was recreated as a Jewish homeland 60 years ago because the very countries now condemning it for its self-defence refused for 1 500 years to treat Jews as human beings. Just six months ago I stood yards from where Israel is now trying to smash the Hamas military machine and asked an Israeli doctor who had been forcibly removed from Gaza be her own government if she was bitter. "No, no, no" she replied. "Not bitter, only resigned. To the fact that the fashion of turning on the Jews and judging them with a unique unfairness and hatred seems to come around every generation or so. Israel will have to return to Gaza, next time with the hand of peace firmly closed." Then she walked away to attend the funeral of a young mother killed by a Hamas terror attack. No journalists bothered to turn up.

MC

Rachel Corrie

North Americans who call themselves peacemakers are extraordinarily fashionable these days. The fact that they seldom actually make and keep any peace appears to be largely irrelevant. Such was and is the case with Rachel Corrie, a 23-year-old American woman who went to the Gaza Strip to show solidarity with the Palestinians and to oppose the Israeli bulldozer.

Quite literally to oppose the Israeli bulldozer. In 2003 She was crushed to death when she stood in front of one as it attempted to destroy the home of a Palestinian doctor, beneath which were tunnels used to smuggle guns and arms to Palestinian militants. Her supporters claim that this was a deliberate murder. Others argue that the driver had no way of seeing her and that, while an accident, the tragedy was caused by Corrie's own irresponsibility.

Thus this angry and arguably somewhat unstable and troubled young woman became a martyr and a cause. Corrie the living and dying icon of selfless devotion to social justice and the personification of sacrifice for an oppressed people. And nobody does icons of social justice and sacrifice for oppressed people better than, well, actors.

A play entitled *My Name is Rachel Corrie*, based on the unfortunate girl's diaries and writings, was created by Katherine Viner from Britain's *Guardian* newspaper and Alan Rickman. Yes, the man from *Harry Potter* and *Robin Hood*. He of frighteningly extended vowel sounds and inexorable thespian malice. Hagiographical and free of context or balance, the play ran in London, England to generally positive reviews and full audiences.

Very few critics wondered why there was no mention, for example, that partly because of Corrie's obstruction of the Israeli army, guns were indeed smuggled to terrorists who then murdered Israeli children in the southern town of Sderot.

Or of the meeting that took place between her allegedly "peaceful" organization and British suicide bombers Omar Khan Sharif and Assif Muhammad. But then nuance does not tell as good a story as reliable old black and white, and good guys and bad Jews.

The play was supposed to open at the off-Broadway New York Theatre Workshop earlier this month but the theatre then announced that the play would not appear. "In our pre-production planning and our talking around and listening in our communities in New York, what we heard was that after Ariel Sharon's illness and the election of Hamas, we had a very edgy situation", explained James Nicola, the theatre's artistic director. "We found that our plan to present a work of art would be seen as us taking a stand in a political conflict, that we didn't want to make."

Which seems abundantly reasonable. The Corrie play is by no means a neutral drama based in Israel/Palestine but a clumsy and tendentious statement in favour of one side over another. But that, naturally, is not how the theatre's decision has been greeted.

"This is censorship born out of fear", opined Alan Rickman, no doubt elongating the word "fear" in that marvelous way he has. Others friends of the play and of Rachel's memory went much further. This was "Zionist pressure winning the day again" said one. "New York's Jews have destroyed free speech", said another.

There is, however, absolutely no evidence that the theatre was pressurized to abandon the play; but ample evidence that activists assumed this to be the case. Which is in itself deeply significant and revealing. They evinced a belief that Jews have the power to close plays and the will to impose censorship. This being the same New York Jewish community that is renowned for its liberalism and for its criticism of Israel and, in particular, the occupation of the West Bank and formerly of Gaza.

More support and money is given by Jewish people in New York to radical Israeli peacenik groups and organizations offering radically liberal solutions to the Israel/Palestine issue than any other city in the world. The *New York Times* is hardly a bastion of right wing Zionism and movies such as *Munich* come from a certain Stephen Spielberg.

While there is no doubt that various Jewish groups, just as various Arab or Christian or Gay or any other group, try to influence the public discourse only someone blinded by anti-Semitism would believe that the community was as monolithic as it was apparently powerful. Outside of the addled minds of conspiracy theorists the world simply does not work like this. Which is why some of the most stridently anti-Zionist literature and drama emanates from Israel itself and is created by Jews as well as Palestinians.

The controversy over the play's cancellation has actually played into the hands of Rachel Corrie's supporters. If it had proceeded as planned it would have been seen by the usual people and ignored by the usual people – the vast majority. Now Rachel is a cause and a controversy once again. Which is, surely, precisely what she would have wanted.

~MC~

Persecuting Chapters

IT WAS A SCENE EERILY REMINISCENT OF GERMANY IN THE 1930S. PROTESTORS OUTSIDE A JEWISH-OWNED STORE WARNING ANYONE ATTEMPTING TO ENTER AND SPEND THEIR MONEY THAT THE PREMISES WERE OWNED BY A CERTAIN TYPE OF PERSON. SEVENTY YEARS AGO THE HYSTERICAL ZEALOTS WERE SA THUGS IN BROWN UNIFORMS AND THEY HAD NO QUALMS ABOUT SCREAMING, "JEWS, JEWS!" ON SATURDAY THE BOYCOTTERS OUTSIDE SEVERAL BRANCHES OF CHAPTERS-INDIGO BOOKSTORES WERE OVERWHELMINGLY OF THE FAR LEFT AND REFERRED TO "ZIONISTS, ZIONISTS! BUT THE MESSAGE WAS THE SAME. DON'T BUY HERE. THESE PEOPLE ARE ...

Actually these people are Heather Reisman and Gerry Schwartz, who may well be Canada's most high profile Jewish couple. They also dare to support the *Heseg* (Achievement) Foundation, which gives scholarships to lone Israeli soldiers. In other words, men and women who have lost their families or whose relatives live elsewhere are given financial help and grants to help them attend university. The money does not purchase arms and has no military purpose. It is purely humanitarian and often goes to the least privileged.

In fact, several beneficiaries have become leaders in the field of social services, conducting aid to Israeli Arabs and Palestinians as well as Israeli Jewish people in need. But facts should never get in the way of a protest. Which is not only daft but extraordinarily lazy, because only a few minutes walk away from various Chapters-Indigo stores are embassies and businesses owned by Arab states directly supporting all sorts of lovely policies. Genocide in Darfur in Western Sudan. The arrest and torture of homosexuals, Christians and labour and feminist leaders. The routine persecution and killing of Palestinians.

Does one detect the stink of anti-Semitism in the double standard? Not at all, respond the organizers of the flaccid boycott. There were, they argue, Jews on the picket line. Which is true. A few. Just as there were blacks that supported the South African apartheid government.

To highlight a tiny, massively unrepresentative minority within a targeted ethnic group is not only fraudulent but, at heart, acutely racist.

Ironically, if the comrades did enter a Chapters-Indigo they would see a large number of books by some of the harshest critics of Israel, with Jimmy Carter's ill-informed anti-Zionist polemic on a major display stand. It's worth noting that there are very few bookstores in the Arab world that stock volumes supporting Israel. For that matter, there are legions of such shops throughout the Arab, Persian and wider Muslim world that sell books alleging Jews drink the blood of Gentile babies and that the Holocaust is a myth. No boycotts there, however.

Indeed the only time the Chapters-Indigo chain did take a political stance was when it refused to sell the edition of *The Western Standard* magazine that ran the famous Danish cartoons of Mohammad. Those that implied the founder of Islam may have been a man of violence and so outraged his peace-loving followers that they shot an elderly nun in the back, fire-bombed a few churches and promised in demonstrations throughout the world to behead anyone who opposed their religion.

The decision was made, presumably with the support of the terrible Zionist owners now being attacked, because the cartoons in question were considered to be offensive to Muslims. Obviously they were. But that means that Muslims rather than cartoons should change. Whatever the merits of the case, it shows Reisman and Schwartz to be extremely sensitive to Islamic sensibilities. None of this appears to matter.

As ultimately risible as Saturday's spasm of Marxist angst may have been, the international attempt by an unholy alliance of Islamic militants, leftist extremists and pure anti-Semites to boycott the Jewish state should not be ignored. In Britain both the National Union of Journalists and the University and College Union have recently passed boycott motions.

Both cases illustrate the crass illogicality and sheer hypocrisy of the boycott kings. British journalists behaved thus even though a

BBC reporter is still a kidnap victim of Gaza Palestinians. They also know full well that while there is an energetically free press in Israel there is enormous state censorship in most Arab countries, including Palestine.

British academics passed their motion while a group of Arab students who attend Israeli universities, supported by Palestinian professors, lobbied the union conference and told delegates that Israel is one of the few places in the Middle East where they have complete intellectual freedom and that there are huge numbers of Arabs at Israel's places of further education. They were, naturally, ignored.

So none of this is rational or fair. But rationality and fairness do not always win the day. The book on the ugly boycott campaign is still wide open or, to put it another way, the last chapter, is yet to be written. Think clearly and, well, spend wisely.

MC

Starbucks Madness

WORKERS OF THE WORLD UNITE, YOU HAVE NOTHING TO LOSE BUT YOUR LATTE WITH WHIPPED CREAM. OR SO LEFT-WING AND ANTI-ISRAEL INTERNET SITES HAVE BEEN EXPLAINING IN BRITAIN, WHERE HYSTERICAL OPPOSITION TO THE JEWISH STATE HAS BECOME A NATIONAL FASHION. SINCE THE BEGINNING OF THE WAR AGAINST HAMAS IN GAZA, VARIOUS ARAB, MUSLIM AND SOCIALIST BLOGS HAVE BECOME OBSESSED WITH THE IDEA THAT STARBUCKS IS SPONSORING THE ISRAEL DEFENCE FORCES, WHICH EXPLAINS WHY ONE OF THEIR STORES WAS SMASHED AND LOOTED DURING AN ANTI-ISRAEL DEMONSTRATION LAST WEEKEND IN LONDON. "STARBUCKS AND MCDONALD'S ARE DONATING THEIR NEXT TWO WEEKS OF EARNED REVENUE TO THE ISRAELI MILITARY. PLEASE BOYCOTT THEM AND FORWARD THIS MESSAGE TO EVERYONE YOU KNOW" WAS A TYPICAL HEADLINE.

The Hamas-supporting thugs who exhibited their commitment to the Palestinian cause by stealing fair trade coffee and travel mugs a few days ago may not have represented the entire demonstration, but nobody in the 50,000 strong crowd seemed to object when one official speaker screamed, "You say you know about the Zionist lobby, but you put money in their pockets every time you're buying their coffee." So, buy a coffee and an Arab child dies. Or buy a coffee and forty camera operators ask a Hamas official to find them a bleeding child to film.

This whole nonsensical campaign is highly illustrative of the current propaganda campaign against Israel and the irksome mingling of anti-Semitism with Islamic and leftist politics. The Starbucks Israel connection is a hoax, originating in an alleged letter from Starbucks CEO Howard Schultz claiming that it was essential to give Israel more money because the country needs to, "pay for all of the weaponry, bulldozers and security fenced." The letter was then repeated in the Egyptian press and found its way into anti-Zionist folklore.

Thing is, it was not written by Schultz at all but by an Australian-German "anti-Zionist" zealot. And here lies the essence of all this. A known fanatic writes a letter and it is accepted by an unquestioning mob. Not because its victim manages a coffee chain, grew up poor in a New York housing project or has won awards for his work helping people with AIDS but because – here we have it – he is Jewish. He is indeed a friend of Israel but then so, we are told, are all those people who criticize it at the moment because they want, "peace for both sides."

None of this should come as any surprise in Britain, where at an anti-Israeli protest earlier this week a man dressed in a mask with a hideously large nose and bulbous eyes – described as a "Jew mask" – stood in front of the Israeli embassy and graphically pretended to eat a baby doll while pretend blood splashed from its plastic body. Not one of the labour union activists, church peaceniks or Marxist egalitarians around him tried to intervene. Jews eat children it seems, just as Jews own coffee shops. Later the same day an attempt was made to firebomb a London synagogue and an armed gang ran down the streets of a suburb with a large Jewish population looking, according to the police, "to beat up people who appeared to be Jewish."

Only a fool would believe that this has anything to do with a moderate and reasoned opposition to Israeli policies, just as only a fool would believe that Hamas is committed to human rights and co-existence and never makes up casualty figures or fabricates evidence. Then again, there are plenty of fools around. Perhaps they need a caffeine fix. They certainly won't be getting it from the Zionist running dogs at Starbucks!

MC

The Pope and the Jews

I SUPPOSE THERE IS SOMETHING FITTING ABOUT THE POPE COMING TO TORONTO JUST A FEW DAYS AFTER A JEWISH MAN WAS MURDERED IN THE CITY FOR, ACCORDING TO SOME PEOPLE, THE SIN OF, WELL, BEING JEWISH. IT IS THE SORT OF CRIME THAT JOHN PAUL HAS SEEN BEFORE IN HIS NATIVE POLAND. WHICH IS ONE OF THE REASONS WHY HE HAS TRANSFORMED THE RELATIONSHIP BETWEEN ROMAN CATHOLICS AND JEWS. IF ANY NON-JEWISH WORLD LEADER HAS SHOWN A GENUINE SENSITIVITY TOWARDS THE JEWISH PEOPLE, IT IS HE.

Not that the Catholic Church had a universally bleak record towards the Jews before this pontiff. John XXIII brought his church out into the light, including in its relationship with the Jews. Other Catholic leaders risked all to save Jews in times of crisis and had a profound love and understanding for their cousins in faith.

It was just that whenever the church reached for the sky in this area, one foot always seemed to stay firmly rooted in the mud.

What Karol Wojtyla possesses in abundance is not so much sympathy, but empathy. Important this. Other Pontiffs of the last fifty years have sympathised with the Jewish people, to varying degrees, and have tried to redress the balance and put right the wrongs. But most had a somewhat cold and clinical understanding.

This man is different. When he sat in the central synagogue in Rome and hid not the tears that bisected his ruddy cheeks as the names of the Jewish slaughtered were read aloud, then the Jewish people knew that this was not an obscure relative who was trying, but a brother who was doing. "The crime which has become known as the *Shoah*", he wrote, "remains an indelible stain on the history of the century."

The Pope's Polish essence is vital here. True, Poland has long had more than its fair share of anti-Semites. But it also had almost four million Jews. Legions of Poles did not imbibe racism – witness the enormous number of Polish names listed amongst the Righteous Gentiles at Israel's Holocaust Memorial, *Yad Vashem*.

John Paul is very much of that tradition. For him the Jews were an integral part of Polish life. His life. Close friends were Jewish. They were there in 1939, and then they were not. In his years as a priest, an academic and a bishop he refined and defined his views on the Jews. Not only did he know them as his friends, but along with many post-Holocaust Christians he came to rediscover the Jewishness of Jesus and the fact that *Yeshua*, Jesus, cannot be understood unless we understand the Hebrew Bible.

Added to this is John Paul's close bond with Jean-Marie Lustiger, the French Cardinal who was born Jewish and whose Polish family died in the Holocaust. It was John Paul who elevated Lustiger to the most important position in the Catholic Church in France, a country that still wears its anti-semitism on its finely tailored sleeve. Indeed, one French bishop observed, "it is sad that we do not have a Cardinal who is truly French."

Nor was this the first, or last, time John Paul would face criticism. No serious observer doubts that the entire Catholic Church has undergone a revolution in its relationship with the Jews. But not all is fresh and sweet. Many in the Vatican civil service and diplomatic corps are renowned for their, shall we say, ambivalent attitude towards Jews and Israel, and there are some in Rome who simply do not understand their leader's love of the Jewish people

One of the largest Catholic newspapers in the United States, *The Wanderer*, seems sourly obsessed with Jewish people and issues, its regular columnist Joseph Sobran referring to his fetish week after week. Closer to home we have had the occasional Canadian Catholic magazine or journalist making painfully crass comments.

Yet these are on the far right and represent the death-throws of a sad and frightened past. John Paul's orthodoxy is less conservative than atavistic, and he appears indifferent to the medievalism that characterises some of his supporters. His friendly visit to Israel, for example, and his even-handedness on the Middle East would have been impossible a generation ago

"It must be understood that Jews, who for 2000 years were dispersed among the nations of the world, had decided to return to the land of their ancestors. This is their right ... The act of establishing diplomatic relations with Israel is simply an international affirmation of this relationship." Pretty significant stuff.

There is, of course, work to be done in this tangled garden. But few have planted as many roses, and killed as many weeds, as the man from Poland. Here oh Israel, the Lord our God, the Lord is one. Karol Wojtyla hears and loves that prayer.

~MC~

Life & Sexuality

Contraception

IN THE MIDDLE OF FEBRUARY MORE THAN TWENTY MEN AND ONE WOMAN WERE ARRESTED IN ONTARIO ON CHARGES OF MANUFACTURING AND SELLING CHILD PORNOGRAPHY. THE POLICE REVEALED THAT THERE WERE MORE THAN 200,000 INTERNET ADDRESSES IN CANADA THAT ACTIVELY DOWNLOAD THE MOST HORRENDOUS SCENES OF CHILD SEXUAL ABUSE AND THAT THE PROBLEM APPEARED TO BE GROWING. GIVING TALK RADIO WARRIORS AND COMPLACENT MEDIA PUNDITS MYRIAD OPPORTUNITIES TO REVEAL HOW OFFENDED, OUTRAGED AND DISGUSTED THEY WERE.

No, no, no! You don't get away with it that easily. Anyone can weep for a child when they are molested by a dribbling pervert. But unless you grasp that paedophilia is merely part of a greater problem and as much a symptom as it is a cause, you will never fully comprehend what child abuse is all about.

We claim to love children but we destroy childhood. Last year in Portland Maine, for example, a middle school made the contraceptive pill available to girls as young as 11. More than this, the school decided that the children's parents would not be asked for their permission and would not even be informed.

The ostensible reason given by social workers and teachers was that there had been 17 pregnancies in the city's three middle schools in the past four years. The authorities were extremely vague about the ages of the girls involved and gave very few details.

If it's true it's extremely disturbing. And if it's true the solution is to stop the girls having sex, not to make it easier for the others to join in. Otherwise it's like assuming that by ignoring the poor we'll prevent poverty. The boys involved should be charged, the parents of the girls investigated and, perhaps, the abused children taken into care.

Because abuse is illegal and it is certainly abuse. Children are not supposed to be having sex, any more than they are supposed to be taking cocaine, driving cars or shooting people. But when it comes to physically and emotionally immature girls having intercourse the lines of what is right and wrong become strangely blurred.

They shouldn't be, because it's quite obvious. Premature sexual activity causes profound and sometimes irreversible damage, it rapes a child of innocence and purity and often has dreadful physical repercussions. We've become convinced that the pill is a force for good. Not so. Even using the very word "pill" is one of the most outrageous misnomers in the modern lexicon. Pills make us better. The contraceptive pill doesn't do anything of the kind but stops the body from doing what it is supposed to do and denies human life.

There is also increasing evidence of the physical harm done to women who use the contraceptive pill on a long-term basis. The mystery is why we would have ever thought otherwise. Chemical intervention alters the natural course and has consequences and side effects. On an ideological level, the pill was supposed to liberate women and give them control over their bodies. Instead it has empowered irresponsible men who can insist on sexual intercourse because, after all, "if you love me you will and anyway you can't get pregnant."

Which takes us back to the truly horrific child pornography case. None of this is at all surprising. Little girls have been dressing like hookers, and boys like pimps, for years. The free market cares not a dot about morality if it can make a profit and its usual opponents, the left, seem obsessed with promoting sexual anarchy and abolishing absolutes.

There is a concerted campaign to sexualise children and as a result, the obscenity of paedophilia has been partly legitimised. The North American Man Boy Love Association (NAMBLA) has marched in some Gay Pride parades and explained its opinions in certain homosexual newspapers. Arguments for what is euphemistically referred to as "inter-generational sex" are now making their way into the mainstream. One such advocate is a journalist published regularly in some of Canada's leading magazines and has been nominated for national magazine awards.

It is in the interest of people who believe in a sexual revolution not only to smash the barriers that inhibit their own sexuality but to shatter barriers that limit any sexuality. When one door opens, all doors open. Beyond the sexual, there is also a concerted campaign to marginalize the established family, encourage universal and communal childcare and increase the rights of the child and thus weaken the authority of the parent.

So in a way it is horribly predictable that children should now become victims of pornography and direct sexual abuse. It's not, of course, that every zealot and every relativist is a child-pornographer. But fellow travellers are what they are. They make it easier for the genuinely evil and the genuinely dark to commit their crimes. Be outraged about the obvious but also be angry at what has been done to our children and our families for the past forty years.

Morgentaler

IT WOULD BE OBSCENE TO CALL IT AN ANNIVERSARY. THAT WORD IS INDELIBLY LINKED WITH CELEBRATION, JOY AND THE MARKING OF AN ACHIEVEMENT. IT IS TWENTY YEARS SINCE THE COURTS BOWED TO HENRY MORGANTALER AND HIS FOLLOWERS AND INTRODUCED THE UNIVERSAL RIGHT TO ABORTION IN CANADA, MAKING THIS COUNTRY UNIQUE IN THE DEMOCRATIC WORLD IN HAVING NO LAWS WHATSOEVER TO PROTECT THE LIFE OF AN UNBORN CHILD AT ANY TIME DURING PREGNANCY.

The decision was based more on current legal opinion and political fashion than it was on moral law, Canadian precedent or a meaningful consideration of the arguments. Although the seven judges gave four different opinions, they agreed that any restriction of abortion was a violation of the Canadian Charter of Rights and Freedoms. And as we know, there is no freedom business like Charter freedom business.

In those two decades almost 2 million babies have been killed in what is supposed to be humanity's safest place, the womb. It has also cost more than one billion public dollars, in that the taxpayer is obliged to finance this elective surgery. In that same period numerous necessary medical procedures have been de-funded by governments that would not dream of removing a penny from state funded abortion, no matter how wealthy the woman who demanded the procedure.

The last twenty years have also seen a curious twisting of the debate around the issue and a monumentally successful campaign to marginalize pro-life opinion. Politicians are told that to even discuss the policy would lose them votes – though polls repeatedly show Canadians as being divided on the subject – and opponents of abortion, whatever their views on other issues, are portrayed as wide-eyed zealots.

The discussion itself, of course, is seldom heard. In the past week alone yet another university student union, this time Lakehead in

Thunder Bay, Ontario has effectively banned a pro-life association and a city council in the same province has removed all pro-life literature from its property, even though the space was legally purchased. It is the love that dare not speak its name. The genuine love that dare not speak its name. The love for children, from their earliest and most vulnerable.

The reasons for the pro-life position are many and obvious. The unborn child is unique from the point of conception, with its own DNA and a genomic character that is entirely separate from any other person. A woman has the choice to do whatever she wants with a tuft of hair or an appendix but not with a distinct person within her. The unborn child cannot survive outside of the womb but then a fully developed newborn child will similarly die if left without care.

The word "fetus" merely means "young child" and, anyway, after three months of growth nothing new develops. At nine months the unborn child is more mature, but then a five-year-old is more mature than a two-year-old. We know instinctively that this is a child, witnessed by how we would react if we saw an obviously pregnant woman smoking or drinking. We've been programmed to think differently if we see a pregnant women opting to end the life of her powerless child.

The reasons for abortion have been explained myriad times – particularly through television drama, where there is no journalistic obligation reason to even pretend balance. More abortion doctors have been killed on episodes of Law and Order than have ever been killed in real life!

Most of these arguments are entirely spurious. Abortion in the case of rape and incest? These tragedies provide less than a fraction of one percent of the reasons for abortion and they are mentioned by abortion advocates simply to make pro-lifers appear extreme. We should ask if those who support abortion in those rare cases would oppose it when rape and incest are not the causes of pregnancy. It would, of course, be a rhetorical question.

Before the Morgentaler decision, enormous numbers of women died in back street abortions. This is mostly propaganda. Of course such horrors occurred but there are no reliable figures and informed sources dismiss most of these claims as nonsense. We do, however, know just how many babies now die in front street abortions.

Only women have a right to comment on this issue. Men are fathers, men are taxpayers, men are citizens. Men are also abortionists. But surely it is the nature and quality of the argument rather than the gender of the individual that should inform our position. Gender bias does, however, lead to far more baby girls being aborted than baby boys. Rather a bitter paradox for feminist ideology.

At the very least we should agree that after twenty bloody years the debate must be resurrected, for the sake of freedom if nothing else. Even, yes, for those who proclaim the love that dare not speak its name.

MC

Killing the Different

EARLIER THIS YEAR IN BRITAIN, JOANNA JEPSON WAS FEATURED ON A CHANNEL 4 TELEVISION SHOW ABOUT CHRISTIAN CONVERSION. THE REASON SHE WAS CHOSEN IS THAT SHE IS FAMOUS. NOT BECAUSE SHE IS A CURATE IN THE CHURCH OF ENGLAND OR BECAUSE SHE IS ATTRACTIVE AND STYLISH BUT BECAUSE IN 2001 SHE FOUGHT FOR THE RIGHTS OF A SLAUGHTERED BABY.

Joanna Jepson was 27-years-old at the time and had particular empathy with disability and deformity because she had been born with a facial defect that required corrective surgery. It was that fact, amongst others, that made her so very angry in the particular case of a child aborted in the sixth month of pregnancy because it had a cleft palate.

The parents decided that they really couldn't cope with the now very common and relatively minor surgery to repair the palate of their child and instead asked obliging doctors to get rid of it. The doctors did. Out it came, cleft palate and all, and into the hospital garbage, along with the rotten organs and the bodily waste. Six months. Meaning it was a fully developed baby, could have survived outside of the womb, was perfect in every other way. How a parent, how a mother or a father, could have requested such a thing is beyond most of us.

Beyond Ms. Jepson too. She felt not only a moral stab on hearing of this but a sense of solidarity with another powerless human being who happened to have a cosmetic deformity. Because Joanna's mum and dad, if callous, could have decided to have had a hit job done on her as well whilst she was still safe in her mother's womb.

The law in Britain is vague on abortion but usually prevents the procedure from taking place after 24 weeks. Anything later than that is very rare, and would usually have to involve danger to the life of the mother. Not a cleft palate to the child.

So Joanna went to the police and the lower courts, who told her to get lost. After all, there were parking tickets to hand out and human rights complaints with which to deal. But this young woman, a feminist who had battled for recognition in church and society, refused to listen. She persevered and finally the High Court in Britain agreed with her arguments and ordered the police to investigate.

The authorities considered the evidence and concluded in 2005 that the doctors had acted "in good faith" and would not face charges. In the past ten years in Britain more than 30 unborn babies with cleft palates have been aborted, three of them after 24 weeks. So Joanna Jepson lost the battle but becomes another of the decorated soldiers in the war that continues.

As soon as she began her campaign the British pro-abortion movement launched a counter attack but even though they won the legal argument they rather gave themselves away and alienated entire chunks of the previously supportive or indifferent British population. One of the reasons being that abortion had always been argued from the standpoint of female liberation and autonomy.

Hard to do that boast when a fully formed, healthy and beautiful child is killed due to a cleft palate. The abortion was considered justifiable as this minor facial problem was classified as a "serious handicap". That is simply a lie. No debate, no argument. A lie. Liar, liar, government grant on fire. Because this case involved lots of taxpayers' money and an entire industry. Just like in good old Canada.

I'd like to think, fool and romantic that I am, that a child with a cleft palate has a right to live. But then I'm an extremist. I'd like to think that children with Down syndrome have a right to live, and that none of us measure up to some artificial notion of perfection. But then I believe in equality, which is something the abortion lobby seems to have abandoned rather a long time ago.

Not Joanna Jepson, though. She knows the pain and knows the truth. She continues to work for unborn children and people continue to listen. But, frankly, she'll probably continue to lose for some time to come. But ultimately not. For all of us, ultimately not.

MC

Killing the Innocent

ROBERT LATIMER, THE SASKATCHEWAN FARMER WHO KILLED HIS DISABLED DAUGHTER, IS TO BE RELEASED ON DAY PAROLE. THE DECISION COMES FROM THE APPEAL DIVISION OF THE NATIONAL PAROLE BOARD AND IS A DIRECT REVERSAL OF THE REGIONAL BOARD'S RULING OF LATE LAST YEAR. LATIMER WAS CONVICTED IN 1993 OF KILLING HIS DAUGHTER TRACY, WHO SUFFERED FROM CEREBRAL PALSY. ALTHOUGH HE ARGUED THAT HIS ACT WAS A "MERCY KILLING" HE WAS CONVICTED OF MURDER AND BEGAN HIS SENTENCE IN 2001.

One of the central reasons why Latimer's parole was originally declined was because he refused to acknowledge that he did anything wrong. He killed his daughter, he argued, out of love. He was putting the girl out of her misery. Perhaps a more candid explanation was that he was putting her out of his.

Tracey Latimer was profoundly ill. But she attended school and, according to the crown presentation during her father's trial, "enjoyed outings, one of which was to the circus, where she smiled when the horses went by. She also responded to visits by her family, smiling and looking happy to see them. The pain she suffered was not unremitting, and her life had value and quality."

In fact, almost all physical pain is controllable. The emotional pain of a parent less so. And when Robert Latimer killed Tracy shortly before her thirteenth birthday he was doubtless in agony. Problem is, personal suffering does not give one the right or privilege to take away the life of another human being. Nor do Latimer's actions indicate even subjective morality. Initially he denied killing Tracy, lying that she had died in her sleep. It was only after an autopsy revealed high levels of carbon dioxide in her blood that he admitted to putting her into his truck and connecting a hose from the exhaust. He also confessed to having considered, "shooting her in the head."

Yet if Robert Latimer had been honest from the beginning, he is still a murderer. A father who placed his able-bodied daughter in a car and choked her to death would provoke unanimous outrage. Because Tracy was disabled, and thus particularly vulnerable, we are ambivalent about the crime and even aggressively sympathetic to the criminal.

The disabled have the same rights as anybody else and Canada boasts notions of equality, derived from universal human concepts, that are supposed to form and define the very fabric of our culture. No person, whether they be parent or stranger, has the moral authority to take innocent life.

There are numerous extraordinary families who care for people just like Tracy Latimer. If her father could not cope – and none of us should judge him for that – he had the option of allowing others to cope for him. At no time did Tracy seek death. She was, however, different. She did not conform to the expectations and demands of normality and others decided that there was insufficient quality in and to her life. But life is either sacred or it is not. If it is, preserve it at all costs. If it is not, we might as well destroy it at will. It is terribly expensive to keep the sick alive and wholly impractical to prolong the life of an ill person who will die anyway.

Teague Johnson wrote the following during the Latimer trial. "I am 11 years old and have really severe cerebral palsy. I feel very strongly that all children are valuable and deserve to live full and complete lives. I had to fight to live when I was very sick. The doctors said I wouldn't live long, but I knew I had so much to accomplish still. I had to fight pain all the time. When I was little, life was pain. I couldn't remember no pain. My foster mom helped me to learn to manage and control my pain. Now my life is so full of joy.

"There isn't enough time in the day for me to learn and experience all I wish to. I have a family and many friends who love me. I have a world of knowledge to discover. I have so much to give. I can't walk or talk or feed myself but I do not need to be 'put out of my misery'. My body is not my enemy. It is that which allows me to cuddle my mom. Life is a gift. My life is going to be astounding." It was. Teague died, naturally, in the summer of 1995.

Not Tracy Latimer. Now her father, who still believes that he is not a criminal, has been given parole. The world today is a little less secure and a little more frightening than it was yesterday for the disabled and those who love and care for them.

MC

Human Dignity

TATIANA AND KRISTA HOGAN-SIMMS APPEAR TO BE ON THE WANTED POSTERS OF EVERY EUTHANASIA ADVOCATE IN CANADA. BECAUSE THE LITTLE GIRLS WERE BORN AS CONJOINED TWINS THERE IS SOME BLOODY, VULGAR RUSH TO ARGUE THAT THEY SHOULD NOT HAVE BEEN ALLOWED TO BE BORN OR, IN SOME CASES, THAT THEY SHOULD NOW BE EXTERMINATED.

Instead of relishing life and praying and hoping that the girls will survive and even be surgically separated, the foot soldiers of the eugenics movement shout for death. But it should not really come as much of a surprise.

The eugenics movement in question became immensely popular in the early 1900s. It was embraced by the socialist left, with famous authors such as Bernard Shaw and H.G. Wells advocating all sorts of extermination policies.

Humanity had to be purified and improved, they argued, and this meant emulating the animal kingdom and removing the weaker of the species. The ideology became intensely racist under Hitler but was at heart no different even from what many Canadian "progressives" were saying at the time.

The list of undesirables included homosexuals, Africans, the "slow and simple" and, according to Wells, the author of *The Time Machine* and *The Invisible Man*, "anybody who doesn't fit into the demands of the modern age."

Which quite clearly these little girls do not. They'll never appear on *American Idol*, never take illegal drugs and be promiscuous, never scream and swear at anybody who challenges them. Never be typical stars of the contemporary mess in which we live. Even worse, they'll be different!

Yet I meet people every day who are not very clever, not very attractive, not very entertaining. They ostensibly contribute very little and may appear to make society less compelling than it could otherwise be. Thing is, according to whom?

It's easy to see that someone like Stephen Hawking expands our knowledge and imagination to an enormous degree but may well have been killed if the social engineers had their way. Yet even if he'd only sat in a chair for his entire life his life would still have possessed an objective quality.

And this surely is the point. Objective quality. If we are subjective and make our own value judgments we might as well wipe out all sorts of people. Or we could simply grow up, develop our compassion and intelligence and realize that existence is a sufficient contribution in itself.

There is an absolute that we have to tackle. Life is either sacred or it is not. If it is, preserve it at all costs. If it is not, we might as well destroy it at will. It is terribly expensive to keep the sick alive and wholly impractical to prolong the life of an ill person who will die anyway.

No civilized person or society, however, considers expense and practicality to be more important than goodness and humanity. If it did, it would immediately wipe out, for example, drug addicts, the homeless and people with AIDS.

Tatiana and Krista will be loved and, important this, will love back. They will smile, laugh, cry, be sad and happy, sometimes frightened, sometimes excited. Just be. Which is quite enough. And God forgive anyone who awards themselves the right to decide who may be and who may not.

MC

The Pope and Africa

THE ATTACKS UPON THE ROMAN CATHOLIC CHURCH IN THE LAST TWO WEEKS FOLLOWING THE POPE'S COMMENTS ABOUT THE DANGERS OF CONDOM USE IN AFRICA IN THE ATTEMPT TO PREVENT AIDS HAVE BEEN AN EXTRAORDINARY LESSON IN APPLIED IGNORANCE AND THE SURVIVAL OF PREJUDICE. TALK-RADIO HOSTS WHO HAVE LONG CALLOUSLY AND NAIVELY BLAMED AFRICANS FOR ALL OF AFRICA'S SUFFERINGS SUDDENLY BECOME CHAMPIONS OF THE CONTINENT. DOCTORS AND ACADEMICS WHO HAVE SHOWN NO PREVIOUS CONCERN FOR THE PLIGHT OF AFRICA INSTANTLY TRANSFORMED INTO EXPERTS AND PARTISANS. IT IS ENOUGH TO MAKE ONE WEEP. THE WEEPING, HOWEVER, SHOULD BE FOR AFRICA RATHER THAN A BUNCH OF ANTI-CATHOLIC HYPOCRITES.

Some context first. AIDS had smashed its way through Africa for almost two generations before many people in Europe or North America had even heard of it. It killed poor black people many miles away and nobody matters less to the wealthy white than poor blacks many miles away. It was only when the disease was brought into the male homosexual community of the United States that the likes of Elizabeth Taylor became so emotional on television and numerous actors, politicians and public figures made it one the most fashionable causes in modern times.

Indeed AIDS is a fascinating case-study in itself in that while politicized statistics and agenda-driven activists try to tell us otherwise, AIDS in the west is still largely a concern for Gay men and intravenous drug-users. Hard to forget the announcement from Canadian health officials that the AIDS rate had doubled in the mainstream community in one particular area. It had. From one person to two. But it is the suffering itself rather than the nature of the sufferer that should motivate us. Problem is, this philosophy was not applied when it was Africans rather than Californians in need.

That, at least, was the attitude of the western elites – the very people now condemning the Roman Catholic Church. Yet it was the Church that was in Africa caring for people with AIDS when

Hollywood and the western media were more concerned with puppies and kittens. Indeed even today almost half of all Africans with AIDS are nursed by people working for the Roman Catholic Church. A Church, by the way, that has also called for all African debt to be forgiven and for a radical redistribution of wealth from north to south.

None of this is mentioned when Pope Benedict is attacked for his condemnation of the condom fetish. If we read the man's statements, however, what we see is a sophisticated deconstruction of western double-standards and a thoughtful critique of the failed attempt to control AIDS.

First, it's not working. In countries where condoms are state-distributed, free and ubiquitous, AIDS has not been controlled and is often spreading. Second, even where AIDS is less an issue, such as in North America, the increased availability and use of condoms has coincided with an annual increase in STDs and so-called unwanted pregnancies. Third, one failure of a condom to work - and the failure rate is significant if not overwhelming - is not a mere mistake but a death sentence. Fourth, condoms enable promiscuity rather than encourage abstinence. And sexual activity is about more than mere intercourse; a cut finger or a small body wound can allow infection to occur.

Fifth, how dare we treat black people as if they were children? They are capable of self-control and all over Africa, most successfully but not exclusively in Uganda, there are elaborate, empathetic and extraordinarily successful abstinence programmes that emphasise humanity rather than lust – a philosophy that runs directly contrary to the sexual gratification cult so favoured by some of the people in the west now so apoplectic at Pope Benedict's comments.

Of course, there is more to this anti-Papal neurosis than television comedians making jokes about celibate clergy and commentators assuming that they know far more about reality than a priest who has worked in an African city slum for forty years. Conventional wisdom has it that Africa has a population problem and that Africans can become "more civilized" if they have fewer children. It's an organised and sometimes quite sinister campaign. Africa is, if anything, under-populated and the problems of the continent are far more about western greed, colonisation, resources exploitation and arms sales than about family size. The Church has spoken out on these issues for decades and was, for example, one of the leading voices at the United Nations that persuaded the multi-national pharmaceuticals to make their anti-AIDS drugs generic and thus affordable in the Third World.

Paradox and lack of understanding rules the day. We applaud an obscenely wealthy American actress when she takes a black baby from Africa but forget that the Hollywood values she epitomizes encourage loveless sex and treating one another as sexual objects rather than distinct individuals – the precise phenomenon that encourages the spread of AIDS. More than this, the solution to children living in poverty in Africa is not to remove the children but to remove the poverty. But there is never a camera crew around for that sort of thing.

It appears these days to be open season on Pope Benedict XVI. In that he leads an organisation that is supposed to be a mirror held up to the world to reflect society's failures and absurdities, the man must be doing a great deal right.

MC

Urban Fun

NEW YORK, NEW YORK, SO GOOD THEY NAMED IT TWICE. THEY ONLY NAMED GENITAL HERPES ONCE, HOWEVER, WHICH IS PROBABLY QUITE A RELIEF FOR THE INHABITANTS OF THE BIG APPLE. OR SHOULD WE SAY THE BIG SEXUALLY TRANSMITTED DISEASE. BECAUSE LAST WEEK IT WAS REVEALED THAT A STAGGERING ONE IN FOUR ADULTS IN NEW YORK HAS THE VIRUS THAT CAUSES GENITAL HERPES, WITH THE RATE CLIMBING TO A COLOSSAL ONE IN TWO FOR AFRICAN-AMERICANS.

Far more women carry the virus than men. 36% percent for the latter and 19% the former. This makes New York the national capital for good old Genital Herpes, something which will surely grace the state's license plates in years to come.

Predictably enough, the city bureaucrat responsible for monitoring all this, Julia Schillinger, opined that, "Using condoms consistently will help you avoid getting or spreading the virus." No, you silly woman!

Not having sexual intercourse with people you hardly know will prevent you getting the virus, not acting like a deranged animal in heat will prevent you getting the virus, having sex only in a loving marriage with your spouse will prevent you getting the virus. A sexually fulfilled and responsible marriage will also, so the surveys show, make you live longer and have a far happier life.

But woe unto us if we tell anybody to keep their private parts private until they meet their life partner. That would involve the limitation of personal choice and freedom. Goodness, it might even offend someone. Better to let them contract a degrading sexual disease or, worse, one that will shrivel them up and kill them.

The whole point about condoms and contraceptives is that they have not liberated anybody but merely empowered and enabled promiscuity. Latex instead of love and instant if soulless and unsatisfying gratification rather than lifelong commitment and pleasure.

Which leads us to the extraordinary success of the movie *Sex and the City*, involving four women in, yes, New York as they smilingly do what they do and, if the figures are accurate, help do their bit in maintaining their home town's place as the Genital Herpes centre of the United States of America.

Not sure if it's a constitutional right or not but it may be in the Bill of Rights. Hey, it must be in Canada's Charter of Rights and Freedoms. How beguiling, though, that while legions of gigglers throw *Sex and the City* parties and while mainstream media revels in the film's success and the lifestyle it champions, we should discover that every third woman one meets in New York is a carrier.

Perhaps it's just me, but that seems more sordid than sexy, more sad than sensuous, more pathetic than pulsating. Strong and independent women defined as such by how many men they are willing to please, and then lying to their friends about how much fun it was for them too. No seriously. Really. No lie. It was fun. No regrets.

There used to be a word for such women. Now there are two words. Genital Herpes. Hard to imagine anybody wanting their daughter to live and act in such a way but as long as Hollywood, the most dysfunctional community in the world, dictates and defines our morality we can look forward to a brave new world where we're all so amazingly, incredibly happy. No, really.

MC

Integrity

IT IS OFTEN TRUE THAT THOSE WHO SHOUT THE LOUDEST ABOUT FREEDOM OF EXPRESSION DO NOT IN FACT BELIEVE IN FREEDOM AT ALL. THEY SUPPORT THE LIBERTY OF PEOPLE WHO THINK AND ACT LIKE THEMSELVES. UPHOLDING THE RIGHTS OF THOSE WITH WHOM THEY DISAGREE DOES NOT SEEM TO COME INTO THEIR INTELLECTUAL PURVIEW. I HAVE SEEN THIS TIME AND TIME AGAIN.

There are exceptions of course, and some genuine civil libertarians out there. But what passes for tolerance is too frequently a case of tolerating those who agree with you. It certainly seems to be the case with American media mogul John Rigas.

76-year-old Rigas is the founder and owner of Adelphia Communications Corporation, the sixth largest cable company in the United States. Adelphia is worth more than $7 billion and includes a telephone company, a small fleet of jets and the Buffalo Sabres.

Rigas recently decided to remove all sexually explicit content from the television stations he had acquired as his cable company expanded into Los Angeles. Simply, anything pornographic would no longer be shown to his 5.6 million customers. There would still be plenty of fairly loose stuff available – standard offering on prime time television – but the obviously prurient material would no longer be available.

One would have thought that this decision would cause little fuss. The masturbation lobby has, forgive me, other things on its hands. And if people want depictions of men and women doing in public what they should only be doing in private, there are a plethora of satellite companies and video stores available.

Not, surely, an issue of free speech. Wrong. Peter Eliasberg, a staff lawyer with the American Civil Liberties Union, declared that, "What Adelphia is doing is illegal." Not contrary to this man's personal opinion, you notice, but actually against the law.

Susan Block, a sexologist whose show was one of those cancelled by Adelphia, stated that, "This old-fashioned moralist from small-town Pennsylvania is trying to dictate programming to open-minded Angelenos and is flouting the rules of public access."

High-ranking executives from the Playboy company visited Adelphia and tried to change policy. No deal, and Rigas says that he has received thousands of letters from all over North American from people who support his position and applaud him for it.

The case is ongoing and it may well be that Adelphia is eventually forced to carry sexually explicit material. Adult movies, as they are called. Pretty ironic, in that the very last thing you can say about porn stars is that they behave like mature, intelligent adults.

But let's look at Ms. Block the sexologist and her opinion. She condemns her foe as an old-fashioned moralist. Do morals, then, change with the times and are there such things as old morals and new morals? Not at all. Different people hold social power and impose their views on others but morals are constant. The defining nature of morality is precisely that is does not change. It is not suddenly right to kill, to steal, lie.

Nor is it suddenly acceptable to reduce sexual love and intimacy into a moneymaking escapade involving the exchange of bodily fluids, put on by the unscrupulous for the exploitation of the needy.

That John Rigas comes from a small town or a big town is irrelevant. Urban population size is hardly a measure for ethical judgement. If it were otherwise, every New Yorker would be deliriously happy. You see, morality is supposed to set us free. It is not an end in itself, but a means to providing a good and righteous life.

Which leads me to ask where are all the happy hookers, the laughing and contented porn stars, the fulfilled porn addicts or, bless my soul, the sexologists with a sense of humour and humility.

Perhaps Rigas is trying to dictate his views. Fine, let's admit it. But this is in no way different from those so-called advocates of civil liberties who have been dictating their views for years now. The only difference is that John Rigas is not trying to stop the pornographers from having their platform. As some have said for so long now, if you don't like it you don't have to watch.

MC

Brave New World

IT HAD TO HAPPEN OF COURSE. AN ASSAULT ON THE LAST TABOO. NEW YORK AUTHOR JUDITH LEVINE HAS WRITTEN A BOOK CALLED *HARMFUL TO MINORS: THE PERILS OF PROTECTING CHILDREN FROM SEX*. IN THE VOLUME SHE WRITES THAT CHILDREN ARE SEXUAL CREATURES AND THAT IN DENYING THIS WE ARE IN FACT HURTING THEM. BRIEFLY, KIDS SHOULD BE HAVING SEX.

"What is a child, sex, consent, pleasure?" asks Levine. Pretty simple questions actually. She goes on to rather predictably attack what she calls the "moral right" who, "boil down very rich, complicated cultural and historical and personal questions to some sort of slogans." Interesting. Someone who dismisses billions of people with an empty political catch phrase, accusing her opponents of using slogans.

Actually Levine almost gets to the truth in spite of herself. Not moral right, but moral and right. Right as opposed to wrong, that is. Because protecting children from adult manipulation is not the preserve of left or right, but the duty of anyone who understands and appreciates childhood.

The author claims that the issue of consent is blurred. Sorry, you're wrong. A clear mind sees clearly. No child can give consent to sex, because no child can give consent to something that is intrinsically adult. The reason is that children, whilst possessing a genuine wisdom and insight in some areas, are still developing morally and intellectually. The exact cause of children falling victim to pedophiles in the first place is that unscrupulous people can deceive and manipulate children, but cannot do so with adults.

Because there can be no genuine consent between a child and an adult, sex with a minor has to be rape. So are we to say that the ethics of rape are suddenly blurred, and will we argue that the victim of rape has sexual feelings and so does the rapist? Would author Levine propose, then, that rape is a valid form of sexual expression and that the raped woman simply has to come to terms with her deeper sexuality?

As to children having the origins of a sexual nature, this is a self-evident truth. Just as little boys have the origins of a beard. But until they grow to adulthood these characteristics, both physical and internal, are potential and not active. A five-year-old boy will grow to be a fine, balanced and sexual being – as long as his parents don't believe Judith Levine. But to pretend to be so at five would be ugly, unnatural and enormously dangerous.

Just as if that same five-year-old walked into the room with a full beard and moustache. We would shudder, and then pity the wretch and wonder who had used diabolical science on him to so horribly damage and twist his little life.

Look, children can fight, but because of this we do not conclude that they should be allowed to take us arms, wear a uniform and shoot and be shot at by the enemy. In fact we have always condemned as barbaric any nation that allows children to be treated in such a manner. Precisely because they are children.

Kids can also drink alcohol. Some do. And become alcoholics who are generally dead long before their time. The person who gives them their first glass is rightly regarded as an abuser. So much greater the abuse when sex is involved.

One of the fascinating aspects of all this is that the liberal academics and radical feminists who are currently championing Levine seem to think that they are sexually liberated, whilst we who oppose them are sexually constipated and missing something. Odd thing is, we're the ones with the large families, the laughing children, the obviously fruitful and enjoyable sex lives. Levine and her people seem so, well, so unhappy.

She describes herself as a member of the "feminist guerilla theatre group known as No More Nice Girls" and as – the cliches get worse – "living with her partner and their cat." Perhaps if the guerilla and her companion lived with children instead of an animal they might get it. Hey, I'm a generous guy. I'm more than willing to let her know how to love life, love a husband, love kids, love childhood. As for the cat – I wonder if it's been neutered?

MC

Pornography

IT WAS THAT OLD FRAUD TRUDEAU WHO TOLD US THAT THE STATE SHOULD KEEP OUT OF THE NATION'S BEDROOMS AND THEN MADE SEXUALITY, MARRIAGE AND PROCREATION SOME OF THE MOST POLITICAL PHENOMENA OF MODERN CANADA. BUT OH WHAT FUN IT IS TO FINALLY REALIZE WHAT HE REALLY MEANT BY THE CLICHÉ. THE STATE SHOULD KEEP OUT OF BEDROOMS BECAUSE THE BEST SEX IS TO BE HAD ON STATE APPROVED TELEVISION.

This is the only reasonable explanation of the recent decision by the CRTC, the state's broadcast police, to allow Canadian TV pornography channel Northern Peaks to broadcast throughout the country. It's the only way, we are told, to guarantee home-grown content in the industry. Debbie will no longer do Dallas but Dundas. And Brandon, Kitchener, Perth, Red Deer and everywhere else in Canada.

It's odd that entertainment aimed at people with extraordinarily immature attitudes towards sex should be described as adult. Pornography is many things, but it is never adult. And the true obscenity is less the simulated or actual exchange of bodily fluids than the fact that Canadians died in North Africa, Dieppe and Normandy for freedoms that we have transformed into moral anarchy.

Canadian content rules demand that at least half of the young women obliged to debase themselves as sex objects and pieces of meat in front of the camera for silly and desperate men will be home-grown. We have not been told who will be monitoring this or how they will recognise naked Canucks. Perhaps a brief reference to socialised medicine or a passing argument in favour of Human Rights Commissions in between moans will suffice.

Which bring us to a magazine that has never promoted female degradation or loveless and exploitative sex but has found itself not praised but punished by another branch of the government's media control bureaucracy. *Catholic Insight* magazine has overwhelmingly Canadian content and caters to millions of seriously Catholic Canadian men and women.

Being seriously Catholic, however, it analyses the issues of the day from a seriously Catholic standpoint. Meaning that those who oppose or are indifferent to serious Catholicism might not be interested. The solution is simple. Don't read it.

But in the nation that encourages nationalist porn, matters are never quite that simple. A Gay activist decided that he didn't like some of the publication's references to homosexuality, assembled everything said about the issue by Catholic Insight for some years and sent them to a Human Rights Commission.

The complaint was rejected by the commission but the magazine was forced to pay several thousand dollars in legal defence fees. The initial rejection has now been appealed so the process, irrespective of the result, will continue to financially punish the magazine.

It has also now been revealed that each issue of the monthly publication will be reviewed by Heritage Canada and if any content is found to be "offensive" it will lose its government funding for postage cost distribution. The amount is not large but is virtually guaranteed to every Canadian magazine as a means of helping local journalism.

So at the same time as a group of porn merchants receive government blessing to make a profit on lust and loneliness an internationally respected journal is threatened because of its Christian teaching on love and sexuality. X-rated lunacy, with more Canadian content than anyone thought possible.

Censorship

A WORRYING TREND HAS DEVELOPED IN CANADA AND IT THREATENS THE VERY BASIS OF FREE SPEECH. CERTAIN PEOPLE NO LONGER SAY "I DISAGREE WITH YOU", BUT "YOU SHOULDN'T BE ALLOWED TO SAY THAT." IT OCCURS IN ALL AREAS, BUT NEVER SO OFTEN AS WHEN HOMOSEXUALITY IS DISCUSSED.

The latest example concerns a stylish and timely book entitled *Divorcing Marriage*. Published by McGill-Queen's University Press, it consists of a series of essays by various scholars and lawyers on the subject of homosexual union, children's rights and related issues. It is edited by Daniel Cere and Douglas Farrow.

Unlike some of writing on both sides of the argument, this is well-documented and highly intelligent stuff from some first-class minds. It is, in fact, just the sort of offering all thinking people should welcome in such a vital and sensitive debate.

Although the premise of the book is that there are inherent dangers in this social experiment, one of the essayists is himself Gay. Another is Margaret Somerville, one of the leading bio-ethicists not just in North America but in the entire world. Philosophy rather than polemic, analysis rather than anger.

The book has supporting comments on its cover from extraordinarily impressive intellectuals. David Novak, Professor of Jewish Studies at the University of Toronto. Mary Ann Glendon, Professor of Law at Harvard. Jean Bethke Elshtain, Professor of Social and Political Ethics, University of Chicago. Janet Ajzenstat, Professor Emeritus, Political Science, McMaster University.

But not according to the student newspaper at McGill University, *The McGill Daily*. "Every now and then, for reasons hard to decipher, the press churns out a text so reactionary you can't believe it was published by educated people."

There's fine writing for you. Then again how would I know? I'm probably not an educated person. The screaming editorial then suddenly realises that it can decipher the reasons why the book was published. And they are all about conservative conspiracy and really nasty people who, one assumes, torture kittens in their spare time.

The book was rushed through, the piece decides, in order to challenge the Supreme Court on the issue of homosexual marriage and, yes, to sell books and make money. My goodness, what swine! Actually the book has been in the works for a long time and it is only fitting that it should be published when its subject is popular.

In one small editorial about a book on marriage, the McGill writers manage to mention not only Hitler but also racism and western populism. Oh, and "right-wing". Twice. Then comes a classic. They also object to the book because "the cover is ugly." Right, yes, see what you mean. After all, I would absolutely adore Kafka and Tolstoy if only their covers weren't so awfully dull.

In all seriousness, this is nothing less than an attempt to censor contrary opinion. What the article does not mention are the threats, sometimes to their lives and families, received by some academics who oppose homosexual marriage and the concerted campaigns to boycott their lectures and even have them fired.

It is worth considering the wider context. There is a veritable flow of books, articles and news shows about the merits of homosexual marriage. Those who oppose the phenomenon tend to be marginalised and often silenced, particularly in our universities.

Within the Canadian academic world it is, quite simply, unwise to oppose any contemporary liberal icons, and none is more iconic that homosexual marriage. "Our university press, especially when it comes to sensitive social issues, should pursue a higher objective: publish only good books" says *The McGill Daily*.

But this is a good book, as witnessed by people who know a little more than student journalists on a college rag. Good or bad, however, has nothing to do with it. It's about right or wrong, politically acceptable or politically incorrect, in the eyes on an increasingly intolerant wave of opponents of free speech.

There is one sure way to defeat those out there who would control what you read and what you think. Buy this book. It will make you a revolutionary comrade in the struggle for a free and open Canada where all rights are cherished and respected. Golly, there's stylish journalism for you. Perhaps I'll get a job at *The McGill Daily*.

TV lunacy

I CAN'T PRETEND TO BE A REGULAR VIEW OF THE TELEVISION SHOW *KINK*. THE ONLY EPISODE I EVER MANAGED TO CATCH FEATURED A JOLLY 350LB WOMAN SQUEEZED INTO A LATEX SKIRT AND BRA BEATING A SIMILARLY OBESE, IF LESS JOLLY, MAN WITH A PADDLE. ENTERTAINING ENOUGH I SUPPOSE BUT A LITTLE REPETITIVE.

I mention this because the programme in question is one of those that currently enjoy a tax credit. In other words, it receives public funding from you and me. It is one of many Canadian television and movie documentaries and dramas that receive public funding and one of several dozen that seem obsessed with perversion, sadomasochism and large people in latex.

There are also some quality products that are given a tax credit but the point about the government's proposed C-10 legislation is that it doesn't threaten anything that's any good. Only cheap trash watched by a handful of people who should really fund their pornography through their own pocket.

None of this, by the way, has anything to do with censorship. That is when the state forbids free speech and expression. Not when the state refuses to fund all speech and expression. But this didn't stop various Canadian actors led by permanently and professionally lugubrious Sarah Polley visiting Ottawa where they explained that the mere "whiff of censorship" was enough to revolt them.

Really? They should, then, be campaigning for magazines such as *Maclean's* and *Catholic Insight*, websites like Free Dominion and Five Feet of Fury and a whole bunch of journalists who are currently under attack by numerous federal and provincial Human Rights Commissions for indulging in genuine freedom of speech without any fatties in latex or government hand-outs.

But we all know that this has never been about defending freedom but all about the chattering classes defending the right of people with whom they agree to exploit our absurdly generous public grants system. Otherwise we would have to ask where Ms. Polley and her comrades were when Rush Limbaugh and Dr. Laura were removed from Canadian airwaves and why all those famous actors didn't support Pat Robertson and Jerry Falwell when there was a concerted campaign to censor them in Canada.

They obviously didn't support these people's view. Fine. But the glorious essence of free speech is that it's supposed to apply to everybody and in particular to those who drive you crazy. I have no time for most of the anti-intellectual, tendentious perversion and bad acting that passes for entertainment in this country but I'm not about to ban it. Nor, however, should I have to subsidise it.

Authentic censorship is a problem in Canada but its champions are not Tories who want to cut taxes but leftist students who ban university pro-life clubs, bureaucrats who persecute editors for publishing cartoons depicting Mohammad and arts councils who for years have only funded projects that fulfil their own Marxist and left-liberal perception of what is acceptable.

It always fascinates me how the first people to cry censorship when conservatives merely suggest a level playing field are just the sort of people who write letters to newspapers calling for people like, well, like me to be fired. By the way, one movie that was given a grand tax-credit by Ottawa was called *The Masturbators*. Abuse yourself or abuse public money – the same thing in the end.

MC

Best Kept Secret

THE PEOPLE OF GUELPH LIKE TO CALL THEIR CITY "ONTARIO'S BEST KEPT SECRET." BY THAT THEY MEAN THAT THEIR HOMETOWN IS SURPRISINGLY PICTURESQUE AND PLEASANT. YES IT IS. BUT DIG A LITTLE DEEPER AND THERE IS ANOTHER LITTLE SURPRISE. FOR THE PAST TWO DECADES GUELPH HAS HOSTED THE ANNUAL CONFERENCE AND TRAINING INSTITUTE ON SEXUALITY, WHERE TEACHERS AND LECTURERS GO TO LEARN HOW TO EDUCATE YOU AND YOUR CHILDREN ABOUT SEX. THIS YEAR'S JAMBOREE RUNS FOR TEN DAYS, BEGINNING JUNE 12TH.

And what a stew it is. Large helpings of perversion, ample chunks of homosexuality and cross-dressing, spices of transsexual nonsense and chunks of indoctrination. All stirred with oodles of public money.

The tone is set by a one day workshop on "Sexual Education in the Classroom", explaining how to teach sexuality to kids. Sounds relatively harmless. But what sort of sexuality? The following day we meet Marshal McLernon, "a 26 year old mid-transitional transsexual man" who is "an activist, trainer/educator, writer/poet and a graphic designer by nature."

He is joined by Rupert Raj, who "is a man and a male – transsexual and bisexual, identifying more as a gay man right now and has been living as a man for close to 30 years. Rupert came out in the queer community in 1971 and was hormonally and surgically reassigned the following year, from female to male." Oh, I see.

If these gentlemen/ladies are not to your taste you could drop in on "Getting together: How and why bisexual women form communities." I would have thought the answer was obvious really. To apply for government grants, share each other's journey and have buddy hugs.

Then there are workshops on "The Joy of Cybersex", "HIV and Lesbian, Gay and Bisexual Youth" and "Awakening your sexual self: A women's workshop series on orgasm and sexual fulfillment." As for the last one, how many conferences does it take before these silly people have mastered the obvious. If you haven't "awoken" yourself yet then buy a bloody alarm clock.

June 20th sees a seemingly useful discussion of "Teachers' Perspectives on Sexual Health Education", but followed the next morning by 'The women's bathhouse experience", where the session "will bring together a group of women who organised attended The Pussy Palace, Toronto's first women's bathhouse."

The final day of the conference should be a joy to behold. "Tribes of Adornment: Piercing, tattooing and other forms of body art." The sessions also explores "scarification and branding" and is led by someone from the "Toronto Raver Information Project." Nice to hear that an "ice cream farewell" will follow. Flavours? Don't ask!

The theme is clear. There are no sessions on normal, healthy sexuality, no affirmation of, God help us, kids who might want to date teenagers of the opposite gender, enjoy themselves, get married when they grow up, have kids. There is no support offered for teenagers who might actually want to remain celibate until marriage. Nothing, in fact, for anyone who is not into body piercing, homosexuality, dressing up in someone else' clothes or running around like chickens with their heads cut off.

Individual teachers are given financial support to attend the conference and many of them have the entire fee, and it's $325 plus expenses for the full conference, paid by schools and school boards. The conference itself is held and partly financed by the University of Guelph, which means from your tax-dollars.

I find it difficult, genuinely difficult, to understand how at a time when student fees are being increased and schools are unable to buy books for their children, neurotics anonymous can gather together to gaze at their own navels (and pierce them) with so much of the cost being paid for by poor, boring old people like us.

This attempt to normalise the abnormal and give an intellectual veneer to the anti-intellectual is bound to fail. But what is so very dangerous is that this conference is supposed to give teachers an education in how to shape and mould the young. Sure it will cost us financially. More important, however, it will cost us morally. Young people desire protection, not demand promiscuity. The organisers of this circus might be forgiven for wasting our cash, they might not be let off for wasting our kids.

MC

Sex and Sensibility

OH FOR THE GIFT OF HINDSIGHT. ONE DAY PEOPLE WILL LOOK BACK TO THE EARLY YEARS OF THE 21ST-CENTURY IN CANADA AND WONDER WHY THE DESIRES OF A SMALL NUMBER OF PEOPLE WITHIN, PERHAPS, 3% OF THE POPULATION SHOULD RECEIVE SO MUCH PUBLICITY AND BE ACTED UPON WITH SUCH ALACRITY BY POLITICIANS AND JUDGES. I REFER OF COURSE TO GAY MARRIAGE.

Numerous legislatures have voted on this issue is recent years and all, including those governed by the NDP, have rejected it. Which is why activists went to the courts and compliant judges read in sexual orientation into a charter of rights that was never intended to include it. So those of us who were opposed to the idea called for a vote. But a free one.

Which is certainly not what will happen when the government prepares a bill on the subject in the extraordinarily short time of two weeks. The Prime Minister has made it clear that he expects his cabinet to vote for the bill. They and their parliamentary secretaries give the proposed legislation an immediate 70 odd votes. Hardly free.

But the issue goes beyond mere politics to the deeper moral and logical issue of what should and should not be. It has to be stated immediately that if there is any hatred in your heart, you have no right to comment on this issue. But if there is love in you, you have a responsibility to do so. I also have to bemoan the fact that the government could not be so enthusiastic and prompt about issues such as, for example, child poverty, third world exploitation and the arms trade. Just a thought.

Marriage is a religious institution. It was designed and devised by faith groups, particularly of the Judeo-Christian kind, several thousand years ago. The argument that it is entirely an economic concept invented in early medieval Europe is nothing more than the tendentious fantasy of radical historians who have not done their homework.

That Gay people will live together, love together and spend productive and generous lives together is axiomatic. Only a zealot would argue otherwise. They should be, and are, protected by legislation that guarantees them employment, housing, benefit and opportunity equality. If abused, they have protection. If insulted, they have recourse. Thank goodness for that.

But when an ancient and, important this, holy, institution is labeled "unconstitutional" by a court and its meaning exploded, we have to take a stand. I have heard people argue that it is of no concern to heterosexuals and will not effect them. Please! As a white man I was not directly harmed by Apartheid, but I still realized the absolute wrong of a philosophy and thus opposed it. It lessened me as a person.

If marriage is suddenly fundamentally altered to include people of the same gender, it loses its genuine meaning to the rest of us. We may include in the cat family the earthworm. Does this make worms feline? Of course not. But it destroys the definition of cat.

Marriage was and can only be the union of a man and a woman. The state intervened some time ago but the origin, and I would argue the essence, of marriage is still rooted in faith. And do not, please, tell me about the vital separation of church and state. Our entire legal code, our entire grasp of right and wrong, is based on Judeo-Christian principles. Let us go further. The very notion that there is such a thing as right and wrong is taken and inspired by Judeo-Christianity. Why not steal or kill if we can get away with it, unless there is a deeper imperative directing our conscience.

It has also become fashionable to deride what has been termed the "slippery slope" approach. In brief, what comes next? But this is a poignant and powerful stance. If we genuinely believe that a man can marry a man and a woman a woman, how can we possibly prevent a man from having more than one wife? Especially as many Muslims believe this to be acceptable. They would have legal precedent as well as freedom of religion on their side.

Incest? Supporters of Gay marriage claim that it is illegal, so there is no argument. Won't do. Homosexuality was illegal not that long ago. The central argument behind Gay marriage is that the only criteria is love. I have no doubt that Gay people can be in love. But then so can a brother and a sister. It may be convenient to say that this will never happen, but it is neither logical nor morally consistent.

Care, compassion, respect all round on this one. But also common sense and thought. One more thing. They used to say the world was flat, and those who disagreed were even arrested. Did it make the world flat?

MC

Same Sex Marriage

WHAT MAKES THE NATIONAL MISTAKE OF LEGALIZING SAME-SEX MARRIAGE UNIQUE IN CANADIAN HISTORY IS THAT TO EVEN DISCUSS THE ISSUE IS CONSIDERED BY MANY, PARTICULARLY OUR ELITES, TO BE AT THE VERY LEAST IN EXTRAORDINARILY BAD TASTE. ALTHOUGH THIS IS A VALID AND VITAL DEBATE ABOUT SOCIAL POLICY, ANYONE CRITIQUING THE STATUS QUO IS LIKELY TO BE MARGINALIZED AS HATEFUL, EXTREME OR SIMPLY MAD. SOCIAL CONSERVATIVES AREN'T JUST WRONG, THEY'RE EVIL.

The discussion, we are told, is over. Which is what triumphalist bullies have said for centuries after they win a battle. In this case the intention is to marginalize anyone who dares to still speak out. In other words, to silence them.

It's important to emphasize that this is not really about homosexuality at all and has nothing to do with homosexual people living together. Opponents of same-sex marriage may have ethical and religious objections to homosexuality but they are irrelevant to the central argument. Which is not about the rights of a sexual minority but the status and meaning of marriage.

Indeed the deconstruction of marriage began not with the Gay community asking for the right to marry but with the heterosexual world rejecting it. The term "common-law marriage" said it all. Marriage is many things but it is never common. Yet with this semantic and legal revolution, desire and convenience replaced commitment and dedication. The qualifications, so to speak, were lowered.

And one does indeed have to qualify for marriage; just as one has, for example, to qualify for a pension or a military medal. People who have not reached the age of retirement don't qualify for a pension, people who don't serve in the armed forces don't qualify for a military medal. It's not a question of equality but requirement. A human right is intrinsic, a social institution is not.

The four great and historic qualifications have always been number, gender, age and blood. Two people, male and female, over a certain age and not closely related. Mainstream and responsible societies have sometimes changed the age of maturity but incest has always been condemned and, by its nature, died out because of retardation. As for polygamy, it's making something of a comeback – and here begin the objections.

Whenever this is mentioned by critics of same-sex marriage we are accused of using the slippery slope argument. Sorry, some slopes are slippery. Polygamy is an ancient tradition within Islam – and was in Sephardic Judaism and some Asian cultures – and when the precedent of Gay marriage is combined with the freedom of religion defence, the courts will have a difficult time rejecting it.

At the moment the Muslim community is not sufficiently politically comfortable to pursue the issue and the clearly deranged polygamous sects on the aesthetic as well as geographical fringes of Canadian society obscure any reasonable debate. But the argument will certainly come and the result is largely inevitable. If love is the only criterion for marriage who are we to judge the love between a man and his wives?

The state, though, has a duty to judge and to do so based on its own interests. The most significant of which is its continued existence, meaning that we have to produce children. As procreation is the likely if not essential result of marriage between a man and a woman it is in the interests of the state to encourage marriage.

Of course lesbian couples can have an obliging friend assist them in having a baby, and Gay men can adopt or have an obliging friend have one for them, but this is hardly the norm and hardly going to guarantee the longevity of a stable society. Just as significant, it smashes the fundamental concept of a child being produced through an act of love. The donation of bodily fluid by an anonymous person, or that obliging friend again, is an act not of love but of lust, indifference, profit or a mere, well, helping hand!

For the first time not only in Canadian but in world history we are purposefully creating and legitimizing families where there will be either no male or no female role model and parent. Anyone who speaks of uncles, aunts, communities and villages raising children has no real understanding of family life. Single-parent families exist and are sometimes excellent and, obviously, not every mother/father family is a success. But to consciously create unbalanced families where children can never enjoy the profound difference between man and woman, mother and father, is dangerous social engineering.

We made a terrible mistake and may not appreciate the full consequences for a generation. We allowed emotion to obscure logic and belittled anyone who appeared out of step with the current fashion. To marry without good reason in regrettable, to divorce good reasoning from public policy is a disgrace.

MC

Books And Authors

Francis Bacon

HOSTAGE TO FORTUNE
Lisa Jardine and Alan Stewart
Hill and Wang, 637pp

THERE IS SOMETHING BOTH DELICIOUS AND COMPELLING ABOUT DECLINE. THE DECAY OF GRANDEUR, THE MELTING AWAY OF GLORY, THE ACHING ABSENCE OF SUCCESS. IF ANY MONARCH EPITOMISED THE SHINING TRIUMPH OF THE ENGLISH WAY IT WAS ELIZABETH, THE FIRST OF THAT NAME. THIS WAS PURE ANGLO-SAXON GENIUS, NOT THE CONTRIVED ACHIEVEMENTS OF LATER CENTURIES. PIRATES AND PRINCES, ANARCHISTS AND GOVERNORS, POETS AND KILLERS. THE SECOND HALF OF THE SIXTEENTH-CENTURY WAS ENGLAND'S ERA. SHE KICKED AWAY AT MIGHTY SPAIN WITH THE PROTESTANT WORLD CHEERING AND EVEN HALF THE CATHOLIC GLOBE ADMIRING THE LITTLE COUNTRY'S CRAZED TENACITY. DRAKE AND RALEIGH, SHAKESPEARE AND MARLOWE.

There is an anecdote that symbolises the quintessence of the age. One of the Virgin queen's greatest sailors is outnumbered five to one by the Spaniards. He sinks three of the enemy's ships but is finally captured. He is mortally injured but the men of Spain still move away from him as he comes on board their craft. They are as frightened as they are respectful. He sits, pours a glass of wine down his throat and then proceeds to eat the glass and laugh at his foe and his predicament. The escapade is turned into a poem back in London, and it glows like a Tudor turquoise.

Francis Bacon has cried out for a thorough and up-to-date biography for thirty years now and in this work he has it. He was born in 1561, and was thus a young man in his prime when the Spanish Armada was defeated, when the London theatres were at their busiest and the Elizabethan Renaissance was splashing over Europe. As the son of the queen's Lord Keeper he witnessed the major events of the day and met Elizabeth herself. But Bacon was of that second generation of Elizabethans, those who stood on the shoulders of the men who had really stared at greatness.

The queen died in 1603 and was succeeded by a dribbling pederast from Edinburgh, James VI of Scotland, the first of England. This was the man who fondled his young boys in court, the king who had Sir Walter Raleigh executed. The year before Bacon died James' son Charles came to the throne. He was to lose his throne and his head to the Puritans under Oliver Cromwell.

Thus, decline. The scene was set for anyone with an eye and a mind. Bacon had one of the finest eyes and perhaps the best mind of his generation. Trained as a lawyer, he entered Parliament in his early twenties and was soon involved with the power blocs at court. He was given generous support by the Earl of Essex, but later played a key role in the trial and execution of the man for treason. Elizabeth never completely trusted Bacon, partly because of his homosexuality, and although he was one of the two or three most powerful men in England by the end of her reign, it was under James that he became first attorney general and then Lord Chancellor.

As a politician he was sly and cold but as a judge he was incisive and deeply clever. He rulings and decisions laid a foundation for constitutional and, to a lesser extent, civil law in England and, by extension, Canada. As the authors demonstrate, his legal abilities could have been the result of his not actually liking people very much, leaving him free to judge with a genuine objectivity.

He was also a scientist, whose theory of scientific classification and work on differentiating between the natural and supernatural world was ahead of its time. And he wrote. Oh how he wrote. His essays, History of Henry VIII and De Sapientia Veterum are astounding even for an age that normalised the brilliant.

He also dabbled in the occult, took drugs, used stolen bodies for medical research and perhaps collaborated with Shakespeare on some works and is one of the candidates put forward by those people obsessed with the idea that Shakespeare didn't write Shakespeare. Bacon didn't write the works of Shakespeare, and even if he did, a movie called *Bacon In Love* would have been dreadful for a whole host of reasons!

What Jardine and Stewart have done is to provide a contemporary analysis of an historic man. Here was a soul trying to make a living. "Francis was obliged to make a working career for himself in the law – a career which constantly interfered with his beloved intellectual pursuits ... The ideal scenario, however, would have involved no demands of employment on Francis Bacon's time whatsoever."

Peppered through the book are Bacon's attempts to find easy money as government employee, royal favourite or high-priced lawyer. An individual version of a legal dream-team, but with twice the wit. He took on cases and stabbed friends in the back purely for money. The book shows how his life became a back-stairs existence, partly because of his sexuality and his dabbling in magic, but also because he was simply better than the mediocrities who peopled the court of James I and had to hide from their resentment. He was, we learn, effectively born twenty years too late.

The cause of Bacon's death is disputed but the most likely, and Good God I hope it is the most authentic, version concerns Bacon trying to stuff a dead hen with snow, to see if it would keep. It did, he didn't. He caught a cold and his weak health let him down. By the time of his death he was financially secure but politically outcast.

He was a nearly man for all seasons. His achievements are mainly in the legal, whereas they should have been in the intellectual. Given a good monarch he could also have been a statesman of historical proportions. Yet nobody more embodies the growing darkness, cloudy intrigue and brilliant if empty philosophy of the age like Bacon. He was, then, perhaps the first truly modern man. Here chronicled by the truly first modern biography of him.

MC

Oscar Wilde & Friends

Bosie: A Biography of Lord Alfred Douglas
By Douglas Murray
Hodder & Stoughton, 374 pp

The Unmasking of Oscar Wilde
By Joseph Pearce
Harper Collins, 301 pp

OH HOW WE HAVE LEARNT RECENTLY THE IMPORTANCE OF BEING OSCAR. FESTIVALS, MOVIES, PLAYS AND UNBRIDLED DEVOTION. THE IMPORTANCE, THAT IS, OF BEING OSCAR WILDE. THE AUTHOR OF, AMONGST OTHERS, *LADY WINDERMERE'S FAN* AND *THE PICTURE OF DORIAN GRAY*. THE ACCEPTED LINE IS THAT WILDE WAS A GENTLE GIANT OF THE INTELLECT, AN INSPIRED WIT AND RACONTEUR WHOSE HOMOSEXUALITY LED HIM INTO BATTLE WITH A CALLOUS BRITISH ESTABLISHMENT. THE BAD GUYS WON AND WILDE WENT TO PRISON, WHERE HE WAS BROKEN BEYOND REPAIR.

Not quite so, says British historian and biographer Joseph Pearce in his new biography of the man. Certainly Wilde was the painted butterfly of the late nineteenth-century, but to view him as some sort of political activist is quite ridiculous. In fact Wilde was not really homosexual at all, only frequenting a notorious male brothel after developing venereal disease and being told by his doctor that he could never again have a sexual relationship with his wife.

His affairs were sordid and sad, often with semi-literate boys who "pleasured gentlemen" for cash and betrayed them as soon as they left the building. If there was perhaps one homosexual love in Wilde's life it was with the son of the Marquis of Queensbury, a spoiled aristocrat known as Bosie. Once again, according to Pearce this is not the tale we have been told in recent years.

That politicised image concerned Bosie's brutal father persecuting Wilde and forcing him into incarceration. It is true that Queensbury was capable of baseness, but he was obliged to watch as the fat, 40-

year-old Wilde paraded Bosie, young enough to be his son, around London as a play thing. Not easy for a father to tolerate. More than this, it was Wilde, not Queensbury, who eventually launched a legal battle for libel. It is simply that Queensbury won.

Another aspect of the life usually hidden to the point of exclusion is that after prison Wilde rejected his earlier ways, apologised for them and embraced Roman Catholicism. Rather than some grand icon of decadence he actually became a gentle knight of orthodoxy. "Much of my moral obliquity is due to the fact that my father would not allow me to become a Catholic", he told a journalist. "The artistic side of the Church would have cured my degeneracies."

Pearce has in many ways given us a life of Wilde for the new century. He celebrates the man's undoubted literary gifts but refuses to bow down to the gods of political correctness. Which is entirely appropriate, because the last person who would have done so would have been one Oscar Wilde.

If the great Irishman is deserving of study because of his genius, his young lover and eventual cause of shame, Lord Alfred Douglas, is of interest for entirely different reasons. The nickname Bosie was merely a play on Boysie, a title given to Douglas when he was tiny. There is something strangely appropriate about it.

There have been books about the man in the past, but nothing of the scope and ambition of Douglas Murray's effort. The youth of the author guaranteed the book celebrity status before it was even produced. Douglas Murray is still at university in Britain, and was hard at work on the book whilst still in his teens. So impressed were publishers on both sides of the Atlantic that the industrious Mr. Murray became a very wealthy young man indeed.

And good for him. Because this is a thorough, well-rounded and startlingly readable account of a severely troubled figure. He was an impressive youngster, talented as athlete as well as poet and thought to be the most beautiful man at Oxford University. Opportunities fell at his feet like raindrops from some loving sky. Until he met the storm that was Oscar Wilde.

There is, according to Murray, mutual exploitation in what happened next. Clearly Wilde devoured Bosie's youth and looks and lived vicariously through this bright young thing. Equally Bosie bathed in Wilde's reputation and also used the notoriety of the relationship to ridicule his father. Wilde was old enough to know better, Bosie was young enough to know best.

Contrary to what has been considered true until now, we are told here that Bosie remained loyal to Wilde through trials, prison and subsequent shunning by fashionable society. But what Murray explains so well is that the entire Wilde episode took up only a few years of Bosie's life. Wilde died in 1900, Bosie lived for almost another half-century. In short, what did he do?

Strangely enough he too converted to Roman Catholicism, but not before rejoining literary society and becoming friends with George Bernard Shaw and the massively overrated artists and writers of The Bloomsbury Group. He launched and edited a small circulation magazine, wrote poetry and occupied a place on the periphery of intellectual society. He also followed Wilde in another way, in that he served a period in prison.

The reason was a libeling of Winston Churchill, against whom he had launched a virtual vendetta some years earlier. By 1924 Churchill, in and out of political office, had turned enough cheeks and decided to sue. Bosie was nothing if not irresponsible and his accusations against Churchill of political corruption resulted in a cell and a badly fitting striped suit.

In a way it was indicative of Bosie's life after Wilde. Attempts at fame and success resulting in failure and sometimes in a quite pernicious darkness. He was intensely jealous of those around him and as his age increased and his looks declined he lashed out with an increasing absurdity. He faced other libel cases, fell headlong into a rancid anti-semitism, became almost permanently and sometimes hysterically unhappy.

He died in 1945, largely forgotten and largely deserving of it. "A deeply flawed personality, perhaps," writes Murray. "A quarrelsome snob or bigot, even. Douglas was a highly complex, but in many ways still loveable figure who, against all odds, has found a place in the history of letters and politics."

Murray is actually being somewhat generous. But then he has a right to be. He has glimpsed through that cloud of unknowing to give us a clear view of a paradoxically significant figure of recent history. We ought to be grateful. So should Lord Alfred Douglas.

Gore Vidal

Gore Vidal: A Biography
By Fred Kaplan
Doubleday, 850pp

THE SCENE IS LONDON'S RIVER THAMES, THE PARLIAMENT BUILDINGS JUXTAPOSED WITH DICKENSIAN WAREHOUSES IN THAT QUINTESSENTIALLY BRITISH PRACTICALITY. A PATRICIAN AMERICAN TALKS TO A CAMERA AS HE GIVES HIS THOUGHTS ON THE NOVELIST ANGUS WILSON. "HIS CONTRIBUTION TO THIS COUNTRY WAS GREAT," SAYS THE MAN IN THE EXPENSIVE SUIT. "COMPARE THIS WILSON TO THE PRIME MINISTER, HAROLD WILSON, AND YOU'LL SEE WHO LEFT THE GREATER LEGACY." UNEXPECTEDLY A PASSING BOAT RELEASES A FOGHORN FART. UNFLAPPABLE, OUR HERO THE COMMENTATOR TURNS TO THE LENS AND SAY, SIMPLY, "SORRY HAROLD." SMILES, TURNS AND WALKS AWAY.

Gore Vidal is clever. No serious person would doubt that for a moment. Less clever than he thinks he is. No serious person "should" doubt that for a moment. But the Americans, for all their protestations, still fall headlong for what they see as class and elitism. Witness the triumph of the Kennedy boys. Vidal detests the reality of the United States, and the Americans love him for it. Fred Kaplan positively adores him for it.

The biographer of Thomas Carlyle and Charles Dickens, Kaplan is more comfortable with the nineteenth-century than with times modern, but with Vidal that will do nicely. Although born in 1925, he has cultivated the manners and morals of the Victorian liberal artist. His speech, his writing, his distance from the people all place him in the school of Washington Irving and Henry James rather than in the club of Norman Mailer and Philip Roth.

He grew up in Washington, an emerging witness to the courtship and statecraft of a maturing super-power. His father was a director of Roosevelt's cabinet, his grandfather, Thomas Gore, was Oklahoma's first Senator. Kaplan is meticulous in explaining the influence on Vidal of his grandfather. The old man's intellect and wit moulded his grandson, the patrician surroundings of home smoothed the edges, a succession of boarding schools probably developed an inchoate homosexuality. Kaplan is a product of his age and never deals with Vidal's sexual preference with anything other than slavish approval. Sad but predictable.

After a non-combatant role in World War Two, a career in literature seemed inevitable. Vidal never seriously considered any other occupation, because unlike most American novelists he was never financially needy. A novel based on his wartime experiences, *Williwaw*, appeared in 1946, followed two years later by *The City and the Pillar*, perhaps the first mainstream work of fiction to deal with homosexuality. He was also earning a reputation as a raconteur and a political commentator, assuming the mantle of the philosopher king who spat down barbs from on high.

He could and can be genuinely witty. On Ronald Reagan, "A triumph of the embalmer's art." On corporal punishment, "I'm all for bringing back the birch, but only between consenting adults." On friendship, "Whenever a friend succeeds, a little something in me dies." Amusing, but not profound. More *Cheers* than Chesterton.

There were big and bigger novels, many of them with a historical context. *Burr* and *Lincoln* were sharp and illuminating, *Live from Golgotha* and *Hollywood* less so. But it was *Myra Breckenridge* in 1968, about a man who dies and returns to life as a woman, that established Vidal as the craftsman he most certainly is. Play-offs level for sure, but not quite Stanley Cup. Kaplan disagrees. "He was writing from deeper, more spontaneous sources than had readily been reachable in previous attempts. For the first time he was decisively and totally liberated from the narrow realism from which he had started."

The reviews were generally positive, and the critics gave Vidal the ultimate literary fillip, they said he was anti-establishment. Vidal ran with it, forming friendships with other famous types who were, apparently, foes of the ruling class. The relationships with Paul Newman and Truman Capote are particularly well chronicled, as is the infamous feud with conservative doyen William F. Buckley. What characterized Vidal and his fellow foes of the system is that, ironically, they were establishment from their toes to their ties.

Vidal ran for office, appeared in movies, wrote more books and essays, and then went to live in Italy. What Kaplan fails to grasp, or to admit, is that his subject is so uncomfortable with America as to actually despise it. Probably because he just doesn't understand it.

Nothing revealed this more explicitly than a nasty little piece he wrote about the relationship between Jews and homosexuals entitled *The Pink Triangle and the Yellow Star*, His tone was so vehement and intolerant that if it had come from, say, a conservative author, he may have been ostracized as an anti-Semite. Vidal displayed a grotesque ignorance of the Holocaust and an equal lack of knowledge of his country. He claimed that American Christians hated both Jews and, his term, "Fags" equally, so that the two groups ought to form an alliance.

Vidal should have known that *The New York Review* would never have published such a fatuous work, but his reaction to their refusal merely demonstrated more, shall we say, ambivalence towards his would-be allies. Vidal didn't understand American Christians, American Jews, American blacks and even American homosexuals. But he does understand himself, and rather likes what he knows.

So does Fred Kaplan, a little too much. "American writers want to be not good but great; and so are neither" said Vidal. Kaplan is actually a good biographer, but in spite of massive research and work, he has let hagiography smother his art. He is not great.

MC

Graham Greene

The Life of Graham Greene, Volume Three
By Norman Sherry
Viking Books, 906 pp

It is worth the weight and the wait. Norman Sherry's life of Graham Greene that is. The former, of course, is beyond doubt at more than 2200 pages of prose. As for the latter, no doubts either really. This British academic who now teaches at Trinity University in Texas has delivered a jubilantly intelligent and surely definitive biography that, 27-years in the making, has set the new standard for the genre. Until now it was Michael Holroyd's massive and massively influential multi-volume life of George Bernard Shaw that held the field. Not now. We must wrap ourselves in flags of Greene.

Truth be told, some of us who have a toe-hold in the world of literary biography wondered if the third volume would ever be completed. There was, after all, a hiatus of ten years between the second installment and this conclusion to the trilogy. But Sherry was in no hurry and his reluctance to take advantage of Greene's death in 1991 and rush into publication was obviously justified. Both decorum and the book itself have benefited.

He said at the time, as he has all along, that reflection on what he writes is as important as the writing itself. In other words he revises and edits to a most extraordinary degree. The result is that the book is soaked in detail but paints the picture of the life as well as it tells the story.

Sherry begins that story in this volume with a summary of his first two books. That being the first part of Green's life. His birth in 1904, his years at university and early successes as a writer. Courtship and marriage, service in British Intelligence during The Second World

War, the triumph of *Brighton Rock*, *The Heart of The Matter*, *The Third Man* and, most of all, *The Power and The Glory*.

He then takes us from 1955 through to Greene's death in 1991. This is the era of declining idealism, both for Greene and for the world at large. In the preceding years the man had been stimulated by the toxins of fascism that flowed into the European bloodstream in the 1930s. Then he had something to hate, something against which to struggle. Now there were so many shades of gray. Thus he searched for causes and never quite found one that completely satisfied.

There was Castro's struggle in Cuba, the hellish conflict in the Belgian Congo and the vicarious Cold War battles fought in Nicaragua and Panama. In Haiti there was, yes, the banality of evil. Equally troubling for Green, there was simply banality. We're given here a man who fell easily into depressive melancholia; as easily as a sweaty crease in a tropical suit.

Always there were the books, and they restored his sense of balance. *Our Man In Havana* was published in 1958 but was based on earlier events. In 1973 came The *Honorary Consul*, in 1978 The Human Factor and in 1988 *The Captain and the Enemy*. In between there were, amongst so many others, A Burnt-Out Case, *Travels With My Aunt* and *The Comedians*.

This was the era when Greene became famous, something he genuinely resented. Not because he was a snob but, as Sherry makes clear, because he wasn't interested in the flummery of celebrity. There were other reasons. Greene was a man of the flesh who seldom tried to curb his sexual appetite and promiscuity. But it was his 32-year relationship with Yvonne Cloetta, whom he had met in French Cameroon in 1959, that is most significant.

Their partnership was sexual, but to describe it as a mere "affair" would be to make meager what was profound. Though an act of chronic infidelity, it cannot be denied that Yvonne was muse as well as mistress. There was genuine love and care here and Greene protected her from exposure and judgment until his death. In so doing, of course, he protected himself from the same.

It was, however, a perverse arrangement in many ways and was never the clean and harmless enterprise that Greene somewhat foolishly hoped it to be. Sherry interviewed Yvonne at length for his book and she told him that, "she loved Graham, and when her husband objected, her answer to him was not delicate but direct. If Jacques loved her still (and he did), it must have caused him acute personal pain: 'If you make me choose between you and Graham, it will be Graham'."

Because of such behaviour critics have, understandably, questioned his Catholic faith. Thing is, so did he; but never abandoned it. Norman Sherry proves that what Greene referred to as "a malign virus from which one can never be cured", religion, was fundamental to the man. He increasingly embraced the Sacraments as he grew older and made regular retreats with an order of Cistercian monks.

Greene was a Catholic novelist, not a novelist who flirted with Catholicism. The safety net of his faith enabled him to walk along some ostensibly irreligious but never atheistic tight ropes. He would also play with his public – claiming, paradoxically, a simultaneous decline of belief but increase in faith. In truth the last three decades of his life saw an expansion of both.

He also spins from these pages as a decent man, and not the anti-Semite, pathological liar and political thug depicted in an infamous biography written by literary journalist Michael Sheldon after Greene's death. Sherry calls Sheldon a "literary terrorist" and the biographical world is still awaiting Mr. Sheldon's response.

Not that it matters very much. Greene is too important to be smashed by urban or even urbane myth. The span, and experiences, of his life are so grand as to provide an alternative history not only of the literature of the twentieth century but of the twentieth century itself. Norman Sherry shows him to be a quintessential "great man of letters", who not only described events but partly shaped them as well.

A George Bernard Shaw, a George Orwell, even a paperback Shakespeare. He would have mocked the latter, because he possessed the angelic quality of never taking himself too seriously. Others did and others should. Norman Sherry has, and thank goodness for that.

Of Greene's death in Switzerland at the age of eighty-six, he writes: "Graham never seemed to die of terrible old age, but faded away – beautiful to the beholder. He was on his way to the land of the dead; perhaps just a heartbeat away. Graham Greene's soul had departed, the Old Fox (his description) was gone; the call to the last hunt sounded."

There may be more to say about Graham Greene. But there is not much more. Not much more at all. Again, let us pause, admire and then wrap ourselves in those flags of Greene.

MC

Jean Vanier

Our Life Together. A Memoir in Letters.
By Jean Vanier
Harper Collins, 578pp, $32.95

SECULARISM IN NORTH AMERICA IS CRUELLY DEFENSIVE OF ITS ESTABLISHED BORDERS. FAITH AND ITS FOLLOWERS ARE MARGINALIZED OR WORSE UNLESS RELIGION IS SO DILUTED AND EMASCULATED AS TO CAUSE NO OFFENCE IN A WORLD INCREASINGLY EAGER TO BE OFFENDED BY ALMOST ANYTHING. BUT EVERY SO OFTEN FIGURES OF BITING HOLINESS MANAGE TO FIND A GAP IN THE FENCE OF MATERIALISM, DECADENCE AND INDIFFERENCE. THEY FIGHT THROUGH TO SHOUT THE TRUTH. SUCH A BURGLAR IS JEAN VANIER.

Probably the closest to a genuine memoir from the man that we will ever have, this collection of letters from the founder of the *L'Arche* and Faith and Life communities covers the period between 1964 and 2007. Vanier's father George was an intensely admired Governor-General and the son of a great family could have chosen almost any career he desired. Instead he developed a means to transform the way in which we live with the developmentally disabled and consequently managed to expunge much of the ugliness that characterized the world of the handicapped.

"A true spiritual family, a network of friendships and fraternity completely oriented towards the poor of our society, towards helping the physically and mentally handicapped" he wrote. Inclusion would replace exclusion, and the *L'Arche* ideal would spread worldwide. This was the Gospel lived to the consummate. He began by inviting two men from an institution to live with him and from this step of personal love sprang a leap of international compassion. The able-bodied would live in community with those who would otherwise be locked away, thrown away. There are now 130 *L'Arche* communities in 30 countries.

By his works rather than his letters should we know him. In other words, the man's humility prevents him from explaining in these messages to friends and supporters just what he actually does. And what he does is not only to love the most humiliated but also to bathe them, put them on the toilet, clean their filth. Clean their filth precisely because the filth of selfishness and rejection has so infected the mainstream world. Yet if he is reluctant to write of his own achievements, he is jubilantly explicit when explaining why he does it in the first place.

"Pray that I may be faithful; that is the only thing that counts. It is true that we can easily turn away from the truth of Jesus and be seduced by prestige. Pray that I remain poor and never fear doing what Jesus asks of me ... pray also for the Church, that the people may be authentic in their commitment to Jesus, that they do not try to escape into a certain piety but remain open to the Holy Spirit and to their wounded brothers and sisters."

He does not look left or right but looks up. A deliberate defiance of the banality of political labels and stylised solutions to complex problems. Vanier works and lives with the handicapped not in spite of his Roman Catholicism but because of it, which is key to understanding the man and his work. Yet this is also the most difficult aspect of Vanier for many of his admirers. Canada is comfortable with decency to the point of being drugged with the opiate of good works. But it needs to understand that those good works are provoked in this case and many others by absolute faith in Christ Jesus and in the Church He founded. Yet while the culture easily embraces Vanier, it tends to reject the institution that made and makes him.

These letters show repeatedly that it is Christ and His church that keep the man balanced and rooted as he travels the world. I had no idea until reading this collection just how many cities and states he has visited over the years. Exhausting and usually admirable, it's also one of the few areas of Vanier's weakness. His views on international politics sometimes take on a jarring partiality.

"I must admit I find it very hurtful personally when I am accused of being anti-Semitic because of my criticism of Israel's actions. I love the beauty of the Jewish people, but I can well understand the anger of biblical prophets who were infuriated and cried out their anger against what their leaders were doing!"

The language is a little condescending, even colonial. Also misleading and unfair. As with many Christian critics of Israel, the approach appears to be that the Jews should be more like Jesus, when one of the main reasons Israel exists is precisely because European Christians did not act like Jesus at all and treated the Jews so appallingly. He is certainly no anti-Semite but he does seem far more able to forgive Arab errors and injustices than Israeli ones.

Similarly with some of his other judgements. "I'm also deeply moved today by the way in which Archbishop Rowan Williams is struggling to maintain unity in the Anglican Communion with such wisdom and prayerfulness." Interesting. Many would argue that the Archbishop of Canterbury has done little to accommodate the views of the majority of Anglicans who are black, poor and conservative; but a great deal to cater to the theology of those for those who are white, wealthy and liberal.

But these are criticisms of the far spokes of the wheel. At its hub is something far greater and deeper than mere political comments made in letters. "*L'Arche* and Faith and Light were founded on weakness, they will continue to grow in their mission and through their fragility, and God will continue to be present." Success in failure, triumph in defeat. The divine paradox lived and died by, and in, Christ and expressed through the work of Jean Vanier. What he has shown in that work and in these letters is the importance of the circular. By embracing the obviously needy we realise our own less visible but still overwhelming neediness. Mutual benefit rather than charity.

Writing of an acquaintance who found it difficult to watch an ailing Pope John Paul II and suggested that he will soon die and thus should retire Vanier writes, "How many times have I heard that said about people with disabilities. It is an attitude that humanly speaking is understandable! It is hard to see and be close to people in pain. Through his physical poverty, the Pope reveals a mystery; he is a living symbol of the presence of God in weakness. Even more than by his words, through his fragile body he is teaching us now the value of human life; he is showing us a path towards holiness."

A burglar has broken through the fence. The alarms scream and the searchlights are turned on. But they reveal and expose not him but us. The perfect crime.

Dorothy L. Sayers

JUST AS WITH ARTHUR CONAN DOYLE AND SHERLOCK HOLMES, POSTERITY HAS SEEN DOROTHY L. SAYERS BECOME A PRISONER OF HER FINEST CREATION. IN THE CASE OF THIS INTENSELY GIFTED BRITISH AUTHOR THE FICTIONAL DETECTIVE IS LORD PETER WIMSEY. DOYLE ACHED TO BE KNOWN FOR SOMETHING OTHER THAN HOLMES AND URGED READERS TO LOOK TO HIS HISTORICAL ROMANCES, NON-FICTION AND VOLUMES ON SPIRITUALISM. SAYERS WAS LESS FRUSTRATED BUT ALWAYS INSISTED THAT AT THE HEART OF HER WRITING AND HER LIFE WAS CHRIST JESUS AND HER FAITH IN GOD.

She was born in Oxford in 1893 and Dorothy Leigh Sayers' father was an Anglican vicar and chaplain of Christ Church College. She herself was educated at Oxford and was one of the first women to receive a full degree. After university she worked as a writer in an advertising company and also began a relationship with an unemployed salesman named Bill White. The affair was sexual rather than loving and Sayers became pregnant.

White abandoned mother and child when he heard the news and Sayers, anxious not to shock her aged parents, hid herself away and disguised her pregnancy. She told her employers that she was suffering from exhastion and asked for an extended vacation. Young, alone and frightened, she went to what was known as a "mother's hospital" where in January 1924 John Anthony was born. She nursed him for three weeks and then arranged for the boy to be raised by her cousin.

In 1926 Sayers fell in love with and married Atherton Fleming. They adopted John Anthony but, submitting to social pressures, Sayers never admitted to being the boy's biological mother.

She began her writing career before her marriage and before her affair. As early as 1921 she wrote to a friend that, "My detective story begins brightly, with a fat lady found dead in her bath with nothing on but her pince-nez. Now why did she wear pince-nez in her bath? If you can guess, you will be in a position to lay hands upon the murderer, but he's a very cool and cunning fellow..."

This was the foundation for the novel *Whose Body*, published in 1923. It was the introduction of Lord Peter Wimsey to the world and he was to entertain for ten books and two volumes of short stories. An aristocrat with a monocle, a pedigree and an accent with which to cut the finest of glass, he was a decorated soldier, a gifted pianist and, most of all, a consummate sleuth. With his faithful butler and helper he re-appeared in *Clouds of Witness*, *Unnatural Death*, *The Unpleasantness At The Bellona Club* and *Lord Peter Views the Body*.

In 1930 Sayers published *Strong Poison*, the debut of Harriet Vane. She was a detective novelist and, inevitably, the object of Wimsey's love. They would marry and in the 1937 *Busman's Honeymoon* set off on their, yes, honeymoon. Where they discover, as of course do so many newly married couples, a mysterious corpse.

The Nine Tailors, *Gaudy Night*, *The Five Red Herrings* and *Have His Carcase*, amongst others, completed the Wimsey and Vane canon and they are still read by millions and televised on a regular basis.

But it was Sayers the Christian whom we need to remember, and the triumph of Wimsey and Vane had often obscured the very real faith of their creator. Sayers always argued that her translation of Dante's *Divina Commedia* was her finest work and she was also justifiably proud of her radio drama *The Man Born to be King*, which C.S. Lewis re-read every Easter. Indeed Sayers made some appearances at the Socratic Club in Oxford with Lewis.

Based on the life of Christ, the play is a cycle of twelve stories presenting various incidents in Scripture. It was originally broadcast on the BBC over a ten month period and provoked opposition from atheist groups. It also led to opposition from some Christians who were offended by Jesus being played by any actor. Yet it was an enormous success, and was turned into a book with accompanying notes from the author.

Sayers also wrote a pageant about the Emperor Constantine, a nativity play entitled *He That Should Come* a collection of essays, *Creed*

Or Chaos and an extraordinary analysis of the Christian creative spirit called *The Mind of the Maker*.

In 1943 the Archbishop of Canterbury offered her a special doctorate in divinity because of her contributions to Christian apologetics and literature. She declined. Seven years later, however, she did accept an honorary doctorate of letters from Durham University. An institution founded, perhaps ironically, by the seventeenth-century Puritan dictator Oliver Comwell.

Sayers was also concerned with the decline of Christian and classical education and her essay The Lost Tools of Learning is still used by many, especially in the home-schooling movement, as a structural guide to classical education.

Sayers died in Decmber 1957, seven years after her husband. Almost forty years earlier she had written, "Christ walks the world again, his lute upon his back, His red robe worn to tatters, his riches gone to rack. The Wind that wakes the morning blows His hair about His face, and His arms and legs are ragged with the thorny briar's embrace."

Remembered mostly and mainly for being one of the greatest of detective writers, she was also a timeless Christian author and a woman for all ages. Her life on earth is over, her words speak on down the ages.

Lord Longford

When the Earl of Longford died in 2001 almost every adult in Britain reacted in some form or another. In North America he was less known, perhaps little known. Even so, he merited half page obituaries in some newspapers and several radio and television discussions. I write about him because Lord Longford, or Frank Pakenham, or just Frank, was my Godfather.

He was 95-years-old and had led a wonderful life. So this is not the time for regrets, but for memories and statements. One being that Frank was one of those rare figures who defied political boundaries and labels.

He was a moral conservative who led crusades against pornography, declining morals and abortion. But also a social radical who called for the release from prison of some of the country's most hated convicts, who opposed the death penalty and who insisted on raising his voice in favour of the marignalised and powerless.

He was a child of privilege, from an ancient family of Anglo-Irish aristocrats. Although raised a Tory and a Protestant, he embraced socialism and Roman Catholicism and served in several Labour governments. He once told me that he had known every Prime Minister since 1930 on first-name terms. He was also a good friend of Presidents Kennedy and Nixon.

He was regarded as an eccentric. Extremely tall and slim, with tufts of hair at the side of his head and a most extraordinary ability to look untidy, he would stand up in the British Parliament and ignore the jeers of political allies and foes alike.

Why the jeers? For one because Frank championed Myra Hindley. This woman was one of the Moors Murderers, a couple who kidnapped several children and then tortured them to death. They tape-recorded the screams of their victims. Hardened policemen broke down in the courtroom.

Frank decided that Hindley had been cajoled by her lover into these devilish crimes and that after decades in prison she should be released. The British public, and successive governments, guaranteed that this would never happen.

For claiming that even the vilest of criminal may be capable of change, and may have been part victim herself, Frank Longford was vilified in the media and even physically attacked. Far from silencing him, however, the vitriol seemed to make him stronger.

Similarly with his campaign against pornography, he was mocked as "Lord Porn" and editorials and cartoonists had endless fun with his supposed enjoyment of or obsession with the stuff. In fact he was a married man with eight children and a very healthy sex life. He simply thought that depicting men and, particularly, women, as pieces of meat for the titillation of the needy and the profit of the unscrupulous was damnable.

He led a government commission on pornography and as such had to watch hours and hours of material. I once asked him if it had any effect. "Yes", he said, giving one of his ironic smiles. "It always made me rather bored, sorry and tired. But I had to admire the stamina of those young people."

He also called for a greater civility in society, for more balance in the media and for a more equal distribution of wealth. He helped establish clubs and centres for very tough inner city kids. There was something abundantly charming about seeing Frank, in crumpled suit and old school tie, chatting with steel hard young men about their former lives as soccer hooligans. He never patronised, always listened.

Frank was at the forefront of the anti-racist movement, as well as the pro-life community. Important this. For him a belief in the sanctity of life meant all humanity, at every stage of development. "I cannot oppose abortion unless I can be there helping that poor, single pregnant woman find a home and a job and support", he said once, over one of our long lunches. "Otherwise I'd be a hypocrite. Can't be that. Just can't be that."

He was active and alert until his final days, even though people often thought him so old as to be out of touch. Not true. He was also proud of his friends, and showed me such pride on more than one occasion. He was a Christian gentleman, in every sense of the phrase. I miss him. So does everyone who knew and understood him.

MC

Paul Johnson

THE FIRST TIME I MET PAUL JOHNSON WAS 25 YEARS AGO. HE ELOQUENTLY EXPLAINED HOW THE WAR ON LIFE AND CULTURE WAS BEING FOUGHT ON VARIOUS LEVELS, ONE OF THEM BEING IN ARTS AND LETTERS. HE ARGUED THAT IT WAS LIBERALS AND ATHEISTS AT THE END OF THE NINETEENTH-CENTURY WHO SOLIDIFIED THE CAMPAIGN AGAINST FAITH AND FAMILY AND PREDICTED THAT BY THE OPENING OF THE 21ST CENTURY CHRISTIANITY WOULD BE THE ONLY ORGANIZED AND POWERFUL VOICE LEFT TO STAND AGAINST MORAL DARKNESS. AS IN SO MANY AREAS, HE WAS BITINGLY CORRECT.

Paul Bede Johnson was born in 1928 in Manchester, England. He went to Stonyhurst College, a private Catholic high school that was also attended by some of Britain's greatest authors and public figures. After Stoneyhurt he attended Magdalen College, Oxford. In the 1950s he made his reputation as a journalist and author, often writing from a leftist standpoint. He edited the *New Statesman*, a socialist British magazine, and covered European and Middle Eastern affairs for various newspapers.

It was his experience analysing politics and culture that obliged him to rethink his poltics. He came to see that it was invariably not the will of the people that was shaping culture and society but the fashionable attitudes of small elites. "Nothing appeals to intellectuals more than the feeling that they represent 'the people'," he would write. "Nothing, as a rule, is further from the truth."

It was this conviction that led him to write a series of history books that are without doubt some of the finest and most important in print. His history of Christianity, Judaism, the twentieth century, the renaissance, the United States and several others are essential reading as independent volumes. As a collective account of world history his more than two-dozen books are simply unparalleled.

As he records the progress and unraveling of the modern world he illuminates deep and revealing truths about our current problems.

Of the rise of Nazism, for example, "It is worth remembering that Hitler was voted into office, quite lawfully and constitutionally, by what was then the best-educated people in the world, and that he and his Nazis always scored higher ratings among the educated young, and among university students and graduates – and professors – than among the population as a whole."

Applied to the chattering classes and the academics who have carved out our abortion, contraception and sexual perversion culture this is a central statement. Establishment wisdom and the ideology of those in power in media and higher education are seldom to be treated as reliable truth.

When Johnson was on the political left he was praised as a great historian and a compelling journalist. When he began to oppose the liberal status quo he was accused of being malicious, bigoted and simply insane. His meeting with the black, homosexual novelist James Baldwin is typical.

"Let me assure readers I am totally without prejudice. I do not prejudge. I have formed my dislikes on the basis of long experience. I tried explaining this once to James Baldwin, who complained to me that it was sheer race prejudice and homophobia which made people dislike him: "No, James, it is not prejudice, it is actual experience of how awful you are." He said, "What experience have you had of prejudice?" I replied, "Listen, old sod, if, like me, you were born in England red-haired, left-handed and a Roman Catholic, there's nothing you don't know about prejudice." At this point he stumped off in a rage."

Stumping off in a rage. The style of so many when presented with pro-life arguments. It's to his enormous credit, however, that Johnson doesn't appear to care. He has been marginalized and attacked for decades but his response is to write, speak and broadcast as much as ever before.

If anything has characterized Johnson's sense of history and politics, however, it is not anything as meager as left and right but the clash between pagan and Christian. He is in the best and purest sense of the term a Roman Catholic historian, seeing in the emerging lines of history the hand of God and the influence of the Church. As such he is an unconventional historian.

"Every good historian is almost by definition a revisionist", he has said. "He looks at the accepted view of a particular historic episode or period with a very critical eye." And, "The study of history is a powerful antidote to contemporary arrogance. It is humbling to discover how many of our glib assumptions, which seem to us novel and plausible, have been tested before, not once bur many times and in innumerable guises; and discovered to be, at great human cost, wholly false."

The most colossal human cost, of course, being the mass slaughters of the twentieth century, when atheist regimes centered in Germany, Russia, China and Cambodia murdered hundreds of millions. It is such social engineering that Paul Johnson was explaining long before mainstream history was prepared to tell the absolute truth.

Johnson remains one of the loudest and finest voices in modern journalism and history. It is to his credit and our triumph that he a man of life who writes about what is all too often a chronicle of death.

MC

G.K. Chesterton

THE *NEW YORKER* MAGAZINE RECENTLY GOT INTO ALL SORTS OF TROUBLE FOR ITS SATIRICAL FRONT COVER CARTOON DEPICTING BARACK OBAMA AS AN ORTHODOX MUSLIM AND HIS WIFE MICHELLE AS A TERRORIST. SOME PEOPLE, IT SEEMS, SIMPLY CAN'T TAKE A JOKE. G.K. CHESTERTON COULD. WHICH IS A GOOD THING IN THAT THE BRITISH WRITER WAS THE SUBJECT OF A LONG AND CRITICAL ESSAY IN THE PRECEDING ISSUE OF *THE NEW YORKER*, IN WHICH THE GREAT MAN WAS ACCUSED OF ANTI-SEMITISM AND HIS CATHOLIC RELIGION PAINTED WITH A STRONG, DULL COAT OF CONDEMNATION.

It goes to Chesterton's reputation and influence that he's still being vilified even though he died in 1936. The dead only matter if they once spoke the truth. And Gilbert Keith Chesterton spoke and wrote the truth of permanent things, of first things. Including in one of his masterpieces, *The Man Who Was Thursday*, the centenary of which was the premise for *The New Yorker* article.

Born in 1874 in London, England, Chesterton grew up in a relatively secular, liberal home and enjoyed the best in British private education when British and private education still meant something. He chose not to go to university, which partly explains his visceral refusal to adopt convention and think and write within partisan definitions. He drifted into journalism but once afloat he sailed perfectly, and often against the wind.

On the fashionable nationalism of the Edwardian age, for example, "My country, right or wrong, is a thing that no patriot would think of saying except in a desperate case. It is like saying, my mother, drunk or sober." On literature, "A good novel tells us the truth about its hero; but a bad novel tells us the truth about its author." On being controversial, "I believe in getting into hot water, it keeps you clean."

Books came early and frequently. *Greybeards at Play* in 1900, *Twelve Types* in 1902, a biography of Robert Browning the following year.

Then in 1904 one of his finest works, a novel entitled *The Napoleon of Notting Hill*. Ostensibly about a London district declaring independence from Great Britain, at heart it explained Chesterton's belief that the state was more often than not a problem rather than a solution and the greater the intervention of government the more profound the damage to the governed.

He married Frances Blogg is 1901 and they had an intensely happy, though childless, life together. She was a steadying influence on his notorious untidiness and lack of organisation. "Am at Market Harborough", he once wrote to her. "Where ought I to be." Her reply? "Home." At a time when H.G. Wells was celebrating infidelity and George Bernard Shaw deconstructing marriage, Chesterton insisted that family was at the epicenter of any civilized society. Family and faith.

In 1922 he became a Roman Catholic. "The fight for the family and the free citizen and everything decent must now be waged by the one fighting form of Christianity", he wrote. And, "The Christian ideal has not been tried and found wanting; it has been found difficult and left untried."

Step forward the grand knight of Church, clan and the notion that small was beautiful – apart from Chesterton himself, who weighed more than 300lbs. With his brother Cecil and the journalist and author Hilaire Belloc he embraced Distributism, an ideology based on concepts of family autonomy and small-scale production leading to authentic democracy. Neither socialist nor capitalist, and never liberal in the contemporary sense, it grappled for a third way. "A citizen can hardly distinguish between a tax and a fine, except that the fine is generally much lighter", and "Too much capitalism does not mean too many capitalists, but too few capitalists."

He possessed a sparkling ability to hold up a mirror to the addled society around him and show its absurd reflection. "Journalism largely consists of saying Lord Jones is Dead to people who never knew that Lord Jones was alive." And, "The Bible tells us to love our neighbours, and also to love our enemies; probably because they are generally the same people."

There were biographies of St. Francis, St. Thomas Aquinas and Charles Dickens, compilations of columns and journalism, autobiography and works of apologetics and history such as *Orthodoxy, Heretics and The Everlasting Man*. There was poetry – *The Ballad of The White Horse* and *Lepanto* – and the creation of the priest detective Father Brown.

He was as witty as Wilde, original as Joyce, clever as Kafka, prolific as Trollope. Yet he remains an icon to too few. Partly, perhaps largely, because he has been accused of anti-Semitism, even seventy years after his death. The charge is not completely lacking in merit but it is horribly partial and invariably partisan. Chesterton was a romantic medievalist, living in a pre-Holocaust Europe. Though never a personal anti-Semite and indeed a close friend to various Jewish people who steadfastly defended his reputation, he never authentically understood the place of the Jew in a non-Jewish society. The offence was one of ignorance rather than malice.

Yet he spoke out against Nazism long before it was politically fashionable to do so and long before many on the organized left thought it necessary. He called for the rescue of European Jews as early as 1934, condemning Nazism as racial lunacy. Rabbi Stephen Wise, one of the most prominent leaders of the American Jewish community and a man who knew his friends as well as enemies, publicly praised this British Catholic as the purest of ally.

In the final years of his life Chesterton predicted that the absolutes of right and wrong would become blurred, religion publicly condemned and that we would care more for animals than babies and would worship sex while mocking love. We would, he said, be governed by whim and fashion. "Tradition means giving votes to the most obscure of all classes, our ancestors. It is the democracy of the dead. Tradition refuses to submit to that arrogant oligarchy who merely happen to be walking around." Even if they be journalists writing for *The New Yorker*.

C.S. LEWIS

AS *PRINCE CASPIAN* RIDES ONTO THE BIG SCREEN THIS MAY THERE IS A GENUINE DANGER THAT HIS CREATOR, C.S. LEWIS, MIGHT BE LEFT BEHIND IN A TRAIL OF OVER-PRICED POPCORN. THE MOVIE IS THE SECOND IN DISNEY'S ADAPTATION OF THE NARNIA SERIES, THE FIRST BEING THE 2005 VERSION OF *THE LION, THE WITCH AND THE WARDROBE*. THERE WERE SEVEN NARNIA BOOKS BUT IT'S NOT ENTIRELY CLEAR HOW MANY FILMS THERE WILL BE. PROFIT WILL DICTATE PRODUCT, WHICH IS ACTUALLY SOMETHING LEWIS WOULD HAVE RATHER DESPISED. NOT THAT HE EMBRACED ANY FASHIONABLE OBJECTION TO CAPITALISM, MORE THAT HE EMBRACED A TIMELESS REGARD FOR WRITING THE PIERCING TRUTH WHATEVER THE COST OR REWARD.

Born in 1898 in Belfast, the author of *Mere Christianity, The Screwtape Letters, Surprised by Joy* and so many others, Jack Lewis – he was never comfortable with Clive Staples – was and remains the most accomplished and successful communicator of the Christian message in modern literary history. But his humility equalled his brilliance. He was, he always said, just an ordinary teacher. Not quite.

In fact this lecturer at both Oxford and Cambridge University was considered one of the finest academic minds of his generation. But it is Lewis the Christian who changed the world. His genius was the ability to convey highly complicated and complex ideas in a straightforward and understandable manner. Like some grand knight of common sense he charged through the ranks of cluttered thinking, double-talk and atheism, seldom taking any prisoners.

"There are two equal and opposite errors into which our race can fall about the devils" he wrote. "One is to disbelieve in their existence. The other is to believe, and to feel an excessive and unhealthy interest in them. They themselves are equally pleased by both errors, and hail a materialist or a magician with the same delight."

Of the increasingly common and painfully banal statement that Jesus might have been a great moral teacher but was not the son of

God, Lewis pointed out that this contradicted Christ's own claims. "A man who was merely a man and said the sort of things Jesus said would not be a great moral teacher. He would either be a lunatic – on the level with the man who says he is a poached egg – or else he would be the Devil of Hell. You can shut Him up for a fool, you can spit at Him and kill Him as a demon; or you can fall at His feet and call Him Lord and God. But let us not come with any patronising nonsense about His being a great human teacher. He has not left that open to us. He did not intend to."

Lewis became a Christian in 1929, "perhaps the most dejected and reluctant convert in all England." It was as though he had tried to avoid the inevitable, considering every argument against Christianity, forcing himself to take on all of the objections his fertile mind could produce. Each one he overcame. By the time his intellect was won over his emotional being simply fell into place.

From this point on everything he wrote was informed and enlivened by his Christianity. But Lewis was too subtle and too clever to knock people over the head with his faith. He knew that talking was far more effective than shouting. In 1950 *The Lion, The Witch and The Wardrobe* was published. The Christian metaphors and imagery are obvious to most adults but not so to children. It is this implicit sowing of seeds of faith that makes Lewis so effective and so hated by atheists. When the first Narnia movie appeared one prominent Canadian critic wrote that, "young viewers should be warned that this is a Christian story."

Mere Christianity appeared in 1952. The title reflected the author's attempt to remove Christianity away from those obsessed with qualifying and editing it. A startling logician, he reversed the equation offered by the secular world, that it is the thoughtless who become Christians, the thoughtful who reject it. "There is no need to be worried by facetious people who try to make the Christian hope of Heaven ridiculous by saying they do not want to spend eternity playing harps. The answer to such people is that if they cannot understand books written for grown-ups, they should not talk about them. All the scriptural imagery (harps, crowns, gold, etc) is, of course, a mere symbolical attempt to express the inexpressible.

People who take these symbols literally might as well think that when Christ told us to be like doves, He meant that we were to lay eggs."

In the 1950s Lewis met and fell in love with Joy Davidman, an American convert from Judaism. The marriage was extraordinarily happy but tragically brief. Joy died of cancer in 1960, but only after her life was prolonged by what Lewis was convinced was a miracle. After Joy's death Lewis wrote a short book entitled *A Grief Observed*, an agonizingly honest exploration of a brokenness he had never assumed possible. "Grief still feels like fear" he said. "Up till this time I always had too little time. Now there is nothing but time. Almost pure time, empty successiveness."

He died in 1963 on the same day as President Kennedy and as a consequence his death received relatively little coverage.Since Kennedy's assassination conspiracy fanatics the world over have pointlessly sought bizarre alternatives to an obvious truth. Oddly enough, since Jack Lewis's death atheists the world over have also pointlessly sought bizarre alternatives to an equally obvious truth – but one that matters just a little more than a lone gunmen and a grassy knoll. All that the new wave of old God-haters have to say was anticipated and countered by Jack Lewis more than half a century ago. Young and old alike should be warned, this is a Christian story.

MC

H.G. Wells

AN EXHIBITION OF THE HISTORY OF THOSE SCIENTIFIC IDEAS THAT GAVE A GRIMY INTELLECTUAL VENEER TO THE NAZI GENOCIDE OPENS THIS WEEK AT THE CANADIAN WAR MUSEUM IN OTTAWA. THE COLLECTION CENTRES ON EUGENICS, THE NOTION THAT HUMANITY CAN BE IMPROVED AND PERFECTED BY SELECTIVE BREEDING AND THE ELIMINATION OF INDIVIDUALS AND GROUPS CONSIDERED TO BE UNDESIRABLE. ENTITLED DEADLY MEDICINE: CREATING THE MASTER RACE, IT REVEALS HOW IT WAS NOT THOUGHTLESS RIGHT-WING THUGS AS MUCH AS WRITERS AND SCIENTISTS, THE INTELLECTUAL ELITE, WHO LED THE MOVEMENT.

It's important, accurate but, regrettably, long overdue. It also fails to stress just how much the socialist left initiated and supported the eugenics campaign, not only in Germany but in Britain, the USA and the rest of Europe. Playwright George Bernard Shaw, English social democrat leader Sydney Webb and, in Canada, Tommy Douglas were just three intensely influential socialists who called, for example, for the mass sterilization of the handicapped. In his thesis *The Problems of the Subnormal Family*, the now revered Douglas argued that the mentally and even physically disabled should be sterilized and sent to camps so as not to "infect" the rest of the population.

It is deeply significant that few if any of Douglas's left-wing comrades in this country or internationally were surprised or offended by his proposals. Indeed the early fascism of 1920s Italy, while unsavoury and dictatorial, had little connection with social engineering and eugenics. The latter German version of fascism was influenced not by ultra conservatism in southern Europe but, as is made clear in the writings of the Nazi ideologues, by the Marxist left.

The most vociferous and outspoken of the socialist eugenicists was the novelist H.G. Wells, author of *The Time Machine*, *The War of the Worlds* and *The Invisible Man*. He argued in best-selling books such as *Anticipations* and *A Modern Utopia* that the world would collapse and from this collapse a new order should and would emerge.

"People throughout the world whose minds were adapted to the big-scale conditions of the new time. A naturally and informally organised educated class, an unprecedented sort of people." A strict social order would be formed. At the bottom of it were the base. These were "people who had given evidence of a strong anti-social disposition", including "the black, the brown, the swarthy, the yellow." Christians would also "have to go" as well as the handicapped. Wells devoted entire pamphlets to the need of "preventing the birth, preventing the procreation or preventing the existence" of the mentally and physically handicapped. "This thing, this euthanasia of the weak and the sensual is possible. I have little or no doubt that in the future it will be planned and achieved."

The people of Africa and Asia, he said, simply could never find a place in a modern world controlled by science. Better to do away with the lot. "I take it they will have to go" he said of them. Marriage as it is known would have to end but couples could form mutually agreed unions. They would list their "desires, diseases, needs" on little cards and a central authority would decide who was fitted for whom.

Population would be rigidly controlled, with forced abortion for those who were not of the right class and race. Religion would be banned, children would be raised in communes and all would be well. The old and the ill would, naturally, have to be done away with and doctors would be given the authority to decide who had a right to live, who had a duty to die.

In the United States socialist writer Margaret Sanger, the founder of Planned Parenthood and the mother of the abortion movement, called for a radical eugenics approach as early as the first years of the 20th century. She wrote of the needs for, "a stern and rigid policy of sterilization and segregation to that grade of population whose progeny is already tainted or whose inheritance is such that objectionable traits may be transmitted to offspring. It is a vicious cycle; ignorance breeds poverty and poverty breeds ignorance. There is only one cure for both, and that is to stop breeding these things. Stop bringing to birth children whose inheritance cannot be one of health or intelligence. Stop bringing into the world children whose parents cannot provide for them. Herein lies the key of civilization."

The key of civilization. Unlocking the doors of a hell once unimaginable but now, after the Holocaust, the Ukrainian genocide, Pol Pot and Mao's mass slaughter, entirely within the grasp of contemporary sensibilities. History is often clouded by fashion and the whims of the victorious. Because some of the most pernicious intellectual criminals of the past century wore red they have escaped condemnation. It is time for the clouds to clear and the fashions to change.

MC

Ronald Knox

HE WAS ONE OF THE MOST REMARKABLE AND IMPORTANT PRIESTS OF THE TWENTIETH CENTURY, AN INTERNATIONALLY ACCLAIMED NOVELIST, AN APOLOGIST AND PHILOSOPHER, TRANSLATOR OF THE BIBLE AND ELOQUENT AND TIRELESS DEFENDER OF LIFE AND FAITH. HE WAS THE AUTHOR OF MYSTERY THRILLERS SUCH AS *THE VIADUCT MURDER*, *THE BODY IN THE SILO* AND *STILL DEAD* AND THEOLOGICAL AND AUTOBIOGRAPHICAL WORKS INCLUDING *A SPIRITUAL AENEID*, *SOME LOOSE STONES*, *REUNION ALL ROUND* AND *THE BELIEF OF CATHOLICS*. MOST OF ALL, HE WAS A PRISTINE FOLLOWER OF CHRIST.

Born in Leicestershire in the English midlands in 1888, Ronald Arbuthnott Knox was an outstanding scholar as a boy at Eton College and then as a young man at Balliol College, Oxford. His father was an evangelical Anglican who became Bishop of Manchester and under his influence Knox became Anglican chaplain at Trinity College, Oxford in 1912. Even as young man he was renowned for his wit as well as his cleverness. "A good sermon should be like a woman's skirt: short enough to arouse interest but long enough to cover the essentials." And, "It is so stupid of modern civilization to have given up believing in the devil when he is the only explanation of it." Or, about babies, "A loud noise at one end and no sense of responsibility at the other."

But his commitment to the Church of England had been waning for some time and in 1917 he entered the Roman Catholic Church, strongly influenced by G.K. Chesterton, even though Chesterton himself did not make the leap for another five years. In fitting paradox, Chesterton claimed that Knox in turn had influenced him. Knox's father, however, was so outraged at his son's conversion that he cut him out of his will and the smashed relationship never completely healed.

Knox taught at a small Catholic school, St. Edmund's College in Hertfordshire, between 1919 and 1926 and then took on the Catholic chaplaincy at Oxford University. For more than thirteen years he inspired a generation of young Christians and shaped the intellectual elite of the Church. He also single handedly translated the St. Jerome Latin Vulgate Bible into English and his translation stands to this day and should be more readily available.

He was a talented broadcaster and reached hundreds of thousands if not millions of people on the BBC. Most of his radio work concerned matters of faith and morals but he could also be mischievous. In 1926 he broadcast a pretend report of a British revolution, with sounds of military attacks and people being lynched in the street. Because of a snowstorm many people didn't see a newspaper for more then a day and they were convinced that Knox was being serious. A minor panic occurred and it's safe to say that Knox was persuaded that it would not be wise to repeat his exercise in radio humour!

He was at the center of an extraordinarily gifted circle of Catholic writers, including Chesterton, Hilaire Belloc, Maurice Baring and Evelyn Waugh. The latter would be named his literary executor and was to write his biography. This group and so many other men and women were attracted to the delicious combination of saintliness and steely, crisp orthodoxy and intelligence that characterized almost all what Knox wrote and said.

He once wrote that, "the study of comparative religions is the best way to become comparatively religious." In other words he was an early and penetrating critic of the relativism that would contaminate Christianity and education in the 1960s and 70s. He was especially perceptive about the modernism that was drowning liberal Protestantism even in the 1920s. To the leaders of the Church of England he stated, "You do not believe what your grandfathers believed, and have no reason to hope that your grandchildren will believe what you do."

He was made a Monsignor and received numerous honours and awards both from the Roman Catholic Church and a number of secular academic institutions. It was a life abundant but a life too short. While staying at 10 Downing Street with his friend the Prime Minister, Harold Macmillan, Knox learned that he had incurable cancer. His body was weakened but his spirit and mind never so. He wrote and spoke and laughed and prayed until the very end and died on August 24, 1957.

His funeral was at London's Westminster Cathedral and was attended not only by legions of his friends and supporters but, important this, by many of those with whom he disagreed. His greatness was thus that the harshest of critics could see that he was righteous if not right. Knox himself would have predicted the fact that for many years he would be out of favour. And, while he would have been far too modest to have ever said so, that the fashion would inevitably change and that today scores of genuine believers would be discovering the great man once again.

J.R.R. Tolkien

HE DOESN'T REALLY FIT THE BILL. J.R.R. TOLKIEN THAT IS. NOVELISTS THESE DAYS ARE SUPPOSED TO WEAR THEIR ANGST ON THEIR FINELY TAILORED SLEEVES, TO BE WHIRLING DERVISHES OF DECONSTRUCTION, DISCONTENT, DEVIANCE AND THE DIVINE RIGHT OF PROTEST. YET THE AUTHOR OF *THE HOBBIT* AND *THE LORD OF THE RINGS* WAS QUINTESSENTIALLY COMFORTABLE; IN HIS LIFE AS WELL AS IN HIS TWEEDS.

When various bookstores, newspapers, magazines and literary societies compiled their lists of all-time greats at the end of last year, however, Tolkien won the contests over and over again. First it was a chain of stores, polling more than 25,000 people. Dickens, Tolstoy and Jane Austen did well, but the bloke with the pipe and friends in dwarfish places came out top.

This annoyed the chattering classes no end, so the highly prestigious Folio Society asked its 50,000 members. Connoisseurs of fine literature, these good men and women were certain to make a different choice. They didn't.

The question was then taken to other countries, other languages, and changed into "Best book of the Century", "Best Author of the Century" and even "Greatest Writer of the Millenium." Like it or not, Tolkien beat Joyce, Proust and Balzac. Prompting one British critic to say that this was why universal literacy and a publicly funded library system were not so desirable. He was joking. Just.

Because nothing is so unpopular with our elites as, yes, popularity. And Tolkien is as popular as they come. In the summer of 2000 the short trailor of *The Lord of the Rings* movie was put on the film company's official website, part of an early publicity blitz for the release of the first of the three productions at the end of this year.

On the first day the trailor was available there were 1.5 million downloads. Twice the number for the previous record, held by *Star Wars: The Phantom Menace*. Informed opinion believes that *The Lord of the Rings* could be the most commercially successful movie ever made.

Why? Or, in the words of those who hate the Oxford University professor with his tales of wizards, elves, battles and mystery, why the hell does this awful man and his awful readers do so well?

The support for Tolkien is fascinating not only because of its size but because of its diversity. Devotees of science fiction, fans of dungeons and dragons, traditional Roman Catholics, zealots on the fringes of the political far right, dabblers in the occult, old hippies and, now, the new wave of people opposed to globalisation and free trade.

The reason for the unholy alliance is really the nature of the man himself. He was a conservative Catholic, never happy with the reforms of the Second Vatican Council and somewhat sympathetic to the aspirations of Franco and his gang during the Spanish Civil War. This needs context. There were many British and North American Catholics who, whilst totally opposed to Hitler and Nazism, were shocked by the slaughter of priests and nuns by the Republicans in Spain and grudgingly preferred the Generalissimo to a left increasingly dominated by Stalinism and the Kremlin's thugs.

Yet Tolkien was an anti-Nazi before it was altogether respectable, and indeed when many on the political left were still ambivalent. Shortly before The Second World War a German publisher wrote to him and inquired about buying the rights to his works. They asked if he was an Aryan. He replied that the word made no linguistic or ethnic sense. But, he added, if they were in fact asking him if he had any Jewish blood he regretted that this was not the case, although he would like to have some connection with such a gifted people. He finished by telling the letter writer that he would never be allowed to publish him and that the Nazis were destroying German culture and the beauty of the northern spirit.

Tolkien's religious conservatism simply did not transfer into political reaction. Indeed it seldom does. He viewed the industrialisation of his beloved Warwickshire, that country in the middle of England that inspired the characters and locations in *The Lord of the Rings*, with unrestrained horror. The working people of his youth had, he thought, a certain autonomy, a special dignity. That had been expunged with the advance of the factory, the collective, the multinational.

As for globalisation, Tolkien believed in the small community. He once said that Belgium was the perfect size for a country. Large enough to be distinct, small enough to feel like an extended family. The idea of universal free trade and a one world corporate government terrified him.

His fame and success was in essence an American phenomenon, or at least it began in the United States. Before American university students took up Tolkien's cause he had been successful on a much smaller scale. World famous in Oxford, so to speak. The new radicalism of the 1960s looked to a most surprising hero. Tolkien's books sold in quite staggering numbers and graffiti began to appear on college walls. Beneath slogans demanding withdrawal from Vietnam would be written, "Frodo Rules" and "Bilbo for President."

No surprise then that the man should be read again now by the pierced ranks determined to bring down Starbucks, Nike and international capitalism.

Science fiction and dungeons and dragons? The appeal is obvious. The issue here is that Tolkien initiated the whole thing. But whereas his emulators fill their books with babes in red leather leotards and muscular chaps in jerkins, Tolkien gave them character and depth and, yes, fundamentally Christian notions of value, virtue and truth.

So the fan base is a delicious mingling of types who would not normally give each other the time of day. The movie, their movie, will annoy as well as delight. There is none so fanatical as a Tolkien fan. By Gandalf's beard they better get, well, better get Gandalf's beard right. And as Tolkien's triumph is largely within the individual imagination, any interpretation will inevitably displease some. But that is the delight of the man and his work. Tolkien gave us the magnificent playing field, we play the game. It never stops. It wasn't supposed to.

MC

People
Politics
&
Culture

Government

THERE I WAS ABOUT TO GO ON A PICNIC WITH MY FAMILY WHEN THE CLOUDS BROKE AND IT RAINED. YET NOWHERE IN SIGHT WAS THERE A MEMBER OF THE GOVERNMENT TO STOP THE STORM, A BUREAUCRAT TO HALT THE WIND OR A CAREGIVER TO SHELTER ME FROM THE COLD. CANADA, YOU HAVE FAILED.

Which is not to say that government has no place in our lives. But when it becomes the problem rather than the solution and when we are emasculated by reliance upon it there is surely a crisis. Which was made clear by two incidents involving young people in the past ten days.

Both took place in Ontario but both are repeated time and time again throughout this country. And both produced a reaction we hear all too often from coast to coast to coast.

First, a 15-year-old boy was shot dead in a troubled area of Toronto. Second, a teenager drove a car at an enormously high speed into a taxi and killed two young women as well as himself.

Whilst it is self-evidently tragic that a young boy should be shot dead, the reaction of members of his family and assorted lawyers has been extraordinary. They have called for a public inquiry into the case and demanded that, "the government does something."

Do what exactly? Stop teenage girls being promiscuous and having babies from various fathers, thus creating legions of sons who have no idea who their father might be and become easy prey for gangsters who frequent the neighborhood?

Force families to stay together, make men raise their children and provide good male role models, transform sub-cultures so that people do not kill each other because they feel in some way disrespected, wave a magic wand and stop school bullying, drug dependency and selfish refusal to work for a living?

No, what the call for action surely means is that government should throw tax dollars paid by law-abiding people into more patronizing social projects; the very programmes that have expunged personal responsibility from under-threat communities and largely caused so many of the challenges they now face.

Public education, public health-care and numerous public support initiatives have clearly failed. It doesn't take a village to raise a child and it certainly doesn't take a government. It takes a mum and a dad who are willing to work at it.

The teen who illegally drove a car and then killed innocent people was, the chattering classes have alleged, a victim himself because he was being pursued by the police at the time. In fact the cruiser was a long way behind him and traveling far more slowly. It's just that cops are supposed to catch bad guys, even in Canada.

The fault was not the cops, not poverty, not lack of self-esteem, not anything other than the criminality of the individual behind the wheel. Yet there are screams for a government inquiry into police car chases. None, however, for a government crackdown on idiots who drive under-age and far too fast.

It is truly insulting to the millions of people who came to this country over the decades with so little and yet achieved so much to assume that individuals can only survive and prosper with government assistance.

Govern yourself. Improve yourself. Respect yourself. To trust politicians at all is unwise. To trust them to solve all your problems is utterly stupid

~MC~

Communism

WE IN CANADA ARE RELUCTANT TO WAVE THE FLAG. WE CRINGE A LITTLE WHEN PEOPLE SPEAK OF OUR VICTORIES, AS THOUGH SOMEHOW THEY DON'T MATTER. BUT THEY DO. IN READING LOUNG UNG'S *FIRST THEY KILLED MY FATHER* I REALISED JUST HOW IMPORTANT IT IS THAT CANADIANS AND THEIR ALLIES BUILD MONUMENTS AND MUSEUMS TO COMMEMORATE OUR GREATEST TRIUMPH OF THEM ALL. THE DEFEAT OF COMMUNISM.

You see Loung Ung is a young Cambodian woman who was a child in 1975 when the Marxist Khmer Rouge took over her country. Her father, a policeman, was the first to be exterminated, followed by most of her family and friends. They were not alone. Millions of Cambodians, including women and children, were murdered in the name of Lenin and Mao, and many liberal and socialist opinion-shapers in the west said that the Khmer Rouge was simply being misunderstood. If only they could have spent some time on the blood red, communist-red killing fields of Pol Pot.

No surprise there. The same sort of people who thought the regime in Cambodia deserved understanding also proclaimed that Stalin was misunderstood and that he was one of the greatest men of all time. So much so, in fact, that when British journalist Malcolm Muggeridge came back from the Soviet Union and wrote of the regime's brutality, he was effectively banned from appearing in print.

We go on, and on, these days about poor little screenwriters and directors who lost their comfortable jobs because of McCarthyism. Well I'm sorry, but remember that many of them did agree with Uncle Joe and wanted a Soviet system in the west. And those on the left were just as harsh, if not more so, in snuffing out opposition as was the Senator from Wisconsin. The difference is, the left is still at it.

But history does not always favour the brave. Muggeridge spoke out against the communist holocaust and was abused as a result. So were other writers and thinkers, men and women who dared to oppose the establishment wisdom of newspapers as powerful as, for example, *The New York Times*.

Yet Stalin was only one communist dictator. True he wiped out tens of millions of his own people, raped and slaughtered Poles, Hungarians, Slovaks, Czechs, Rumanians, Germans, Bulgarians, Christians and so many more. But he was not alone.

Mao exterminated entire regions and classes. He fired his simple and bloody followers with the sort of hatred that even Hitler failed to achieve. Mobs ran through towns and cities ripping their opponents apart. Unlike the monster in Berlin, the communist dictators did not have the means of mass killing. They used whatever was at hand.

Beyond Russia and China there were puppet regimes in Asia and Africa, repugnant little quagmires of darkness where, according to one eye-witness, "the smell of blood drenched your clothing." But, again, whilst during the war against Nazism the press condemned Hitlerism, so many people of influence not only refused to criticise communism but even praised it. There are still political parties in Canada that praise Lenin and Marx.

When Lenin launched his campaign against the Kulaks, wealthy peasants, he and his people said that there were "sub-humans who stank and lived like animals. Even their children are scum and no mercy must be shown them. Like flies they must be exterminated."

The communists said this because they wanted the Kulaks' land and property, and they got it. You'll be pushed to find a memorial to those poor souls anywhere in the world. As you will to many other such victims. Which is particularly distressing. Because while the Nazi holocaust, which must never be forgotten, ended more than half-a-century ago, the embers of the Communist one are still alight. Witness North Korea and China. And if you doubt me, ask a refugee from Tibet.

Canadian streets bulge with people who fled communism, people whose parents, children, husbands and wives were expunged from the earth simply for being who they were. Loung Ung knows this, and Loung Ung will never forget it.

Which is why I would be more than willing to give a contribution to erect a statue in every Canadian city to the victims of communism and our victory over that evil creed. Why, I wonder, are our leaders so reluctant to do the same?

~MC~

The Christian Right

THIS LAST WEEK HAS BEEN A DISGRACE FOR JOURNALISM. ESPECIALLY FOR CANADIAN JOURNALISM. ESPECIALLY FOR LIBERAL CANADIAN JOURNALISM. UNABLE TO TOLERATE LOSING IN THE GAME OF DEMOCRACY, LEFT-LEANING PUNDITS DECIDED TO BLAME THE PARTICIPANTS. WELCOME TO THE HELLISH WORLD OF THE CHRISTIAN RIGHT.

I've never seen such flummery and nonsense in all my life. A toxin of ignorance and bitterness suddenly flowed into the media bloodstream and poisoned the body politic. The very nature of free speech and political expression was challenged.

Why? Because the left lost. They had to find a scapegoat because they couldn't come to terms with their own failures. Just as with minorities of old, the best type of scapegoat is someone you don't really know but really know you're supposed to hate.

One rather glib Canadian pundit opined "Half of the United States wants to be like Canada, the other half like Iran." How awfully clever. Yes that's right, 150 million Americans want to amputate limbs as a form of punishment and sponsor international terrorism.

But in Canada this is accepted as intelligent analysis. It is what we have come to expect from the influential minority group known as The Secular Left. They dominate political parties, are well organised and are vehemently intolerant. They are also incapable of listening to the inherent contradictions in their own arguments.

It needn't be that way. The public square should be a place for civil if heated debate. No voice need be marginalised and no viewpoint silenced as being extreme or unacceptable. The reality, however, is fundamentally different.

The Secular Left may advocate, for example, Gay marriage, abortion on demand, the removal of prayer from schools, more state intervention in the family, lowering the age of consent and full access to pornography on television.

The Christian Right may advocate, for example, no Gay marriage, no abortion on demand, prayer in schools, less state intervention in the family, raising the age of consent and limited access to pornography on television.

I have views on all these issues but I do not see one as extreme and one as moderate or one as intelligent and one as stupid. It is surely acceptable, indeed laudable, to have differing view on such vital topics in a thriving democracy.

What we have been told in the last week, though, is that the people who hold one of these sets of opinions are righteous and the others are fascists who want to stone people to death for watching The Simspons.

Let me tell you about some members of the alleged Christian Right. The following are real but I have altered their names. The Van Pelts have six children. Their fifth child is a Downs Syndrome boy, Timmy. "You never quite stop grieving for the normal child you lost, even though he never existed", says Jean Van Pelt. "But the love is overwhelming. It's like being drowned in love."

The Van Pelts are not wealthy but their sixth child is adopted. He is black. And, like Timmy, he is also Downs Syndrome. "He needed us more than other children", says Jean. "If we're not here to help, there's no point." The Van Pelts voted for Bush.

The Burmans lead their church mission to the inner city. They never discuss Jesus unless asked, but they do work with alcoholics, drug addicts and the abused. Both Dean and Cindy Burman have been physically attacked during their work but they wouldn't abandon their friends for anything. They both voted for Bush.

Rick Kelly is a widower. His wife died five years ago and since then he has raised their four children alone. The tears are less common now but they never completely stop. Rick's church has raised millions of dollars to help fights AIDS in Africa and also supports an AIDS hospice in the United States. Rick voted for Bush.

The Christian Right. Some are saints, some are the contrary. They can be intolerant and annoying. Just like, in fact, The Secular Left.

But we all have a right and a responsibility to have an influence over our political system. How outrageous that the smug and powerful encourage one group but despise the other. Thing is, Jean, Dean, Cindy and Rick will forgive them. Perhaps it's this that makes them so very angry

MC

Frightening

A GOVERNMENT GRANT AND AN ORDER OF CANADA TO THE NEXT PERSON WHO TELLS ME THAT SOMETHING CONNECTED WITH STEPHEN HARPER, GEORGE W BUSH OR CONSERVATISM IN GENERAL IS "FRIGHTENING." BETTER STILL, GIVE THEM A YEAR OR TWO IN ONE OF FIDEL CASTRO'S LABOUR CAMPS OR A LONG VACATION TO THE PEOPLES' SOCIALIST PARADISE OF NORTH KOREA.

A few examples from the past ten days. From a Liberal MP: "I find what the Tories just said about health care to be truly frightening". From a publicly funded school teacher, perhaps working to rule: "I just read an article on the Christian right in a magazine and, frankly, it's frightening."

From a 23-year-old social worker with a degree in media studies: "The idea of the Reform Party, and that is what they are, government is nothing less than frightening." And from an e-mail to me: "You are one of the most frightening people I've ever read."

Yes, I suppose I am. Certainly hope so. In fact if ever I lose my career in journalism for being, well, too frightening I might find work terrifying children at birthday parties.

It's a fairly new cliché but it's doing extremely well. It follows on from the "why are you threatened?" line used to silence anybody who had any sort of disagreement with the homosexual agenda. Before that was the "I find what you say to be nothing less than racist" screamed at anyone who dared to be a conservative.

It's all about marginalizing the opposition. That is, rather than taking on the substance of an argument the new left and the old leftovers would rather simply dismiss opponents as being beyond rational concern.

Like a vampire or ghoul or figure of science fiction, those who are not socialists or liberals must, by their very nature, be frightening. President Kennedy, for example, sent American troops into Vietnam, opened the doors to the military-industrial complex and had sex with almost any female with a pulse who stepped into The White House.

Yet he was never frightening. President Bush, on the other hand, is so frightening that babies cry at the mere mention of his name. Perhaps not babies but certainly adults who act thus. And if we want people who act like children, Canada is a living museum of such individuals.

The economic policies of Paul Martin and Stephen Harper are fundamentally quite similar. Harper is a right-of-centre pragmatist while Martin is a banker with a red tie. At least he was. He has suddenly become a New Democrat obsessed with giving money to Jack Layton's favourite causes.

But a Tory government would not be radically different from a Liberal administration. Less corruption, more original thought, less dead wood on the backbenches and more listening to the people. Apart from that, no radical changes.

The notion put forward by the "it's frightening" crowd that the Conservatives would somehow sell the country to the United States is ludicrous. One assumes that they mean by this that there will be more free trade and a greater alliance with the south.

Yet when he was Finance Minister Paul Martin led the charge on free trade and has made it abundantly clear for many years that he embraces in the policy root and branch. More than this, many experts believe that he favours a joint missile defence policy and would dearly love to jettison some of his less pro-American colleagues.

Yes, it's frightening. Also frightening that people don't think, frightening that they speak in sound-bites, frightening that they have lost the ability to question the status quo, to be offended by the abuse of their own money, to move out of their tired little political comfort zones.

Frightening that they are so complacent, frightening that they still believe that Canada is respected, frightening that they assume that the Americans even care about this country. Frightening that they watch reality television while the reality of Canada increasingly resembles a down-market soap opera

Frightening. Publicly frightening. Public education, public health, public childcare, public radio, public lunacy. What is actually frightening is how this great nations became this way. Frightening.

~MC~

Flags

I FEEL RATHER ASHAMED. FOR YEARS NOW I'VE TREATED APRIL 28 AND DECEMBER 6 AS ORDINARY DAYS OF THE WEEK. LITTLE DID I KNOW THAT THE FORMER IS NATIONAL MOURNING WORKERS DAY AND THE LATTER THE NATIONAL DAY OF REMEMBRANCE AND ACTION ON VIOLENCE AGAINST WOMEN. WHAT A BLIND FOOL I AM. THE FLAG WAS AT HALF-STAFF AT GOVERNMENT BUILDINGS AND BUSINESSES – MY GOLLY, WASN'T IT OBVIOUS?

I mention this because of the fuss about lowering the flag each time a Canadian soldier is killed. Which is a very bad idea indeed. If we'd done so 65 years ago the thing would never have been raised at all! We have become maudlin, pathetic and obsessed with "sharing pain", "closure" and the rest of the neurotic lexicon.

It is self-evident that every Canadian life lost in Afghanistan is a tragedy. But they are soldiers. Soldiers sometimes die in war. It's part of the job description. Remember them, honour them, revere them. But don't turn them into shadows from an Oprah show or political footballs to be tossed around by weak-minded and weak-kneed Ottawa types.

Even the flag itself is something of a joke. It's not the great, grand standard upon which this country was built and for which so many died in two bloody world wars. That one boasted the emblem of a great world faith. The new one pictures vegetation and is in the colours of the Liberal Party. The sides of the thing are supposed to represent sea and the only red sea I know is a long way from Canada and will certainly not part for National Mourning Workers Day.

One day a year should be set aside for lowering the flag of our nation. Better than Remembrance Day it should be the anniversary of Vimy Ridge, when this country came of age. Before Vimy we were a colonial outpost, after it a universally known nation-state. That, however, will mean that Canadian children will have to learn what and when Vimy Ridge was. They're more likely, however, to be taught about domestic abuse and the evils of imperialism than Canada's glorious war record.

To lower our icon of identity too often is to cheapen it and obliterate the very meaning of both the flag and what is signified when it is flown at half-staff. To compare fallen soldiers to workers dying on the job or a madman murdering women is absurd and obscene. It is nothing more than the product of political pressure from the labour movement and the feminist lobby.

We might as well have National I've a Headache Day or Stephen Lewis's Birthday or, best of all, National I'm Offended Day. No I'm not minimizing the reality of people dying at work and certainly not the horror of violence against women. But both involve crime, neglect and immorality. Government, courts and police are dealing with them.

To single out any group's suffering is inevitably to ignore other groups. The pain of a dead worker's family or a beaten woman is no different from the agony of, for example, the parents of an assaulted child or the wife of a man killed by a drunk driver.

And none of these experiences compare to the individual and collective sacrifice of Canadian men and women for their country and, yes, for their flag. That is why it should be lowered. One very special time a year.

MC

God Bless America

THE UGLIEST ASPECT OF CANADA IS ITS OBSESSION WITH NOT BEING THE UNITED STATES. AND TO DISGUISE THIS OBSESSION ITS HITS OUT AT ITS NEIGHBOUR, LIKE SOME LITTLE BOY WITH A CRUSH WHO TEASES A PRETTY GIRL. IT'S POINTLESS AND SAYS FAR MORE ABOUT THE TEASER THAN THE TEASED.

What every Canadian should really be saying is God Bless America.

For leaving half-a million men on the battlefields of Africa, Asia and Europe during the Second World War, a conflict the United States could easily have sat out. God Bless America.

For that farm-boy from Nebraska who had never even heard of Normandy or Sicily, who wanted so much to walk back from the hill but continued on. For his determination to do his duty and for his dedication to freedom. For his mother and for the stars and stripes flag she hung in her window. For his life, and for the fact that he gave it. God Bless America.

For being prepared to rip the country apart in a bloody spasm of civil war because, however delayed and reluctant in some quarters, the leaders and people knew that slavery was wrong. For seeing the future dawn when others could only see the enveloping night . God Bless America.

For the legion of Nobel Prizes won with grace, for the medical breakthroughs celebrated with decorum, for the sporting records, the intellectual triumphs, the moral victories, the glory. For embracing yes rather than hiding behind no. God Bless America.

For jazz and pluralism, baseball and religious tolerance, burgers and equality. For inventing and pursuing an ideal that, though not always achieved, is still glorious in the making and pristine in the chasing. God Bless America.

For the Marshall Plan and Marshall Dillon, for *Tom Sawyer* and Tom Hanks, for New York and for the New Deal. God Bless America. For not minding when foreigners actually show more ignorance about American culture than Americans ever do about theirs. For in fact being more polite and sensitive when abroad than many other peoples but merely smiling when described as ugly. God Bless America.

For inviting Irish, Jew, Italian, Pole, German, Hispanic, black, Asian, man and woman, all and every into the highest levels of government. For being the first nation in the world to treat the outsider as a guest rather than a problem. For being a melting pot rather than a melting society. God Bless America.

For allowing God and prayer and faith to enter public life and for not running scared of gratitude to the almighty for all that He has given us. God Bless America.

For your comedies and your dramas, for your movies and your novels, your sentimentality and glamour, your self-parody and self-criticism. For your splendour and for your silliness. God Bless America.

For being right more often than being wrong. For being the nation that still leads the way in so many ways, still lights the path on so many days. For being you. For being. God Bless America.

MC

Draft Dodgers

DAYS BEFORE GEORGE W. BUSH COMES TO TOWN THREE OF THE PRESIDENT'S COMPATRIOTS HAVE BEEN DEALT A BLOW IN THEIR CAMPAIGN TO RECEIVE REFUGEE STATUS AND BE ALLOWED TO LIVE IN CANADA. THE THREE ARE FORMER MEMBERS OF THE US MILITARY WHO REFUSE TO FIGHT IN IRAQ.

The federal refugee board has declared that it is irrelevant whether the Iraq war is legal or illegal. It does not, they claim, have any bearing on the rights of the three men to stay in this country or be declared valid refugees.

The board is quite right of course. What it should also say is that these three men should stop wasting Canadian time and money and be sent back to the free and democratic United States where their punishment will be moderate and appropriate.

Appropriate because they were, indeed, members of the American military. They may go to prison for a while and then receive a dishomnourable discharge from the armed forces. One would have thought that any person with principles would welcome such a fair conclusion.

I happen to be opposed to the war in Iraq but that is not the point. The United States has a volunteer army and nobody is forced to serve. More than that, some of those applying for refugee status also volunteered for advanced units such as the airborne.

Forgive my cynicism, but surely by the time you complete basic infantry training and then advanced paratroop training you might have just the hint of an idea that your role is to fire guns at the enemy and obey orders.

It's particularly troubling because there are thousands of deserving refugee claimants, many of them black and brown and poor, who are desperate to enter Canada and who face torture and execution in their homelands.

Their welcome has never been as generous as that given to people who run away from the United States. And it is this attitude, surely, that characterises the hostility being directed towards President Bush as he prepares to visit Canada.

It may well be that Bush's foreign policy is unfair and unwise but that has relatively little to do with it. He is despised by the chattering classes in Canada for the same reason that a bunch of deserters are so lionised. Because it's a way of screaming at the United States.

And why do they scream at the United States? Because they are jealous, smug and bitter. I'd like to sound more understanding, I really would, but the evidence does not allow me such an indulgence.

For decades various Soviet leaders visited Canada and we heard barely a whisper from labour leaders, Canadian nationalists, television personalities and newspaper columnists. Yet these men directed a foreign policy that made the clumsiest of American excesses appear generous.

When the Soviets invaded Hungary and Czechoslovakia and murdered so many of their people, when half of Europe was imprisoned, when grotesque terrorist movements were sponsored and trained, there were no mass demonstrations in Canada or calls to indict assorted Soviet bosses.

Similarly with China and its rape of Tibet and subjugation of its own people. Maoist leaders visited Canada and only members of the Chinese diaspora protested. The Canadian left and its media representatives found these various Marxist thugs to be meaningful rather than monstrous.

The hypocrisy runs deep, and so does the guilt. Canada's immigration policy, for example, was inherently racist for more than half-a-century. During these years the Americans opened their doors to people who because of their race or class were considered to be beneath Canadian standards.

None of this makes Canada a bad country. It does, however, make Canada a lesser country. Like a child who constantly measures his self-worth by how nasty he can be about his big brother, even when the sibling has done nothing wrong.

American policies deserve to be criticised but only by those who have a moral right do so, based on their own consistency and integrity. As for the American deserters, they can go home, face their punishment like men and then write best-selling books about the horror of it all. Books that will no doubt become best sellers in good old Canada.

~MC~

Guns

IT'S BECOME AS REGULAR AND PREDICTABLE AS A HALF-WITTED CANADIAN POET APPLYING FOR A PUBLIC GRANT. ASSORTED LEFTIST POLITICIANS, MISNAMED PEACE ACTIVISTS AND FELLOW TRAVELING DUNDERHEADS CALLING FOR A TOTAL BAN ON HANDGUNS. IT HAPPENS EVERY TIME SOMEONE IS KILLED ON CANADA'S STREETS BY AN EVIL PUNK WITH A PISTOL.

Which should lead us to call for a total ban of evil punks. But no. That would require original thought and original policies. To adapt the words of the great and now greatly missed Charlton Heston, they'll take my welfare cheque for having yet another child by an anonymous father from my cold, dead hands.

Because that is what so much of this is all about. The killing that provoked the latest spasm took place in Toronto. Where so many murders and shootings are carried out by young men who have never known their father and barely their mother.

We're force-fed the urban myth that all of these single mums are crosses between Mother Theresa and Mary Poppins, but the truth is that while some may be sacrificing darlings, others are entirely indifferent to their kids. If they weren't, they'd have been careful to make sure they gave themselves to men who might hang around a little longer.

We can quote statistics all day about the violent crime rates in Britain where there is a handgun ban and the safety of Scandinavian nations where there is no ban at all but the zealots base their arguments not on facts but on raw emotion. A crying cousin of a victim is worth a hundred informed arguments.

These gun-haters, ironically, tend to be the very same people who also campaign for more rights for criminals, shorter sentences and emptier prisons. In other words, we'll ban hand-guns but only slap you on the wrist if you break the ban anyway.

They also tend by their nature to be state-control freaks. Yet ifevery cop who spends dozens of hours setting up and manning speed-traps for harmless people driving marginally over the limit, giving out tickets for minor infringements and generally playing social worker actually targeted gun-carrying hoodlums we'd be a far safer country.

One brief example of the nonsense. Last year a child was shot dead in a Toronto school. He was immediately painted as an angel by everyone around him and that may be true – it's odd, however, how so many young people involved in gang violence, whether victims or perpetrators, turn out to be so saintly.

I covered the boy's funeral live on radio. After a few speeches a young person stepped to the microphone and announced that "the youth" would now be in charge of the ceremony and they would play the dead boy's favourite song.

It was a recording from a convicted felon and used so many obscene and violent words in the first stanza that we had to hurriedly cut away. Leading us to ask why there was no adult supervision of this part of the funeral and what sort of message a filthy, misogynistic, gangster-glorifying song was doing at such a time and place.

Perhaps a total ban of hand-guns would have transformed the culture and climate of this event and the community around it. Then again, perhaps that's total garbage. Let's not disarm the law-abiding but arrest the lawless. You'll take my ability to think away from my cold, dead mind.

MC

Racism

MICHAEL RICHARDS WAS UNDOUBTEDLY MASTER OF HIS OWN DOMAIN LAST WEEK, WHEN THE FORMER *SEINFELD* STAR DELIVERED A FOUL-MOUTHED AND RACIST TIRADE AT A LOS ANGELES COMEDY CLUB. BY NOW WE'VE ALL HEARD HIS EXPLANATION. HE'S NOT A RACIST, HE SAYS, AND WAS SIMPLY ANGRY AND FRUSTRATED AT TWO BLACK AUDIENCE MEMBERS WHO DID NOT APPRECIATE HIS ACT.

Well, we all get angry and frustrated at times but unlike Mr. Richards we're not professional comedians whose have years of experience of dealing with hecklers.

Seems to me that after delivering the initial line about black people being lynched fifty years ago he tried to cover himself by mock hysteria, becoming increasingly extreme and absurd as if to pretend that he was some sort of shock jock. It only made matters worse.

Even when the immensely talented, though not always funny, Lenny Bruce was using this shtick to show the hypocrisy of language and the foolishness of racism, it was sometimes misinterpreted. And Michael Richards is no Lenny Bruce.

So he dug his grave ever deeper and is now trying to crawl out of it with a shovel full of apologies. They seem heartfelt and there is a clear desperation and confusion about the man. It took only moments, however, for has-beens such as Jesse Jackson and Sinbad to climb on the soapbox and opine to the world.

The same Jesse Jackson, of course, who described Jews as "Hymies". My golly, the speed with which these activists appear on television after such incidents is extraordinary. "Got racism? Call Jesse. Fast, furious. Satisfaction guaranteed."

As obnoxious as racism may be, there are many racists who have never harmed another person and many men and women who are not racist who have spent their lives hurting all sorts of people. In other words, racism is always to be condemned but is not necessarily the human trait that causes the most damage.

Richards messed up big time. What he did was horrible and merited a good dose of humiliation. At least the man didn't blame drugs or booze or abuse but admitted that he was a total twit and needs to work on his attitudes.

Thing is, racism exists all over the place but is officially condemned in North America and Europe. In many African and Asian countries it is virtually encouraged and little is said because of the patronizing and itself racist attitude that only white people can be racist.

When Kenya and Uganda expelled their south Asian populations the western world merely opened their doors to the refugees. When hundreds of thousands of Jews were thrown of out of the Arab nations the usual liberal suspects said hardly a word but Canada, the United States and Israel opened their doors to these poor souls.

In Britain almost half of all racist attacks are now committed by black or brown people on white victims. In Canada there are all sorts of racist beliefs held by all sorts of ethnic groups. In the United States, white people are frequently the subject of sometimes extremely cruel jokes told by black comics.

So we have to be honest. And we have to ask whether a brief if vile racist scream is a greater sin than the refusal to forgive someone's uncharacteristic behavior. The answer reveals a great deal.

MC

Sudan

"WOMEN AND CHILDREN ABDUCTED IN SLAVE RAIDS ARE ROPED BY THE NECK OR STRAPPED TO ANIMALS AND THEN MARCHED NORTH. ALONG THE WAY, MANY WOMEN AND GIRLS ARE REPEATEDLY GANG-RAPED. CHILDREN WHO WILL NOT BE SILENT ARE SHOT ON THE SPOT. IN THE NORTH, SLAVES ARE EITHER KEPT BY INDIVIDUAL MILITIA SOLDIERS OR SOLD IN MARKETS. BOYS WORK AS LIVESTOCK HERDERS, FORCED TO SLEEP WITH THE ANIMALS THEY CARE FOR.

"Some who try to escape have their Achilles tendons cut to hamper their ability to run. Masters typically use women and girls as domestics and concubines, cleaning by day and serving the master sexually by night. Survivors report being called Abeed (black slave), enduing daily beatings, and receiving awful food. Masters also strip slaves of their religious and cultural identities, giving them Arabic names and forcing them to pray as Muslims."

Thus says one leading slavery abolitionist group. A former slave writes of, "The rape of girls and boys alike, the forced circumcision of boys and girls, often with them fully conscious and screaming and having to be held down by many people. Sodomy and sadistic torture are common. Living hell."

Another says. "Families were broken up, with children sometimes murdered in front of their mothers as a warning and because they were too much trouble. We cried out to the west, to the countries who said they believed in human rights, but they were indifferent to our agony."

Thank goodness, of course, that this is the stuff of a dark history that can now be comfortably condemned in the privilege of a civilized and complacent modernity. Oh what awful times they were.

Problem is, it's not some description of the ancient world or an example of the worst excesses of American slavery in the early nineteenth-century. No, it's happening right now, and some of those who have escaped this evil have found sanctuary in Canada. They are willing to tell their stories if anyone will listen.

This is the reality of Sudan, a country with which Ottawa has good relations and a nation that is accepted in every major international organization, where it regularly votes to condemn liberal democracies. Because it possesses oil, many foreign governments who scream freedom seem to become deaf and dumb about the obscenity of slavery.

There has been a civil war going on in Sudan for years, and after years of pain and struggle a peace treaty was been signed between the Islamic government in Khartoum and the black, largely Christian groups in the south. A referendum has been guaranteed to decide whether the south wants independence. The yes vote would be almost unanimous, but the Arab rulers in the north have enforced a several year waiting period until this plebiscite can take place.

One can only imagine what they will try to do in the time they have left, particularly as war has once again broken out in the region. They are backed by Muslim groups and governments the world over and even have supporters in Canada. Major newspapers have featured articles denying that slavery exists in Sudan. Almost akin to Holocaust denial in its vile spirit. Then again, several Muslim states bathe in those stagnant and infected waters these days.

This horror has taken place for two major reasons. The people of southern Sudan are black, and they are not Muslim. At a time when we hear so much about Islam's treatment by the world, we ought to consider that one of the greatest crimes of this generation has been committed by a Muslim fundamentalist government and army against a black and Christian people who want only their dignity.

In fact millions have been enslaved, murdered, mutilated and abused in this campaign, far more than have suffered in, for example, what are known as the occupied territories in Israel. Odd, then, that so much media time is given to that situation, so little to this. Even now, with a new civil war raging, international bodies are doing too little, too late.

The world ought to look very closely at what takes place in Sudan in the months and years to come. There are very powerful and very bad people who will resist ceaselessly the creation of a separate African and largely Christian state on the edge of the House of Islam. Let us hope that the world does not play the role of hypocrite once again. The stench of the blood is becoming overwhelming.

Slavery

THIS WEEK WE COMMEMORATE THE 200TH ANNIVERSARY OF THE ABOLITION OF THE SLAVE TRADE BY THE BRITISH PARLIAMENT. ANGLICAN LEADERS IN BRITAIN HAVE MARCHED AROUND THE COUNTRY OFFERING THEIR APOLOGIES AND EVEN PRIME MINISTER TONY BLAIR HAS SAID SORRY, AS IF HE WAS SOMEHOW PERSONALLY RESPONSIBLE. HARDLY A DAY GOES BY WITHOUT ANOTHER CONFUSED AND CONFUSING EUROPEAN OR NORTH AMERICAN SCREAMING CONTRITION AND INDIRECTLY BLAMING THE CHURCHES AND WHITE CIVILIZATION FOR THE USE OF AFRICAN SLAVES BETWEEN THE LATE SIXTEENTH AND MID NINETEENTH-CENTURIES. PROBLEM IS, IT DISPLAYS AN ACHINGLY FLAWED UNDERSTANDING OF HISTORY AND OF HUMAN NATURE.

It's surely a self-evident truth in the opening years of the 21st century that slavery is an intolerable evil. Also self-evident that earlier cultures did not share this opinion and that the most sophisticated of them, of all races and religions, thought it inevitable and even ethical that the powerful would enslave those whom they defeated or those who could not effectively resist capture. One culture and one religion, however, are distinguished for condemning and concluding slavery when it was easier and far more lucrative not to have done so. The culture is Anglo-Saxon and the religion is Christianity.

Europeans certainly enslaved Africans, often buying them from local African warlords or simply transforming local customs into something far more repugnant and far more widespread. The same Europeans, of course, were themselves used as slaves when captured by the Ottoman Turks and would continue to be such victims until the seventeenth-century.

But there is no doubt that the white use of black men, women and children as slaves was organized, brutal and grotesque. And enormously profitable. Which makes the grand opposition to it by the 1780s so profoundly impressive. To put it simply, there was a great deal to lose, nothing to gain and no need to change anything. The only dynamic behind a series of boycotts of slave-produced products, campaigns to expose the cruelty of slavery and eventually successful legislation to abolish the trade was that in Christian eyes it was wrong.

There were certainly church figures who supported slavery but there were people from all area of life who supported it. What is important is that the only opponents were monks, priests and Christian laity. Secular and non-Christian resistance was almost unheard of.

This was one of the reasons why Christian missionaries were so vehemently opposed by many African chieftains. The famous Dr. Livingstone spent much of his time in central Africa preaching against slavery, much to the chagrin of the local Arab slave-dealers, and their indigenous partners, who made a fortune out of selling Africans to other parts of the continent and to the Middle East. The Sultan of Zanzibar was forced to end slavery as late as 1873 when the British arrived. In an act that would today be called barbarically imperialistic the British occupiers built an Anglican cathedral on the site of the destroyed slave market.

In 1843 the British took Karachi from its Muslim leaders and demanded that the slave trade be stopped immediately and the slave market be torn to the ground. They built in its place a huge fruit and vegetable market that operates even to this day. The notion that Islam rejects slavery and Christianity encourages it is, frankly, laughable.

It is beyond dispute that in the eyes of African and Arab leaders in the nineteenth-century Christian expansion signified an end to slavery, which is one of the reasons why British ships so regularly battled Muslim pirates around North Africa and why Anglo-Celtic culture was seen as a liberating force by contemporary liberal movements.

The real axis of evil that was slavery connected Africa, south Asia and Arabia and lasted far longer than that in the white, Christian world. Indeed it still exists. According to anti-slavery groups there are still millions who are enslaved servants and concubines. In Sudan Animist and Christian tribes are raided by Arab militias; the men are killed and the women and children taken as slaves. There are cane-workers in leg-shackles in southern Pakistan and hundreds of thousands of women and children are sold from Benin and Togo to wealthier African nations such as Nigeria and Gabon.

The criminals who operate these multi-national enterprises are seldom reprimanded and in the case of Sudan are applauded by a government that is, in turn, supported by several leading Arab states. They must be laughing at the post-Christian westerners beating their breasts and crying for forgiveness for something, which their ancestors worked so hard to stop. Did so only because their Christian faith and European enlightenment convinced them that it was wrong. Those dead white guys certainly knew a thing or two.

MC

Ukraine

THEY CALL IT A HOLOCAUST. AND THEY ARE RIGHT. BECAUSE A HOLOCAUST IS WHAT IT WAS. THEY ALSO WONDER WHY SO FEW PEOPLE SHARE THEIR PAIN AND ANGER AT WHAT HAPPENED TO THEIR PROUD, BEAUTIFUL NATION.

The cold, stiff children still cuddled by their mothers long after death. The mass piles of corpses frozen by the cold into a twilight picture of agony. The seemingly endless suffering, driving a blood-red knife into the weeping heart of an entire country.

I refer to the forced starvation, murder, rape, slaughter and mass destruction of the Ukrainian people by the Soviet Communists in the early 1930s, a man-made catastrophe that is remembered at this time of year by Ukrainians the world over. In sorrow. In deep, deep sorrow.

The issue is particularly relevant this year because of the work of two great Canadians. One is Lubomyr Luciuk, whose latest book *Searching for Place* chronicles the story of the Ukrainians in Canada and the reason that so many of them came here.

The other is Professor Ian Hunter, a man with no Ukrainian blood but with an inner need to speak out for justice. He is a warrior for truth who writes and speaks on behalf of the millions who died like animals in ditches.

No, correct that. Not like animals in a ditch. Animals would have received more sympathy and their fate would not have been denied. The attempted genocide of the Ukrainians is one of the great horrors of the world. The manner in which it has been forgotten or ignored is almost worse.

In 1932 and 1933 between 7 and 10 million people, mostly Ukrainian, died in what was known then as the Soviet Union. Joseph Stalin and his gang decided that the culture and spirit of Ukraine had to be smashed and that the farmers and peasants of the northern Caucasus and the lower Volga River must be forced into docility.

They decided to demand 44% more wheat from the Ukrainians as part of the national quota, knowing that this would cause a massive shortage of food and starve millions. They made it an offence to feed the Ukrainian peasants until the new quota was met, and killed anybody who disobeyed.

More than this, Ukrainians were suddenly refused permission to move out of their region, making it impossible for them to search for food. Soviet soldiers and secret policemen stored grain in huge silos and stood guard outside, sometimes only yards away from where families were dying of starvation. Any attempt to find food, approach the silos or hide grain was met with execution of "culprit" and family.

"I watched the babies and the old and the sick die first", wrote a witness who managed to survive. "Then the others, then everybody. When we men protested they shot us down like flies. Not that they needed a reason. They killed as sport. We were nothing to them. Entire families dead, lying there, with fathers on top of the heap as they tried to protect their children from the bullets of the communists."

But the Ukrainian genocide has its deniers and revisionists. Unlike the madmen who deny the Jewish Holocaust, however, these people are often treated with respect and authority. For many years and still today there are university teachers, media figures and politicians will minimise or even dismiss the suffering of the Ukrainian people.

They argue that if the starvation did happen it was a natural occurrence. Or they somehow imply that the Ukrainians brought the whole thing on themselves because of their sense of national pride or because they stood in the way of progress. Statements and attitudes that are grotesque and horrible but for some reason have been allowed and even encouraged.

All holocaust denial is wrong. All denial of human cruelty is wrong. All feelings of racial superiority are wrong. To be blunt, a dead baby is a dead baby. White, black, Jewish, gentile, Ukrainian, Canadian. We now know that Soviet Communism was a hellish ideology that had as little concern for life and love as German National Socialism.

Ukrainians have known this for a very long time. They simply want the rest of the world to know it as well. Not a lot to ask.

MC

German Resistance

NOTHING SAYS CHRISTMAS MORE THAN A MOVIE ABOUT A FAILED ATTEMPT IN 1944 TO EXPLODE THE LEADER OF NATIONAL SOCIALIST GERMANY INTO HUNDREDS OF BLOODY CHUNKS. THAT, AT LEAST, APPEARS TO BE THE VIEW OF HOLLYWOOD, AS IT RELEASES THE FILM *VALKYRIE* ON DECEMBER 25TH. THE IRONY IS INESCAPABLE. LIKE SO MANY OF THE MOST ACTIVE OPPONENTS OF HITLER, COLONEL CLAUS VON STAUFFENBERG WAS A CHRISTIAN WHO WAS MOTIVATED BY HIS ROMAN CATHOLIC FAITH. AS SUCH HE MAY HAVE BELIEVED THAT CHRISTMAS DAY WAS BETTER LEFT TO MATTERS OTHER THAN EATING POPCORN IN A THEATRE. STILL, WE CAN ALL SIT BACK AND FEEL JUST A LITTLE BETTER ABOUT THE WORLD AS TOM CRUISE PLAYS THE GOOD GERMAN TRYING TO KILL THE BAD GERMAN. ACTUALLY BAD AUSTRIAN, BUT THAT IS BESIDE THE POINT.

What is not in dispute is that von Stauffenberg was a heroic character who, while he initially applauded the Nazi Party's German nationalism, was disgusted by its anti-Semitism and was committed to replacing Hitler by 1941. His final words before execution were, "Long live our holy Germany." His iconic stature in contemporary Germany is well deserved.

Yet what disturbs some of the families of those persecuted and murdered during the Third Reich is the thesis that domestic resistance partly expunges German guilt or, important this, empowers the Germans as fellow victims of fascism. This was the East German argument. As Communists, they claimed, they were victims rather than perpetrators and Nazism was a bastard child of the west. Total claptrap of course, but systematic mythology shapes nations and cultures.

In fact the denial of the former East Germany made the rise of neo-Nazism in the new eastern Germany far more possible. West Germans, however, were reminded daily of the stains of their past. It worked. They still look at their eastern cousins in disbelief but are proud that Germany had its martyrs and believe that this gives the country an historic lifeline to the civilized world.

Count Clemens August von Galen, Bishop of Munster, Martin Niemoller, Pastor Dietrich Bonhoeffer, the White Rose student group in Munich, the Red Orchestra organisation, former Mayor of Leipzig Carl Goerdeler, Prussian Finance Minister Johannes Popitz, the Kreisau Circle, Julius Leber, the Social Democrat and Communist underground, Catholic and Protestant secret opposition movements. As early as November 1939 Georg Elser, acting alone and with the most extraordinary dedication, tried to assassinate Hitler with a homemade bomb. The plan almost worked. There were also two attempted suicide bombings of Hitler as well as numerous plans for conventional armed attacks.

We should be surprised not at how few but at how many and varied were the resisters. Especially after Hitler's early military successes when even moderate Germans who had never voted Nazi were euphoric at the reversals of the 1918 humiliation. By the end of 1940 the internal security system was intensely sophisticated and meaningful opposition, particularly under a war economy, was often effectively impossible. Punishment for even the mildest rebuke of the government was swift and grotesque. We have never properly honored those who were killed for their stance, in Germany as well as in occupied Europe.

No serious person in Germany denies the past and no country could have done more to acknowledge what was, is and should be. All that informed, studious Germans argue is that we ought not to be confined by war comic mentality and that while never forgetting that the bridge of understanding was made filthy by Hitler and his grimy gang, it was kept in one piece by the very people depicted in a big budget American movie. Even one released on Christmas Day.

MC

Animal Rights

THREE MEN ARE FACING 12-YEAR PRISON SENTENCES IN BRITAIN AFTER ADMITTING LAST WEEK TO A PROLONGED TERRORIST CAMPAIGN AGAINST THE OWNERS OF A GUINEA PIG FARM IN STAFFORDSHIRE IN THE ENGLISH MIDLANDS. THE ANIMALS WERE SOLD TO LABORATORIES AND UNIVERSITY MEDICAL FACILITIES FOR VIVISECTION AND EXPERIMENTAL PURPOSES. THE FARM OWNERS, BROTHERS CHRIS AND JOHN HALL, WERE THE VICTIMS OF SYSTEMATIC THREATS, ABUSE AND VIOLENT ATTACKS ON THEIR PROPERTY. ANIMAL RIGHTS EXTREMISTS EVEN USED EXPLOSIVES IN AN ATTEMPT TO SO FRIGHTEN THE VILLAGE COMMUNITY THAT THE OWNERS OF THE FARM WOULD BE OSTRACIZED AND HAVE TO SELL THEIR BUSINESS.

The brothers and their families became virtual prisoners and their neighbors were afraid to be seen even speaking to the Halls in case they too would be targeted. One man who merely supplied fuel to the farm had a brick thrown through the window of his home at his head and his clients received letters accusing him of being a pedophile.

The final outrage occurred when activists dug up the body of Chris Hall's mother-in-law, Gladys Hammond, and stole it from St. Peter's churchyard. The remains have never been returned and the body is thought to have been cut into a number of separate pieces. The Hall brothers surrendered. Another victory for the animal rights movement.

Johnny Holmes, a spokesman for the campaign, told reporters that, "This is the most fantastic day of my life. It' a victory for the animals and it's a fundamental victory for the animal rights movement." There was no comment from those suffering, or dying, from chronic respiratory diseases, many of which are being treated with medication developed from research on guinea pigs.

Here lies the quintessence of the debate. It is entirely rational and laudable to have compassion for animals and even a moral, emotional and intellectual objection to the abuse of powerless creatures for the sake of human want. But there is something fundamentally different, and fundamentally dysfunctional, about obsessive opposition to the responsible use of animals for the sake of human need.

Once the difference is obscured it is a short leap to use violence against people for the sake of guinea pigs, dogs or, for that matter, earthworms. In fact it is only logical. If humanity has no right to use animals at all, animal supporters have every right to use any means necessary to achieve their ends.

Which is why the sort of people Lenin referred to as useful idiots – Pamela Anderson, Paul McCartney and the like – are not merely eccentric and foolish but downright dangerous. While they might not applaud the extremism of animal rights zealots, they help create a climate where such repugnant behavior is not only possible but inevitable.

People for the Ethical Treatment of Animals, PETA, was at one time on the radical fringe of the movement but is now in the mainstream. When it compares the killing of chickens to the Holocaust, as it did in 2003 with its "Holocaust on Your Plate" exhibition, there might be occasional outrage from the public but little if any dissent from within the animal rights community.

The relativist slide began more than thirty years ago when militants in Europe planted bombs in stores that stocked fur coats. Their defence was that the buildings were empty and thus nobody was harmed. Not quite the case. Night staff and security guards were put in danger, as were the firefighters called to deal with the situation. It also meant that a life-threatening emergency in the same area may not have received the speedy response it required.

Thirty years has seen a colossal numbing of western culture and an exponential growth in the feelings industry. We are no longer asked what we know but how we feel. And kittens and puppies make us feel just like we're supposed to feel when we see them staring at us from glossy calendars or PETA propaganda.

Neurosis has smothered thought. We find ways to explain away starving Africans or the homeless but insist, to use the animal rights line, on speaking for those who cannot speak for themselves. It's also a bourgeois conceit. Impoverished Peru, for example, actually produces more fish than any other nation in the world but most of the catch goes to North America as cat food. A fish equals a cat equals a Peruvian child.

In 2002 Ontario MPP and current provincial Immigration Minister Mike Colle broke down in tears at a press conference because his proposed legislation on puppy mills had been rejected by the legislature. Not once but several times did this man lose his composure because a draconian bill demanding extraordinary punishment for people who raise dogs for sale in dreadful conditions failed to become law.

Of course people who run cruel puppy mills should be punished. Yet this particular law may well have meant that a convicted rapist would receive a lesser sentence than a thug who abuses a dog. When did we last see any politician crying in public because a home for mentally challenged children was being closed or because a woman had been murdered by her ex-husband due to inadequate state protection?

New, sensitive North Americans and Europeans define themselves by what offends them and, increasingly, what moves them to tears. It's certainly not the plight of people, let alone guinea pig farmers and their deceased relatives. The only thing worse than a fool is a fool with weapons. Or a fool who doesn't realize that meat isn't murder, meat is tasty.

MC

The 1950s

SOMETIMES WE IN THE MEDIA MERELY PLAY A GAME. MAKING LITTLE RIPPLES AT THE SIDE OF THE WATER RATHER THAN DIVING RIGHT IN TO MAKE AN ALMIGHTY SPLASH. IN OTHER WORDS, WE RUN AROUND THE EDGE OF VARIOUS PROBLEMS AND DEBATES BUT ARE AFRAID TO SHINE LIGHT ON THE AUTHENTIC DILEMMAS OF OUR AGE.

Whether it's politics, economics, culture or morality the culture, society and various pundits always assume that things are getting better, that we're making progress and that what we have and what is to come is superior to what was. Problem is, it's mostly nonsense. If anything, North American society is slipping into the abyss as the years go by.

Yet if any of us point to the past and argue that just half a century ago the world was more civilized, gentle, kind and moral we are dismissed at best as nostalgic cranks. Facts, however, are more significant than abuse.

A few examples. Those much-despised 1950s were, we are told, oppressive, confining and prudish. Yet since then teenage suicide in North America has increased enormously. The allegedly dark days of half-a-century ago seldom saw young Canadians and Americans try to and often succeeding in killing themselves. Not now.

In 1958 a broad cross-section of school principals was asked what were the five most challenging problems they faced in dealing with students. The answers were as follows. Not doing homework. Not respecting property, such as throwing books. Leaving lights or and doors and windows open. Throwing spitballs in class. Running in the halls.

In 1988 the same question were asked to a similar group of teachers. This time the answers were a little different. Children having abortions. Young people infected with AIDS. Incidents of rape. Widespread use of soft and increasingly hard drugs. A fear of violent murders and guns and knives in class.

We were told in the 1960s that the almost universal availability of the contraceptive pill and condoms would liberate women, increase marital happiness and lead to sexual fulfillment. In fact there has been a steady increase in so-called unwanted pregnancies, sexually transmitted diseases, divorce, the use of anti-depressants and reliance on pornography

Rather than empowering women, contraceptives have had the opposite effect and are used by men to have sexual intercourse without responsibility. Every serious survey reveals that young girls today feel far more pressurized to reluctantly agree to sex than their mothers and grandmothers did twenty and forty years ago.

More children are raised by single parents now than was thought remotely possible by even the most pessimistic analysts thirty-five years ago and those children sufficiently fortunate to have both parents in the home see their fathers and especially their mothers substantially less often than was the norm in the 50s and 60s.

In schools we spend more than ever before but genuine literacy levels have declined to such an extent that university teachers now complain that student essays are indecipherable. We abolished uniforms so that children could express their individuality and they dress in identical baggy pants and baseball caps.

There has been a concerted attempt to paint the generation following the Second World War as a false dawn. Entire television drama series have been dedicated to the premise that behind the façade of contentment and stability was a firestorm of grief, promiscuity and confusion. It's simply untrue. Nostalgia is pointless but an intelligent analysis of what we had and what we have lost can teach us a great deal.

It's not about turning back the clock but learning how to understand the time. These times are bleak. Instead of a New Jerusalem the country and culture resemble the new Gaza Strip. Good grief, if decadence made people happy there would at least be some hedonistic and purely selfish argument for it. But this is not the case. No serious person believes that people are happier today or that the cult of gratification provides anything more than a brief spasm of pleasure.

The deniers are still in positions of power but increasing numbers of young people have realized that the promises of their liberal parents were merely a cloud of smoke. Cannabis smoke at that. These men and women in their teens, twenties and thirties don't yearn for an era they never knew but for a moral code and a set of ethical assumptions that they know will give them peace and happiness.

The great writer Gilbert Keith Chesterton, who himself had dabbled with the occult and fallen into near despair when he was a young man, referred to the democracy of the dead. Listen to the past a little, it's amazing the wisdom and common sense you might hear. Allow the success of the past to inform and shape the future and those sounds will become a glorious song.

MC

Money and Happiness

JUST AS IT'S USUALLY ONLY BEAUTIFUL PEOPLE WHO PRETEND THAT GOOD LOOKS DON'T MATTER, IT'S GENERALLY THE RICH WHO TELL US THAT MONEY ISN'T PARTICULARLY IMPORTANT. IT IS IF YOU DON'T HAVE ANY. AND THOSE DROWNING OR SWIMMING FOR THEIR LIVES IN THE CURRENT ECONOMIC STORM KNOW THAT UNEMPLOYMENT, PAY CUTS AND EVAPORATING SAVINGS ARE MORE THAN MERE DENTS IN THEIR HOBBIES. SO WHEN, FOR EXAMPLE, VARIOUS ANGLICAN AND ROMAN CATHOLIC LEADERS IN BRITAIN SAID RECENTLY THAT THERE WERE IN FACT "POSITIVE ASPECTS TO THE RECESSION" THEY WERE DISMISSED AS RELIGIOUS CLOWNS AND OUT-OF-TOUCH DREAMERS.

Actually some of them are. It's the churches, however, that will be at the forefront of caring and coping in all this mess and all that these men were correctly saying is that such a massive shock to the system might deliver a spiritual reboot; might force us, perhaps kicking and screaming, to revaluate the meaning of life, the universe and the banking system.

Nietzsche said that what doesn't kill us makes us stronger. I know this because it's up there on the movie screen at the start of Conan the Barbarian. In fact what doesn't kill us makes us poorer. Then again Nietzsche said that God was dead. He's not, but Nietzsche is. And this is the essence of what the bishops were trying to explain. The sudden realization that material wealth is transitory and that earning, spending and saving are as much symptoms as they are solutions should lead us to grapple for the greater and grander things in life. Such as God, faith, family, community, the spiritual and the knowledge that this is the land of shadows and that real life hasn't begun yet.

At its most cynical it's a suburban version of the bunker syndrome. There are said to be no atheists when bullets are flying and death appears imminent. In other words, the propinquity of eternity obliges someone to consider where they will be spending it. A ravished economy is not the same as a filthy battlefield but it still lunges at complacency. The foundations of our very being – purchasing power, pensions, the car and the vacation and, at its most severe, a roof over our head and food for the family – are shaken if not destroyed.

The inherent danger is the appearance of exploitation. The ugly spectacle of the evangelist failing with the healthy but converting the sick. A liturgical dance through the ruins of people's lives. Yet that is not really what the argument is about. It's using, not abusing, the change in climate to readjust focus and lead people to ask the most profound questions. Questions about first things, permanent things. Whether God exists may be more significant an issue than whether GST should be lowered by a percentage point and whether we are made in the image of God to love our creator and love our neighbour as ourselves more relevant than any debate over selective import controls.

If nothing else the fundamentally contrary opinions of internationally respected economists regarding how to respond to the financial crisis has shown us that even the most informed do not know what to do. No compelling responses either from the social scientists, the politicians or the modernist gurus. We look elsewhere. We look. We see. See meaning instead of motive, people instead of crowds. The economy will surely recover and the buttons will be turned back on. After the forced hiatus the world will probably be a very similar place. What is infinitely weightier - the weight of glory - is whether we will be the same people. It's about the economy of grace rather than the economy of money. Always has been, always will be.

MC

Art?

I'VE WAITED FOR THE HYSTERIA ABOUT THE GREAT CAT TORTURE INCIDENT TO SUBSIDE A LITTLE BEFORE MAKING COMMENT. FOR THE UNINITIATED, TWO MEN IN TORONTO WERE CHARGED WITH MAKING A VIDEO OF THE TORTURE AND KILLING OF A CAT. THE PAIR CLAIMED THAT THE FOOTAGE WAS A WORK OF ART AND HAD A SPECIAL ARTISTIC AND SOCIAL MESSAGE.

The usual animal rights zealots have had a field day with this one, but in fact the gruesome episode has little do with cats at all. It does, however, have everything to do with how an addled society has come to regard art, and how artists now regard themselves.

A little background. A few years ago I wrote about a young man whose exhibit consisted of dozens, if not hundreds, of pairs of boy's used underwear. As I said at the time, great artists change the world, this fellow changes underpants. The response of some of his supporters was interesting. They drove up to one of my outdoor radio broadcasts, shouted something about artistic freedom, and then threw an egg at me. It missed. Well, at least they weren't starving artists and could afford to waste good food.

In western Canada we had in the past ten years both Piss Pope and Piss Christ, in which pictures of the leader of the Roman Catholic Church and of Jesus were depicted soaking in urine. Then there was a graphic portrait of the crucified Jesus having forced sexual acts performed on him by a clergyman. That one managed to win an award.

In Ontario there was an exhibition consisting of hundreds of children's pictures of penises. I can only assume that the children were told to make these drawings and paintings and have long wondered why there were no criminal charges. The gallery in which this nonsense was shown, by the way, received public funding.

Toronto saw another example of tax-payers' generosity when a sado-masochistic exhibit was put on. A large rack was present, one apparently used for tying up men who want to be chastised. Hey, just try being a genuine art lover, there's punishment enough in contemporary Canada. Next to the rack was a picture of a naked woman pulling a scroll through her legs.

In a small glass case alongside the picture was the scroll itself, covered in dried menstrual blood. This, the guide assured me, was dangerous and hard-hitting art. No it wasn't. It was the neurosis of the under-achiever and the pampered pervert.

Even the relative mainstream of modern art shows a gaping lack of creativity. Piles of bricks, dead cows, candies piled up in a heap, enormous canvases painted entirely in one colour, so-called living art with people taking their clothes off in mass parades of silliness. Goodness me, do they not have lives?

There is, of course, a need for art that challenges and provokes. But we don't have that. By pandering to pornography, homoeroticism, hatred of religion and anti-intellectualism these people are actually merely floating along with the cultural and moral tide. They are riding the waves, not battling them.

What this is all really about is the absence of good. And when there is an absence of good the subsequent vacuum does nor remain empty. It is filled, and filled with bad. By that I do not mean that the people who create rancid and repugnant art are necessarily bad themselves, but that they inhabit an artistic world that has abandoned goodness and, inevitably, opened its very being to all that is bad, dark and destructive.

We should be surprised not that a cat has been tortured in the name of art, but that this did not happen earlier and that the same has not yet occurred to vulnerable humans. Babies, or the old and the weak.

If the people who are accused of this crime are convicted they must be punished. But they are merely symptoms. For the causes and the root we must look deeper, and perhaps closer to home. Magazines, books, television, radio and movies. So bursting with dumbed down decadence that they drip filth over us every day. Cats may have nine lives, but a civilised society has only one.

MC

In The Eye of the Beholder

A DECADE AGO I SPENT AN AFTERNOON WITH JUDY SGRO, NOW A LIBERAL MP. SHE WAS THEN A CITY COUNCILOR AND SHE AND A MEMBER OF HER STAFF ASKED ME TO ACCOMPANY THEM ON A TOUR OF VARIOUS PUBLICLY FUNDED ART GALLERIES IN TORONTO. IT WAS, SHALL WE SAY, AN ENLIGHTENING EXPERIENCE.

The four galleries we visited received hundreds of thousands of dollars in direct grants form various levels of government and through generous tax breaks. Was this, Judy wondered, an appropriate use of public money?

The first thing we noticed was that at no time was there anybody in any of these galleries apart from the curator and ourselves. Actually no. The first thing we noticed was an enormous photograph of a man being crucified on a Volkswagen. Hard not to notice such a thing really.

The "art work" was part of a larger display involving sadomasochism, with pictures of men and women being tied, bound, strangled and beaten for sexual stimulation. And not even on good old Canadian-made cars but on a German import!

The same gallery featured a six-foot high photograph of a naked woman pulling a long piece of paper between her legs. She was menstruating at the time. We knew this because the caption by the picture told us so and because that same paper, soaked in dried blood, was proudly placed alongside the exhibit.

The other galleries were of a similar quality. One was particularly disturbing in that its main exhibit was of children's drawings of men's penises. Certainly appalling and probably illegal. Judy Sgro was rightly shocked.

I assume, then, that she and the rest of the Liberal caucus will be supporting the government's new amendments to the legislation that gives tax credits to Canadian movies. Because some of the films that enjoy these financial handouts are just as wretched, repugnant and, frankly, banal as the trash at the galleries.

The Conservatives have announced that they will be, "expanding slightly the criteria for denying tax credits to Canadian films that include gratuitous violence, significant sexual content and that lack an educational purpose, or involve the denigration of an identifiable group."

Hardly draconian stuff. Merely arguing that if people want to produce pornographic garbage they should do it on their own dollar. Nor is this censorship – nothing is being banned - but an intelligent use of tax-dollars.

The screams of protest, however, can be heard from cocktail parties coast to fashionable coast. "How dare a tiny minority of people dictate what we can see and how dare the government control art."

Quite so. The government should not be involved at all. If you want to make it, write it, record it, fine. Do it. Yourself. As for the tiny minority, it is indeed time that the usual types with their radical sexual agenda and hatred for what they see as orthodoxy lost their special privileges.

Canada may, just may, be able to survive without your money subsidising yet more movies about Gay angst on the prairies, dads abusing their Marxist feminist daughters, the evils of religion and how Americans are lizards from Mars waiting to eat our healthcare system.

If Judy Sgro and her Liberal MP friends want a remider of what we are funding they only have to ask me. I can't send the pictures by e-mail though – I'd probably be arrested.

MC

Woodstock

Sometimes, as they say, fact is far stranger than fiction. And what is supposed to be serious is actually much funnier than comedy. Such as this official media release from The Woodstock Art Gallery in Woodstock, Ontario. It is worth, I think, quoting in full. Forgive my comments, I couldn't resist.

"Ed Zelenak is a process artist who has remained emphatically anti-allusionary. In fact, there are few artists who are as admired for their sophisticated use of physicality. Every mark, every bit of physical evidence is a document, an intentional gesture recorded, witnessed and made specifically to be itself."

A free picture of dogs playing poker if you can tell me what that paragraph means or identify the writer's high school English teacher. Because he should be fired.

"Yet, although Zelenak uses processes we normally associate with minimal process, seriality and progression, (Zelenak's work is done in series which last several years), a strategy that embodies a cognitive model with pragmatic primacy, Zelenak has a deep distrust of conventional empiricism. Conversely, his work is all about the inability of physical process to fix meaning. He believes that expression is only a place pointing to a shifting reality."

Okay, I take my last comment back. The opening paragraph was easy compared to this one. Perhaps it's a translation from Hungarian or Finnish? No, it's just clever artsy people being, well, clever artsy people. Odd how their supposed cleverness seems to normal people to be so stupid.

"In his latest series of works being shown in the collective flow exhibition, Zelenak repeats and reworks one common symbol: a divining rod (the Y-shaped stick that dowsers use to find water). It might be easy to read the symbol literally and conclude that water, or the search for it, is a material/process that significantly reflects the nature of the universe. But Zelenak contends that (his) symbol meaning constantly morphs and becomes a site of perpetual re-signification."

Sorry, still can't follow it. It seems to be that this guy paints a bunch of sticks and calls it his constantly morphing symbol. A medical complaint I wouldn't wish on my worst enemy.

"In this recent work, Zelenak includes some symbols from previous series such as his 'boat map' series and his 'basin map' works. A lot of his previous work involved constructing voids and connecting us to the ominous nature of the negative or the other by engaging us with the mystery of existence by mapping its opposite. Now, Zelenak has allowed energy and existence into this void by allowing symbols into these spaces. Perhaps this is what happens when you create voids: nature (or our belief in perpetuality) rushes in to fill that space."

Oh I see. Now it's all crystal clear. I can't understand the brilliance of all this because of my belief in "perpetuality" and because I refuse to be engaged by the mystery of existence by mapping its opposite. I'm a philistine who still thinks Titian and Leonardo were real artists.

"Alternateively, Zelenak creates maps leading us to and focussing on the 'big' questions, but he knows enough not to try and answer them. Instead, he invokes the ever-present effect of paradox on our everyday lives."

I have to agree. Certainly my everyday life has just been hit by a great big paradox. Or we could call it a contradiction, or an enigma, or even a conundrum. No, it's just a plain old question. Why are horribly pretentious and silly people encouraged to pollute our art galleries and why are their buddies allowed to rape the language?

But the funniest part of all this I've kept until last. By funny, however, I mean funny in a grotesque way, in that the last laugh is on us. Because at the bottom of the release we are told that "The Woodstock Art Gallery is a cultural division of the Community Services Department of the City of Woodstock", and that "we gratefully acknowledge the assistance of the Ontario Arts Council".

In other words, you're paying for it. Paying through your tax-dollars and paying through the dumbing down of our country and culture by the chattering classes. By the way, stories such as this can be found in virtually every gallery in Canada. An embarrassment, and a disgrace.

Mary Poppins

So another Harry Potter book is about to be published and the critical e-mails are already doing the rounds. But those who wrote the entire world about the hellish horrors of HP may well be correct. Harry, Hermione and Ron could simply be lulling us into a false sense of security before they turn us all into collective newts. Thing is, the problem goes much further than JK Rowling and all her sordid works.

Take Mary Poppins for instance. The woman is unmarried, strong-willed and independent. Thus a feminist and almost certainly a lesbian. She uses magic, witchcraft and levitation to tidy houses, do dishes, make beds and the like. She also flies around holding some sort of umbrella and a large bag. One can only imagine what is contained in that carpet full of hideousness.

She has a very close relationship with Bert, the leader of a gang of chimney-sweeps, a radical special interest group or, let's be candid here, a labour union. In short, Mary Poppins is in love with a dangerous Marxist-Leninist intent on world revolution and enforced atheism. Comrade Bert's ties to the NDP or worse are frightening to say the least.

I refer you to "What Is To Be Swept? The Radical Solution To The State of the Chimney-Sweep", by Bert. The pamphlet calls for an alliance of sweeps, sidewalk artists and merry-go-round operatives to fight the system and bring down capitalism and bad cockney accents. Enough said.

Poppins' employer is Mr. Banks, who is a highly placed banker and thus part of a huge Masonic conspiracy dedicated to one-world government and allied to Satan in his efforts to take over the world. Experts believe that the bank donates money to the United Nations and has purchased black helicopters in readiness for, well, for when the time comes.

Banks' wife, Winnifred, is a radical suffragette and thus may well be a lesbian as well. The fact that Banks cannot control his spouse and make her stay at home with his children shows that he himself is weak and effeminate.

That Mrs. Banks, or is it Ms. Banks, is out campaigning instead of making dinner for her family makes her a disgrace as a mother and, now I think about it, definitely a lesbian. Perhaps she and Poppins know one another as fellow members of some secret and perverse cult.

The Banks children became lost at one point in the story and had to be brought home by the police. They are obviously not being beaten frequently enough by their so-called parents, who no doubt believe that there are alternatives to a good spanking with a stick. For all intents and purposes this is Communism. "Suffer the children." Precisely.

Those same children's reference to "Let's go fly a kite" is not as harmless as it seems. Various Internet experts have informed me that the phrase is in fact an esoteric reference to devil worship. The word "Kite" in an ancient tongue meaning, "One who is frightened by everything new, ignores real problems and obsesses about nothing."

Then we have Uncle Albert. This reprobate seems to be drunk all of the time, and drinking alcohol is a sin arguably worse even than feeding the birds without parental permission. His uncontrollable laughter is the work of the evil one, an old weapon of Lucifer. Put simply, anyone who laughs is a friend of Beelzebub. I personally have never laughed and never intend to do so. Indeed my wife has strict instructions to hit me over the head at even the merest hint of a giggle. Can't be too careful.

A final word. On my way to protest outside the local bookstore selling copies of the new Harry Potter I had to detour around several homeless people living on the street, a drug-ridden prostitute standing on the corner, an unemployed individual offering to do absolutely any job for money and a preacher talking about love, humanity and understanding.

The fact that thousands of unborn children are being aborted, that genuine marriage is under attack by the courts, culture and addled politicians, that materialism and decadence combine to rape what is good and noble, all this is irrelevant compared to the tragedy of a children's book.

And just in case you think I'm over-reacting and find what I say to be amusing, be very careful and mindful. Remember, they laughed at Donald Duck too. Ha!

MC

Actresses

WHAT A BUSY BEE LITTLE DAKOTA FANNING HAS BEEN LATELY. WHILE STILL IN THE THEATRES HAVING CONVERSATIONS WITH A TALKING SPIDER CALLED CHARLOTTE THE 12-YEAR-OLD ACTRESS IS ABOUT TO PREMIERE ON SCREEN PLAYING A LITTLE GIRL BEING RAPED BY HER FATHER.

Which has led quite a few people to question the ethics and legality of the movie *Hounddog*. Alleged defenders of free speech have, predictably, replied that their opponents haven't even seen that which they are criticizing.

A dumb thesis. I wasn't in a death camp but I know that The Holocaust was ghastly. I never met Saddam Hussein but I know he was a thug. In the final analysis, you don't have to step in excrement to know it stinks.

Fanning is not raped of course. She's just acting. Acting as she puts on a body suit for the scene and makes all the right noises that little girls apparently make when they're being brutally sexually assaulted.

Raising the question of who told Ms. Fanning all the gory details of what little girls might do in such a situation. The director of course. Because, say the makers of the movie, we need to understand the horrors of incest.

Thing is, we already assumed that incest was horrific. Hard to imagine some potential pedophile saying, "Oh, I was going to rape a child but after that movie, well I've completely changed my mind."

The issue has often been discussed and should be so in the future. But with skill and craft. When Shakespeare writes of Richard III's murder of the princes in the tower, for example, we do not have to see the deaths. The writer is sufficiently gifted to convey the horror. Playwright Bertolt Brecht revealed the whole sordid world of torture in his "Life of Galileo" with the simple line, "They showed me the instruments."

But great minds the makers of *Hounddog* are certainly not.

At heart it's about what we should label shock kudos. Nothing is more trendy in the movie business than the apparent shocking of what these patronizing dunderheads think of as middle North America. And as every form of adult perversion has been already been used, let's try the kids instead.

Then they'll sit back and look smug and caring and enlightened when moral and religious types argue that it's emotionally and sexually unhealthy to use child rape as a form of titillation for witless audiences.

Some have argued that it's fine because Fanning's mother was present during the ordeal and approved of her daughter's work. Oh, well that's okay then. After all, there has never been a neurotic mother of an actor child in Hollywood, living her life vicariously and enjoying the money and glamour of being mum to a star.

It really is extraordinary that the same sort of people who routinely attack traditional parenting and vehemently oppose even mild spanking are so supportive of a mother's right to allow her 12-year-old child to behave in such a manner.

Frankly, any criticism will only encourage the chattering classes and inflate still further their sense of self-righteous paranoia. A child here, a moral code there, a broken generation somewhere else. Doesn't matter, as long as you're the center of attention at a fashionable party.

MC

Lights, Action, Nonsense

A SURPRISINGLY BRAVE AND ORIGINAL PERIOD FOR THE ENTERTAINMENT INDUSTRY. AT THE TORONTO INTERNATIONAL FILM FESTIVAL ONE OF THE HITS WAS A MOVING DRAMA ABOUT AN INNOCENT FAMILY TORN APART BY THE FORCED STARVATION OF MORE THAN A MILLION UKRAINIANS BY STALIN. THE MOVIE DEPICTED THE SOVIET POLITICAL MURDER MACHINE THAT KILLED MORE PEOPLE THAN HITLER AND THE SATANIC EVILS OF INTERNATIONAL COMMUNISM.

Another hit was a biting documentary that exposed the link between abortion and cancer and also the medical dangers of long-term use of the contraceptive pill. It pulled no punches as it took on the enormously wealthy and powerful contraceptive and abortion movement.

The third big winner was a charming film that showed a husband and wife and their five children in a loving, happy and fulfilling relationship. It was subtle and stylish and also managed to tell audiences that children raised in common law homes were 450 times more likely to see their parents split up than were children whose parents were married.

It also revealed the agony of divorce, tbe pain of promiscuity and the overwhelming joy and love that was so typical of committed families – especially those with a strong faith life.

Just a few days later at the Primetime Emmy ceremony in Los Angeles Mel Gibson received a special award for his work and also a heat-felt apology for the persecution he had been forced to endure. It was a truly emotional moment as various producers and actors begged to be forgiven.

Then there were some particularly funny and courageous speeches. A leading comic made fun of the hypocrisy of super-rich actors who preach environmentalism but travel in private planes and live in mansions that use breathtakingly large amounts of energy.

Particular fun was made of Michael Moore, with jokes made about his former employees who claim he treated them so badly while making lucrative movies about employees being treated badly. And about how he is the champion of hard-hitting documentaries but refused to cooperate with a Canadian couple making a hard-hitting documentary about him.

Michael was seen to he taking it all in his usual good-natured way and telling reporters that it was only correct that the left was mocked as well as the right.

But we know it didn't happen. None of it. Never will. Because the denizens of the house of Hollywood and its little suburbs across the globe are extreme, cowardly and slow. Complacent, greedy and terrified of being left out of the fashion that dictates their career and their future.

So at the Toronto festival old David Cronenberg gave us yet another film where people get naked and kill each other. Then he looked all cross as he stared at the camera and made some pretentious comment about not being a pornographer.

So did director Alan Bell, who was apparently completely unable to discuss the horror of child abuse without showing an eighteen-year-old actress pretending to be thirteen pretending to be raped and sodomized by a grown man.

All, of course, in the best possible taste and not in any way to arouse perverts, make money and get people to discuss what would otherwise be a completely ignored piece of rubbish made by posing mediocrities.

The grotesque Emmy night? The usual Christian-bashing. And vacuous attempts by actors to shock the very people who buy theatre tickets make them so rich. How pathetic, how privileged and how utterly banal and predictable.

Oscars

I'VE WON AN OSCAR! THANK YOU MY BEAUTIFUL PARTNER, MY BEAUTIFUL THERAPIST, MY BEAUTIFUL BANKERS. THANK YOU TO THE MEMORY OF AN OVER-INDULGED PLAYBOY WHO WAS CONSIDERED A GREAT THESPIAN BECAUSE HE PUT WHITE MAKE-UP ON HIS FACE, OVER-ACTED AND THEN FILLED HIMSELF WITH DRUGS AND TOOK HIS OWN LIFE. THANK YOU. FALSE EMOTION. PREPARED SPEECH. GO OBAMA! THANK YOU TO THOSE DOCUMENTARIES ABOUT WORTHY SUBJECTS THAT WE'VE NEVER ACTUALLY SEEN AND DON'T CARE ABOUT BUT WILL THEN CHEER REALLY LOUDLY SO THAT THOSE WATCHING THE SHOW WILL ASSUME WE HAVE SEEN THESE THINGS AND ACTUALLY DO CARE ABOUT KIDS WITH CLEFT PALATES AND POOR PEOPLE. GO OBAMA!

Banal liberal comments, predictable and safe gestures towards homosexuals and sweeping generalizations about peace, liberty and the arts. Thank you. Praise for my fellow actors who didn't win but they should have and I don't deserve this and actually I hate you and couldn't care less because I won and you didn't and I'll be even richer and more successful than you.

Mindless comment making fun of President Bush laughed at and applauded by mindless millionaires who mindlessly claim to be radicals when they couldn't spell the word and would no more embrace a dangerous cause than come to an award ceremony without a suit costing more than most working people earn in a month. Thank you. Tears. Thank you. Go Obama! Thank you. Obligatory attack on religion. Crying. This is so very important.

Thank you for giving statues to movies that have the right politics and thank you for allowing us to make speeches from positions of enormous privilege abusing people who dare to disagree with us. Act like a spoilt little fascist. More false emotion and false liberalism. Yes, yes, yes! I love Hollywood, it's the real America. Laws don't apply to me, being arrested for drugs and alcohol is a career boost and I'll never have to worry about not being able to pay the bills or not being able to send my kids to a school that's safe and good and clean. Thank you.

This is such a wonderful occasion. Having no idea who the foreign filmmakers are and not caring – where did she get that awful dress? Describing arch mediocrities who can memorise other people's words and sleep with the right people as geniuses. Tears, marriage is wrong, tears, another attack on religion, go Obama! I have no idea who most of these dead people from last year are and don't care either. Thank you.

Punch a photographer, scream at a cameraman, swear at a child, act like a whore, behave in a way accepted only in Hollywood and then pretend that you are just like anyone else. Be part of the most neurotic and dysfunctional community in human history and then tell other people how to live, behave, think and vote. Thank you. Tears. False emotion, bad acting.

No to war, yes to war movies. Yes to freedom, no to you having the freedom to take issue with me and my super-rich friends. Tears. Go Obama! Batman 5, Spiderman 6, Superman 7. Such quality. We're great, you're not. Hide Charlton Heston away in the middle of the list because even though he campaigned for civil rights before you were born, he dared to be a Republican. Crying. Thank you. Where's my cheque? I love you all.

MC

Don't Get the Joke

When sane people read about a comedy show called *Little Mosque on the Prairie* made by a notoriously liberal public broadcaster they assumed it was a clever self-parody. The CBC had at last found a sense of humor, they assumed, and was making fun of its own reputation for political correctness and plodding leftism.

A spoof, they thought. A clever ploy to fool us into believing that our national broadcaster would be so predictable and crass as to actually run with such a weak and cringing idea. But then they realized that this was Canada and this was the CBC.

Then they saw it. The usual visual drudgery. Awful Canadian actors mouthing lamentable dialogue packed with clichés and telegraphed attempts at humour. The bland leading the bland. And all paid for by your tax dollars, including the huge advertising campaign for the project. Public money that could otherwise been spent on something trivial like a nurse in an intensive care ward.

The obvious first. It goes without saying that no such comedy will be made in this country where Christians are portrayed as a misunderstood community and all of the non-Christians around them as buffoons and extremists. Also goes without saying that we'll never see an episode of Little Church in the Desert on Saudi TV.

From beginning to end the show thumps us over our non-hijab wearing heads with a clumsy hammer. Any fears about Islam, we are told, are based on our own ignorance and bigotry. Everyone is a caricature in Little Mosque, but some caricatures are more obnoxious than others.

The Muslim characters are nice and kind and ordinary in that quintessentially Canadian way. Some of them may be silly and old-fashioned but they'd never hurt a fly, let alone kill an infidel. The non-Muslim caricatures, however, are repugnant. Especially if they're cops.

You know cops. The poor fools who have to put their lives on the line during a terrorist attack. A terrorist attack which, naturally, could never have anything to do with Islam. By the way, in the month of December alone there were 249 jihadist incidents around the world, resulting in 1794 deaths and 1589 people being critically injured.

About the only compassionate and apparently informed non-Muslim anywhere to be seen in the programme is an Anglican priest. The usual witless literary device who makes us feel good because we're obliged to identify with his good sense and humanism.

Does he, one wonders, ask his Muslim friends if they follow the Koran's teaching that apostates from their religion should be killed? A concept that is taught throughout Islamic jurisprudence and practiced all over the Muslim world.

He might also want to ask them if the Koran allows a husband to beat his wife? Something which is not denied even by those Muslims who are uncomfortable with the passage.

Or he might want to monitor the sermons in the Little Mosque to make sure that, unlike many of those in Gaza, Cairo, Jerusalem, Damascus, Islamabad and even a few in Canada they're not applauding the 9/11 massacres, calling Jews monkeys and pigs who should be slaughtered, demanding that Christians be killed in a holy war or that homosexuals should be put to the sword.

Genuine understanding might be possible. But only after genuine truth, genuine criticism and, well, genuine comedy.

MC

Pagans

FASCINATING NEWS THAT WICCA PRIESTS AND PRIESTESSES ARE TO BE CHAPLAINS IN OUR PRISONS. JUST LIKE REPRESENTATIVE OF CHRISTIANITY, JUDAISM, ISLAM AND OTHER FAITHS, CANADIAN LAW AND THE CANADIAN CHARTER WILL GIVE WITCHES FULL ACCESS TO OUR INCARCERATED CRIMINALS. ONE CAN ONLY HOPE THAT THEY WON'T BE TEACHING THEM HOW TO MAKE THE CELL DOORS DISAPPEAR OR THE WARDERS INVISIBLE.

Knowing that every good Canadian would delight in this oh so progressive adventure, one that the public will have to pay for of course, I thought a trip to the Pagan Federation website might be in order. What fun it turned out to be. The organization represents witches, druids, goddess worshippers and various others. As for Satan, visitors to the site are given an essay praising Satanism and providing a link to the church of Satan website.

Then we are treated to a whole variety of sub-groups. The Pagan Firefighters Association unfortunately has "no info at the moment, but will post when we do." This is very good news indeed. The average speed of a broom is several miles an hour faster than that of even the most advanced fire-truck. There is also the chance of communing with the god of fire and asking him (or is it her) to be reasonable and simply put the flames out without any human intervention.

Then we have The Pagan Bar Association. Oddly enough, I'm not surprised. I think I may have met some of the members. "Like many good projects, the Pagan Bar Association started for selfish reasons. I wanted to communicate with other attorneys who, like myself, follow the way of the Witch." Right. Lots of nose-wiggling I suppose, and stopping your mother from getting cross with poor old Darren.

Next come the Pagan Alliance of Nurses, and, most amusing of all, Pagans in the Auto Industry. "Automative Pagans is a networking group for all Pagans who work in the automotive industry – no matter where they live, or which company they work for, whether they work for manufacturers or suppliers, hourly or salary."

I just know that CAW members all over Canada have been counting the days until they can have the union fight for crystal manipulation lessons. Look out Buzz Hargrove, you could be replaced by Harry Potter. Mind you, is Harry a socialist? Goes to a private school, speaks in a posh accent. No, it's Ron Weasley who's the member of the proletariat.

We also have the great North American disease of being offended. "SciFi Channel actively misrepresenting pagans specifically in two programmes" announces the site. The two to watch for in case Mr. Warlock or Ms. Goblin is moved to tears are "Evil Witches" and "Declassified Evil". Stay tuned for Buffy with a bad hair day.

In the noble words of the Monty Python team in the *Holy Grail* movie: "How do you know she's a witch?" Reply: "Because she looks like one." In that case the local peasants had put a false big nose and a funny hat on the woman.

My experience has been that such people tend to have a little too much time and money on their hands and a feeling that they are superior to the "ordinary people" around them "who don't quite understand." Also a contempt for and crass ignorance of what is referred to as "organized religion" and a total lack of contextual knowledge of ancient and medieval history.

A liking for dark make-up and black clothes, often mingled with Hollywood witch fashion and celtic jewlery. A habit of staring a lot and speaking in a slow, deliberate manner that is supposed to indicate authority and wisdom. Oh, and a fair helping of middle-class neurosis.

In all seriousness, this absurd situation could be problematic. Whilst nobody would allege that all pagans break the law, people proudly calling themselves pagans have been involved in child abuse circles and grotesque dark cults. Would a prisoner genuinely benefit from a pagan visit? Is it healthy that a pagan group called the "Officers of Avalon" is listed and claims to have police members in the USA, Canada, Britain, Ireland and Australia?

To quote the divine Python again. "She turned me into a newt … I got better." Let us hope the same for these poor misguided souls. And that we don't have to finance the treatment.

Not Funny

I JUST COULDN'T HELP IT. MAKING FUN OF THE FUNNY, THAT IS. LAST WEEK I RECEIVED THE FOLLOWING E-MAIL.

"Peace and Release is a series of weekly 'coffee house' performances and teach-ins. These will bring together members of the local music scene with the peace activist community in a bid to bring the people of Toronto closer to current events in Iraq.

"Presented by a wide range of organizations including Christian Peacemaker Teams (CPT), Friends Peace and Social Action Committee, The War Resisters Support Campaign, and Artists Against War, the series is greatly inspired by the courage of Toronto's own Jim Loney and the three other CPT hostages, as well as the 16,000 unjustly detained Iraqis.

"The teach-ins will include concise, up to date reports from members of organizations working in Iraq as well as short documentaries, slide shows and testimonies from people who have experienced the effects of the war directly i.e., families of hostages/detainees, AWOL soldiers, journalists etc."

I replied, being just a little mischievous. "Sounds wonderful. But I do have a few questions. Do you guarantee a smoke-free environment and an atmosphere where members of the Gay, Lesbian, Bisexual and Transsexual community will feel welcome and empowered? Also, is there a childcare area provided where single mothers may leave their children? Finally, would my Wiccan friends enjoy these evenings or face any Christofascist discrimination – regrettably, it does still happen. Thanks again, and I do hope to hear back soon."

The reply was delicious. "Hi, I don't know you, but I thought I'd answer that as one of the organizers, a long time wiccan, a long time friend of one of the CPT ers, I can answer in the affirmative to all your queries, except we are too small a skeleton crew to set up a child care area. This is taking place in the El Mocambo, a bar, even my 15-year-old daughter can't come. Any childcare would have to be off-site. However, if you're volunteering ..."

Courtesy demanded that I respond once again. "That's good to know. What about the general atmosphere? Friendly towards the transgendered? I so much want these poor guys who have run away from Bush's Nazi state to find peace and love here."

The reponse. "I'm not a X-ian ....I think we are all struggling to re-kick-start the protest movement in T.O. in the face of rampant apathy, rampant sexism, rampant plutocracy, no f*****g, no fun. If you wanna bring Tamara and the Wiccans from her famous bookstore down, be my guest but they were always a little too ay-political for my taste. The Radical Fairies I used to know in the U.S. were a lot more into demonstrations. Did you ever meet Ken Quayle? He came to ACT for Disarmament demonstrations in a pink bloody tutu. Now, that's my kind of man. (He's retired to a small island on the West Coast now.) As for the actual soldiers who have run away, I don't know what they look like so I don't know if they were there.

"Pax, and all that shit, Smokey"

Unfortunately I didn't meet Mr. Quayle or see his pink ballet skirt. My loss I'm sure. One last e-mail. Would it be okay, I asked, if I brought my guitar along? "It's not a bother if you are serious. But someone in our group thinks you are the M.Coren who writes for the *Sun* and has hosted some talk shows. Is this the case?"

Absolutely not. Rock on comrade, rock on. And thank goodness that when it comes to a situation as serious as Iraq we never have to deal with caricatures.

Natives

ANOTHER OCCUPATION BY NATIVES OF DISPUTED LAND. THIS TIME THE BATTLE LINES ARE DRAWN IN CALEDONIA, ONTARIO BUT THEY COULD BE ANYWHERE IN CANADA AND MAY WELL BE REPEATED ALL OVER THE COUNTRY BEFORE LONG. AGEING AND ACHING CONFLICTS, DUSTY WITH HISTORY AND RUSTY WITH LEGAL WRANGLING.

As with most of these incidents, there are compelling arguments on all sides. Residents argue that the police are not doing enough to protect their freedom of movement and property. Police complain that their hands are tied by cowardly politicians. Aboriginals argue that the land was stolen from them in the first place.

At least some of them do. Elected leaders, traditional elders, young activists all have their own views and agendas and often they are in sharp disagreement. Within white Canada, however, the debate over native issues is smothered by political correctness and the fear of being labeled a racist.

What is so ironic about this is that the bulk of this country is composed of people who suffered just as much as the First Nations. Highland Scots, Ukrainians, European Jews, Irish Catholics, Black Africans, Chinese and Vietnamese victims of Communism, for example, all experienced massacres, mass starvations, rape, pillage, destruction and attempt at genocide.

Many of them have never received any compensation and are never likely to do so. Those devastated by Communism have to remain silent as teenagers wear T-shirts emblazoned with the hammer and sickle or portraits of Marxist killers.

Yet they move on. As we all do. I watch each day as my eighteen-year-old son leaves for work with his heavy backpack, working forty hours a week and more and often coming home so tired that he collapses into bed. He does this so as to pay for at least part of his university education.

If he were native, much if not all of that education would be paid for by the state. Yet my wife's family lost their property and safety in India and had to flee their homeland. My family was deprived of everything in Eastern Europe and had many relatives slaughtered. Nobody is offering to pay for our children's further education and, frankly, none of us would expect it.

Is it time for the native world to put its own house in order and stop relying on undoubted past wrongs to explain current problems? Should we be compensating people for the experience of residential schools when many of these institutions were not the vile caricatures painted by activists and the mainstream media?

Do the land claims have any relevance in the modern world and is it not time for a new vision to be created? Have we idealized and idolized native culture and history and blackened the reality of the European and Christian legacy? Are we willing to hold individuals accountable for dependency and addiction problems?

These are questions being asked by millions of ordinary, compassionate and generous Canadians who wish only peace and happiness for their native brothers and sisters. Within the answers there may be truth, or just more political nonsense.

MC

School Bullies

LAST FRIDAY WAS JUST AN ORDINARY DAY UNTIL MY LIFE WAS DRAMATICALLY TRANSFORMED BY THE NEWS THAT THE CHILDREN OF ONTARIO WOULD FROM NOW ON BE HAPPIER, MORE INTELLIGENT, MORE ENLIGHTENED AND CERTAINLY MODEL CITIZENS. BRIEFLY, THE TORONTO DISTRICT SCHOOL BOARD ISSUED A DRAFT HUMAN RIGHTS POLICY BANNING DISCRIMINATION AND TAUNTING.

The fact that Toronto's schools are producing waves of children who know more about Keannu Reeves than about Keats, more about hairstyles than about history and have never read a book in their lives is, of course, irrelevant. As long as they all grasp the fact that we are all in every single way exactly the same and that nothing is better than anything else.

The board lists 14 areas of discrimination, including sexual orientation, ancestry, citizenship, gender, socio-economic status, unwanted or practical jokes, intrusive comments about a child's clothes, shunning or exclusion and condescension or paternalism.

"Mummy, Jimmy was paternalistic to me in gym class today. I feel really threatened and offended."

"There, there Crystal-Star. I'll make you a vegetarian sandwich and we can sit down together and watch a rerun of that marvelous CBC documentary about feminist truckers in Northern Manitoba."

"Thanks mum, you're a real comrade."

What is so apparent from this document is that the people who claim to know how to educate our children in fact know absolutely nothing about children. Kids will exclude, will tease, will joke, will sulk and will form cliques. Violence is never acceptable and nor is racism or genuine nastiness. But in a school system with such elevating levels of drug-dealing, under-age sex, smoking and drinking it is shocking that a bunch of naïve ideologues would waste time and money on such a fantasy as this.

Obviously a great deal of the material is driven by a homosexual lobby that would have us believe that if any young boy is mildly effeminate he must be given Gay awareness training and protected from everybody around him. The policy devotes several of its entries to banning homophobia and "outing", as though Canada's schools were bursting at the seams with tiny Gay activists.

As for shunning, groups of children will always form clubs and groups and they are usually quite delightful. Will, I wonder, the school board reprimand, say, black or Vietnamese students for hanging together, or will this be an example of "racism" or "cultural insensitivity". Or even, God save us, "condescension."

And what happens if a Christian or Muslim student makes polite objection to the homosexual lifestyle of a fellow student. The board will be "homophobic" if it sides with the religious kids, "disparaging of specific religious and cultural groups" if it favours the Gay chap.

Another section of this policy outlaws the false teaching of history, obviously meant to prevent denial of the holocaust, which is of course occurring every day in every classroom in Canada. But what of the now common teaching that our native peoples were always in the right, or that French-Canadians are oppressed? Some of this stuff is actually in writing in the curricula.

Violence, insults and racist taunts are already prohibited in our schools and no further policy is needed. This is all about the social engineers on the school board who actually do not like kids very much. What they want are little robots that will confirm to their gruesome dream of the model Canadian. Know your rights and love your neighbour, unless your neighbour isn't as liberal as you.

There's more. A ten-year-old daughter of a friend of mine came home from school recently with an official noted explaining that she had "committed an assault" on another child. In fact the girl in question had been involved in a pushing match and her opponent had fallen over. If signed, the form will forever be on the tiny felon's record. What was a natural childhood disagreement that should have been dealt with in minutes by a teacher worth the name was transformed into legalistic nonsense

So it has come to this. To paraphrase the philosopher Voltaire after he had received a nasty letter. "I am sitting in the washroom and your note is in front of me. Shortly it will be behind me." Wipe on man, wipe on.

My Grandpa

IT WAS SIX YEARS AGO BUT STILL SEEMS LIKE YESTERDAY, ALWAYS BROUGHT BACK TO ME BUY LAST WEEK'S REMEMBRANCE DAY. THERE WAS NO OBITUARY OF COURSE, NO NEWS. THE DEATH WAS PRIVATE AND SO WAS THE LIFE. WHAT COMMEMORATIONS THERE WERE CAME IN THE LOCAL PUBS AMONGST HIS FRIENDS IN THE LYRICAL TRADITION OF LONDON ENGLISH THAT CHARLES DICKENS ALMOST CAPTURED.

I speak of the death of my grandpa. He was eighty-nine, it was time. He would have been the first to say so. Blind, unable to walk, a shell of the great man who was. What a bloody lark, he would have said. That great, untamed, kind, strong, wise, gentle man.

He worked at many jobs, never settled for one and never made much money. He and his wife were cockneys and they would have had it no other way. His life was interrupted in 1939 when His Majesty gave him a gun and told him to kill the nation's enemies. He must have been quite good at it, because he survived for six years. He didn't talk very often about his time in North Africa or Italy and never, ever boasted about it.

If the war arose in conversation it was usually the subject of mockery. "Me a soldier? Blimey." And he would tell us jokes about stupid officers. "The Krauts? Well, we hated 'em. But I tell you, we respected the bastards." Then he stopped. I knew he didn't want to say any more. Yet my mum remembered that every time he came home on leave he had another stripe on his arm.

One year we managed to take him on holiday to Italy and we surprised him with a trip to a southern battlefield. Mum told me that I should leave him alone for a while, but after a few minutes I went looking for him. I saw him, but he didn't see me. I was so shocked. He was kneeling by a wall with some flowers around it and looking at a photograph held in his large, callused hand. And he was crying. My Grandpa was crying.

Then one day I was looking in his bedroom for a watch he had lost and I found his medals, tucked away. So many of them. I was fascinated by the different colours and the accompanying letters speaking of courage and honour. I supposed at the time that he had misplaced them, just as he had his watch.

He drank a great deal. An alcoholic? No. He enjoyed it rather than needed it. And when he drank, he was a nice drunk. Playful, affectionate. He would dismiss men who were made brave by drinking as "not real men. Liquid courage. Easy, that." He was also a smoker, sometimes swore and even told dirty jokes. Working-class men did that, do that, thank goodness. He had no tolerance for those who were offended by his ways. Better still, he hardly knew or cared they even existed.

He gave me an allowance every Wednesday afternoon when I was small. Sixpence. Worth nothing now, worth little then. It always seemed more important to him than it was to me. It used to confuse me, embarrass me. But I know now just how little money he had and just how reluctant he was to accept charity. Sixpence. A million dollars.

His home overlooked and overheard the railway track and when I slept on the sofa in his living room I was kept awake by trains making their way to parts of the world I had never seen. Adventurous places to me, small industrial towns in reality. But in his home everything seemed exciting, anything possible.

A quarter of a century later my mother telephones to tell me the news. She isn't crying but she has been. She explains that her dad has left me a note and a small box. The note says: "You've never seen these before Mike, so here they are now. Not much, but all for you. Just put them away somewhere, safe keeping. They don't matter. You know I love you, Grandpa." They were his medals.

Goodnight, Grandpa. I know that the drinks and the smokes and the jokes will be even better in your Heaven. Goodnight soldier, goodnight man. I loved you too. And I still miss you.

MC

Dad

My dad died in August. There, I've said it. He would have been 74-years-old at the end of October. But he didn't make it. And I can't pretend that I'm not angry at that. But first let me introduce you to him. My dad, Phil Coren.

When I was a boy I would stand next to him as he washed his hard, calloused hands and he would chat away, telling me tales of his own childhood and letting little drops of moral tuition fall into my lap. Simple, and quite marvelous. "A promise is a promise." It was. He never broke one. He was my father.

He drove a London black taxi for more than forty years. It was a job that attracted waves of poor young men after the Second World War, a job that paid a decent wage if you were willing to work a seventy-hour week and not complain or give up.

When I was small and we were driving back from soccer matches he would sometimes pick people up who were hailing cabs along the way. He wasn't supposed to, not with me there. But I was six or seven and sat in the hollow space next to the driver's seat where the luggage was stored and where he had placed a special little seat. I was barely noticed.

I could never understand why the passengers treated him with such contempt, such patronising disregard. He was "cabby" and "driver" and "you!" No he wasn't, he was my dad. But he smiled and said nothing and did his job. They weren't good enough to walk in his shadow. I knew that, and he knew I knew that. Which is what really mattered.

And then he told me more stories from his past, such as about the times he boxed for the RAF. Oh, the pride. And about how his German cousin had gone back to Berlin in the 1930s to rescue his family. The family did not escape and the cousin never came back. A long time ago, said my father, and not for you to worry about. He winked, a wink full of confidence. Never again, he said. I believed him. He was my father.

He always looked so strong, so able to protect me, so powerful. Powerful enough to cry when he felt the need. I heard him weep when my grandmother died. Confusing. How should I react, what should I do? Just be there, as he was for me. He came into my room, saw the fear on my face and recited a short prayer with me for my grandma. He kissed me, held my hand and then drove me to school before putting in his ten hours. No grumbles, no moans. Of course not. He was my father.

I remember his sheer joy when I went to university, the first in the family to do so. Of course he took too many photographs when I graduated and of course he didn't understand the Latin that was spoken before the meal. Who cares? His wisdom was born long before the Romans imposed their language on the world.

He felt a little out of place, but all that concerned this working man in a smart suit was that his son would not follow in his footsteps. "Do you know why I work such long hours?" he would ask me. "So that you won't have to push a cab around and tip your hat to everybody." Then he'd pause. "So that you won't have to." Not said with bitterness but with resolution. There is dignity in labour, he told me, but shame in sloth.

He didn't come on vacation with us to the English coast very often, just didn't have the money. He stayed behind, ate his cheese sandwiches when he got home, and worked. We'd telephone him and tell him we loved him. He already knew. When my first child, Daniel, was born my dad said little. Just sat and stared and smiled. A circle had been completed, a story had been told, a great knight had won his battles. He spoke through his eyes. And what eloquence he had.

When I went to see him in hospital after his death I saw not my father but merely the vehicle in which his soul and spirit had lived. I apologized to him for not loving him enough, I kissed his forehead and said goodnight. Then I cried. Because he was, in every sense, my father.

MC

Mum

Last year I wrote about my mum and the fact that she was suffering from dementia. By the time you read this column I will be in Britain, spending two weeks with her. She's 74-years-old now and, well, the illness has got worse recently. Words haven't made sense for some time, and she's sometimes not sure where she is. She needs help to dress, to take her medication, to eat.

She is now doubly incontinent, and we're building a washroom for her on the main floor so that she doesn't have to climb the stairs in a hurry. She's already had one fall. She doesn't seem to remember dad, who passed away more than a year ago now, and I'm not sure if she's going to know me this time. I know her though. Oh how I know her.

My sister is there a lot of the time and my cousin is an angel with a cockney accent. There's also a professional caregiver who mum, I think, has grown to love. We had mum in Canada for a couple of months, but the strangeness made things even worse. My sister and I discussed me going back to Britain for good, but I have a family here and can't suddenly pick up a job in London.

I used to be able to phone mum every few days, but she doesn't know how or when to pick the phone up now. Even when she was well, and my dad alive, the idea of answering machine or e-mail was like asking them to build a nuclear reactor in the kitchen. New technology? Not quite.

We're doing all we can to keep her at home for as long as possible. A nursing home may have to come, but not yet. No, not yet. Let her be surrounded by memories, good memories, her memories, our memories.

She wanders a little, though not too much. Golly, there was one funny incident last year when she decided that she simply had to visit her best friend at dawn. Off she went for a walk to Ros's house.

Then she knocked on the door, loudly. But Ros is rather deaf. So here we had a woman with dementia shouting and knocking for a friend who is too deaf to hear at 5.30am. The neighbours were very understanding.

I call this "funny" because that's what mum would have called it. A sense of humour, especially when things were at their darkest, was one of the gifts she gave me. But there were so many, many more.

Most of all she taught me love. Values, virtues, responsibilities, respect, common sense, a low tolerance for the bullies and the boasters, a high tolerance for the hurting and the hated. Most of all, though, love.

I cry a fair bit. For her but also for me. I'm being honest with you. Some of the pain is selfish. I had a lovely childhood. Not much money but lots of warmth, safety and affection. Dad's gone and now mum's a different person. Part of me weeps because I'm losing that childhood, the part of my background that made me.

It's partly a realisation of my own mortality. More a realisation of the mortality of my origins. I want to know that those early years will always be there, somehow symbolised by my parents. It always seemed to be Christmas, always the smell of cake and toast and tea. Yes it will always exist in my consciousness, but somehow it's not the same.

Obviously the relationship is different. She's now the child, and needs the care of her children. But let nobody tell me that there is no dignity in life for people who are suffering or handicapped. Quality of life? Who are we to judge! Mum is happy in a way we do not understand, and I defy any galloping, able-bodied millionaire to tell me that they have a "better" life than Sheila Coren.

She loves therefore she is. This is not some life that should be ended, not someone who should be "put out of her misery." Just as with my handicapped niece, I've learned that it is we the so-called healthy who need to listen, look and learn. Mum, teach me. I'm here.

MC

Lizzie

LIZZIE WAS SIX-YEARS-OLD LAST WEEK. OUR YOUNGEST, ELIZABETH ANNE MIRIAM. CHILD NUMBER FOUR SUDDENLY A LITTLE GIRL WHO GOES TO SCHOOL AND WRITES AND READS. I LOVE HER GROWING UP, BUT PART OF ME DOESN'T WANT IT TO HAPPEN. SO MY LAMENT IS ENTIRELY SELFISH. I'M SLOWLY LOSING THAT BRIDGE TO THE WORLD OF TOTAL INNOCENCE THAT I'VE RELISHED ALL THESE YEARS.

That, of course, is the sweet quintessence of being a parent. To see the world through the eyes of a being who knows neither hatred nor lust nor greed. And whose little statements so delight. "Daddy, I don't think I can do my homework because I've got short-term memory loss!" She got this from the *Finding Nemo* movie.

Or, disputing whether she really does have to stop watching television. "Dad, I need to watch it. You just don't know how hard they work us at school. It's terrible."

Then there are the traumas that make the whole world impossible to tolerate. "She's my best friend ever and now she doesn't like me and I don't like her and we don't like each other and it's not nice." Tears to float a battle fleet. Until a massive ten minutes later and the alliance is restarted and the sun shines once again.

I sometimes wonder what sort of world this little person will be given. A better one than we have now I hope. One that respects both extremes of life. Allowing childhood to flourish and old age to bloom. How odd it is that we seem intent on turning children into miniature adults yet run in shame away from our senior years.

A perverse desire for a perennial state of being in our mid 20s perhaps. This, surely, is neurosis at its worst. Be happy at every stage of life, and don't try to make it anything other than what it is. There's a purpose behind it all.

I recall when my dad died and I was sitting on the bed crying. Because 43-year-old men are allowed to cry, and should cry more often. Lizzie came into the room and I tried to hide my face, convinced that she would be confused and frightened by the sight of a weeping father.

What a fool I was. The fear was mine, not hers. Tears for a child are an entirely natural way of showing emotion. It's the alleged maturity of adulthood that makes us so afraid. She put her little head on my chest and hugged me. "It's okay dada", she said. "Grandpa hasn't gone far. I can still see him when I close my eyes."

A pause and a slant of the head. "But I don't think he'll get me a birthday present this year. Never mind dada, never mind."

Never mind indeed. I couldn't stop cuddling her then, and I find it hard to stop now. Wish dad could buy her a present though. Wish he could speak to her on the phone and tell her about what it was like when he was six.

It was better in some ways, worse in others. Those who long for the good old days never knew them. Nothing good about premature death, inferior medicine, too many hours at work and a frequent denial of justice.

But neither is modernity the great triumph so many of us proclaim. The decline of community, the worship of the sound bite, the attempted perversion of natural law and a world rape by materialism and fashion.

Lizzie is one of the perfect tribe of royalty who stands firm against all that is bad. A princess and a warrior. No spear or sword, but a heart and a soul uncluttered and unblemished. She stands in the gap and evil simply evaporates at her feet.

I tell her something like this one day and she laughs at me and wonders if she can play Barbie again on my computer. I say she can, because I always do. She knows it, which is why she asks. "Dada", she says as I leave the room. "Grandpa loved you, you loved grandpa, you love me, I love you. It's like a story."

Yes. A story. One I will tell for all time to all people. Taught me by my new little six-year-old.

MC

Ezra Levant

MUCH HAS NOW BEEN WRITTEN ABOUT EZRA LEVANT, THE FORMER PUBLISHER OF THE NOW DEFUNCT *WESTERN STANDARD*, AND HIS DECISION TWO YEARS AGO TO PUBLISH A SET OF CARTOONS DEPICTING THE ISLAMIC PROPHET MUHAMMAD. FOR THOSE WHO PREFER TO FORGET, THEY WERE THE DANISH CARICATURES OF THE FOUNDER OF ISLAM, IMPLYING A CONNECTION BETWEEN MUSLIM FANATICISM AND TERRORIST VIOLENCE.

In response to the appearance of the said pictures and their claim that Islamic extremism led to violence, Islamic extremists killed people, promised to decapitate their opponents and firebombed churches and embassies.

Not all Muslims behaved or thought thus. But anyone who argues that it was a mere handful is a liar, a fool or a Canadian leftist. Some Canadian Muslims took a different path and simply complained to the Human Rights Commission that the cartoons transgressed their, here we go, human rights.

Human rights are a funny old thing. They tend to change shape and meaning depending on the day and place. Most of us, however, would agree that the right to life, freedom and movement were pretty obvious ones. But the human right not to be offended? The very idea, well, offends me.

So a handful of people complained and as a result journalist Levant is obliged to hire a lawyer and spend a great deal of time with an unqualified official who will decide whether freedom of the press is a good or bad thing.

Actually the real disgrace here is that the *Western Standard* was the only magazine or newspaper in Canada to publish the cartoons. They should have featured in every media outlet in the country, in that they made international news. The ostensible reason was that they were, yet again, offensive.

So bloody what! Canadian newspapers publish cartoons that are offensive to Christians, for example, dozens of times a year. Tolerating that which offends is part of being an adult, being sensible and being part of am adult, sensible county with an adult, sensible culture. Or at least it was.

The genuine reason why the cartoons were not published, of course, was that people were terrified of the consequences. In some cases editors had private security companies give them estimates of how much it would cost to protect the building. Which is not only cowardly but deeply insulting to Canadian Muslims, who are some of the most moderate in the Islamic Diaspora.

The good old *New York Times* pretentiously explained why they wouldn't publish pictures of Muhammad with a bomb in his turban. They could, they said, adequately explain the cartoons in words. Odd, then, that in the same week they printed a photograph of an alleged artwork depicting the Virgin Mary covered in excrement. Suddenly their ability to describe had abandoned them.

The stench of double standard and fearfulness is as heady as the perfume from an Arabic harem. We know they're lying and they know they're lying. And we and they know that Ezra Levant has become an icon of hope in this nation. The mere fact that he has been called to account is obscene and it must be stressed that the outcome of this witch-hunt is absolutely irrelevant.

Freedom seems so trivial when you possess it but it's like water to a man in the desert when it is taken away. Drink deeply, and loudly condemn those who would have you die of thirst.

MC

Castro

PIERRE TRUDEAU MUST BE ROLLING IN HIS GRAVE. HIS GOOD FRIEND FIDEL CASTRO HAS STEPPED DOWN FORM POWER, HANDING THE DICTATORSHIP OVER TO HIS BROTHER. THERE'S DEMOCRACY AND PEOPLE'S CHOICE FOR YOU. THEN AGAIN, THAT OLD CHARLATAN TRUDEAU HAD A THING FOR AUTHORITARIAN THUGS THE WORLD OVER. THANK THE LORD HE WASN'T PRIME MINISTER IN 1940.

Cuba is an open wound, bleeding away the integrity of Canada and any other country that refuses to condemn Havana's brutality, oppression and imperialism. It is dominated by a cruel, hypocritical junta that has arrested, tortured and killed more people than most of Latin America's leaders combined.

But still Canadians visit, sing the praises of Castro and wear their Che Guevara T-shirts. Guevara, by the way, was a middle-class dental student who became physically aroused when he watched people being butchered. He personally murdered or had killed numerous ordinary, apolitical men and women simply because they had been denounced by Marxist officials. He was a perverse, manic little man who would fulfill any rational definition of a war criminal.

Guevara was also a coward. He was killed after being found hiding behind a tree, urging his followers to fight to the death. He surrendered, begged for his life and told his captors that he was famous and worth more money alive than dead.

According to Castro, however, the potential dentist in a beret is a hero of the revolution. And what a revolution it has been. Castro opposed all of the Soviet Union's modern reforms, praised the show trials and gulags of the 1950s and condemned Premier Khrushchev for removing nuclear weapons from Cuba. World war and mass destruction were worth the price, Castro said, for the victory of Communism.

On two separate occasions the United States offered the Cuban leader a new relationship that would have ended the political and economic embargo. Both times Castro not only rejected the offer but tried to provoked Washington, once shooting down an aircraft and killing even more innocent people.

He proposed the imprisonment of men with AIDS, built internment camps for political prisoners, rounded up hundreds of thousands of people merely for disagreeing with the government or holding a specific religion and banned almost all forms of free speech, movement and assembly.

He initiated a system of political oppression that has outlived Stalin, Hitler and Mao. Secret policemen abound, interfering busybodies on the street have the authority to condemn people to prison and any independent thought is seen as dangerous and threatening.

Cuban soldiers have been sent to fight and die all over the world on the orders of their leader and his sordid attempts at extending his power. In Africa un-educated, under-trained Cubans fell in enormous numbers but also extended civil wars and thus caused the deaths of Africans particularly in Angola and Mozambique.

Cubans have been forced to risk their lives in the open seas to escape Marxist persecution, and have then been libeled as criminals and gangsters by Castro and his fellow travelers in North America. Many of them did not survive the trip and drowned as martyrs to Communist barbarism.

But barbarism in the sun, with a touch of the sexy and the exotic. Which is why Canadians vacation there and why fools like Trudeau so adored the place. Have faith. Liberation is not far off now, then the real party on the beach begins.

MC

Trudeau

IS IT OVER? IS IT REALLY FINISHED NOW? CAN I ACTUALLY READ SOMETHING INTELLIGENT AND NEWSWORTHY IN THE NEWSPAPERS? BECAUSE I AM TRULY SICK AND TIRED OF THIS ADULATION FOR THE RICH MAN FROM MONTREAL WHO DID MORE THAN MOST PEOPLE TO RUIN CANADA.

I haven't written a word till now because I thought it fit that he was buried before comment. And yes, he was bright, massively charismatic and had style coming out of his ears. He was also a fine father and a fascinating man. But it's time to point out that the emperor was absolutely and insultingly naked.

Trudeau divided this country as never before. He had no time for the west and literally gave its people the finger. The twin solitudes that exist between western and eastern Canada became far deeper and more hostile during his reign. I'm not here to sell your grain, he said. And he believed it. There were no photo ops in grain selling.

The bilingual campaign was noble but achieved little. It did nothing to appease the separatists and Canada is little more bilingual today than it was before Trudeau. As for arresting 500 people after what was, relatively speaking, a minor disturbance - if this happened in London or New York we would accuse the government of being authoritarian.

He knew nothing of economics and left this country with a debt so deep that we may never recover. While the world attacked inflation Trudeau merely panicked. He promised not to introduce wage controls but did so immediately once in office. The result? Working people lost jobs, lost homes, lost out.

He said that the state had no place in the bedrooms of the nation, and then proceeded to push the state into every bedroom in Canada. Suddenly sexuality was to be an issue when it came to benefits and status, leading to the mess we have today. He liberalised the laws on divorce, abortion and homosexuality. Well, the number of unwanted pregnancies, fatherless children and sexually transmitted disease have multiplied quite staggeringly in the last thirty years.

The Charter of Rights took away the rights we already had and gave most of them back in a different form. But now those in charge were not our elected representatives but a set of unaccountable judges appointed by Trudeau and his heirs. This was elitism at its purest, and Trudeau was nothing if not the consummate elitist.

There was the little incident of wearing a Nazi helmet and driving around Montreal screaming that the war against the Axis was "an English war." Interesting. Try telling that to the prisoners of Belsen and Dachau. While Canadian boys were being tortured by Japanese soldiers and killed by stormtroopers, a wealthy kid back home managed to avoid fighting for his country and effectively gave support to the enemy war effort. Imagine if any other politician had acted thus.

But then Trudeau was not like any other politician, in that the media loved him. Loved him because they lived through him. You see, we who write and broadcast are generally a pretty dull lot. Particularly in the 1960s. The world was becoming hip and modern but Canadian journalists were still grey and old. If you doubt me, just look at the photographs of the time.

Then came Trudeau, and these good old guys in the press could stand up proudly as Canadians, because suddenly Canadians were all mini-skirts, affairs with absurdly young women, swearing in public and self-promotion. Maybe I wear a dark suit and sensible shoes, but my Prime Minister dances with babes!

Some say that he gave us our identity. No. The men who left their limbs and blood at Vimy Ridge and Dieppe knew who they were. The women who carved a country out of prairie dirt and Atlantic mud knew what it meant to be Canadian. They did not need Pierre Trudeau to tell them

He lived eighty wonderful years, having all the money and prestige he wanted from the very beginning. Yet we cry for him as though he was some sort of victim. Not at all. If anything, we were the victims. He was and remains a media creation. And now, perhaps, we can get on with our lives.

MC

Kennedy

THAT WAS THE WEEK THAT WAS. IN THE UNITED STATES POLITICIANS OF ALL STRIPES TOLD LIES ON CALL AS IT WAS ANNOUNCED THAT TED KENNEDY WAS GRAVELY ILL AND WILL LIKELY SUCCUMB TO A BRAIN TUMOUR. HE WILL BE MISSED, THEY ANNOUNCED, AND IS A STATESMAN OF INTEGRITY AND SKILL.

No. He is a long-term alcoholic who drove a car off a bridge and left a young female campaign worker and "friend" to drown in what must have been despair and agony. He waited until the following day to report the incident but received only a suspended two month sentence. A coward, a fraud and a very lucky man indeed.

But then just being a Kennedy makes one lucky. JFK the President was a repeat adulterer with probable ties to organised crime. He used women like slices of meat but got away with it because the liberal media – meaning most of the media – loves a Kennedy. The Kennedy clan's father, Joseph, was a bootlegger and vulgar anti-Semite who as US Ambassador to London relished telling his superiors that Hitler would beat the British.

Closer to home the Toronto District School Board issued a press release in reaction to school violence. The one page document contained a spelling error and more socialist clichés than an NDP annual conference. No problem – it was paid for by tax dollars so nobody will be reprimanded.

"The Leadership Action Team identified major themes and actions that could be taken to affect real change in each area" it said. "Those six themes are: equity, gender-based violence, partnerships/integrated services, support for marginalized youth, silence and safety."

Much as it may please a kid being beaten half to death to know that his attacker is marginalized or may not enjoy full equity, the solution to gang violence, murderous teenagers and the mass decay of inner-city public education is, for a start, to dismantle school boards that issue absurd and pointless press releases.

More importantly, punish rather than reward irresponsible behaviour. Just as an example, cut off welfare payments to women who have several children by several men before they've reached twenty years of age. Expel kids with knives and guns immediately, admit that it's not empty stomachs but empty homes that lead to bad behaviour and stop pretending that poverty has anything to do with thuggery – that's an insult to the poor.

Also in Ontario the Health Ministry decided to restore full funding for sex change surgery, while simultaneously refusing to fulfil its election promise to finance special and crucial education to autistic children. If only those annoying Autistic youngsters could prove that they were born in a body of the wrong gender!

At a national level no Canadian labour union or left-wing church called for a boycott of either China or Iran, after it was exposed that these two countries alone account for the vast majority of the world's executions and torture. In fact there was an eerie silence surrounding the figures.

Those of us who believe that these two authoritarian and corrupt regimes should indeed be boycotted have come up with a foolproof way of producing action from said unions and liberal churches. From now on both Iran and China will be known as Israel. Motions of boycott and condemnation are being written as we speak. Yes, that was certainly the week that was.

MC

Obama

A YOUNG STUDENT FRIEND E-MAILED ME ON TUESDAY NIGHT. "HAVE LOCKED MYSELF IN MY ROOM BECAUSE THE PLACE IS FULL OF LITTLE IDIOTS - WHO CANNOT SPELL BARACK OBAMA'S NAME AND COULD NOT NAME ONE OF HIS FOREIGN OR DOMESTIC POLICIES – RUNNING AROUND SCREAMING OBSCENITIES ABOUT GEORGE BUSH, CONSERVATIVES AND HOW SARAH PALIN IS A BITCH. I LOVE DEMOCRACY!"

Even so, the people spoke. A victory for the hysterical Oprah Winfrey, the mad racist preacher Jeremiah Wright, the mainstream media who abandoned any sense of objectivity long ago, Europeans who despise America largely because they depend on her, comics who claim to be dangerous and fearless but would not dare attack genuinely powerful special interest groups. A victory for Obama-worshippers everywhere.

A victory for the cult of the cult. A man who has done little with his life but has written about his achievements as if he had found the cure for cancer in between winning a marathon and building a nuclear reactor with his teeth. Victory for style over substance, hyperbole over history, rabble-raising over reality.

A victory for Hollywood, the most dysfunctional community in the world. Victory for Streisand, Spielberg, Soros and Sarandon. Victory for those who prefer welfare to will and interference to independence. For those who settle for group think and herd mentality rather than those who fight for individual initiative and the right to be out of step with meagre political fashion.

Victory for a man who is no friend of freedom. He and his people have already stated that media has to be controlled so as to be balanced, without realizing the extraordinary irony within that statement. Like most liberal zealots, the Obama-worshippers constantly speak of Fox and Limbaugh, when the vast bulk of television stations and newspapers are drastically liberal and anti-conservative.

Senior Democrat Chuck Schumer said that just as pornography should be censored, so should talk-radio. In other words, one of the few free and open means of popular expression may well be cornered and beaten by bullies who even in triumph cannot tolerate any criticism and opposition.

A victory for those who believe the state is better qualified to raise children than the family, for those who prefer teachers' unions to teaching and for those who are naively convinced that if the west is sufficiently weak towards its enemies, war and terror will dissolve as quickly as the tears on the face of a leftist celebrity.

A victory for social democracy even after most of Europe has come to the painful conclusion that social democracy leads to mediocrity, failure, unemployment, inflation, higher taxes and economic stagnation. A victory for intrusive lawyers, banal sentimentalists, social extremists and urban snobs.

Also a defeat for one of the weakest Presidential candidates in living memory. Why would anyone vote for a man who seemed incapable of outlining his policies and instead repeatedly emphasised a noble but, if we are candid, largely irrelevant war record? Joined by a woman who was defended so vehemently by her supporters when it was cuttingly evident that she is years away from being and perhaps never will be a serious candidate for senior national office.

Most of all it was a terrible defeat for democracy and the United States. A politician of nothing defeated a nothing politician and a credulous electorate screamed in adoration. I fear we will all suffer very much indeed.

MC

Cindy Sheehan

CINDY SHEEHAN WAS ARRESTED LAST WEEK. NOT VERY IMPORTANT IN ITSELF BUT SYMBOLIC OF A FUNDAMENTALLY IMPORTANT DIVISION IN NORTH AMERICAN SOCIETY. THE INCREASINGLY HOSTILE CHASM BETWEEN THOSE WHO SUPPORT AND THOSE WHO OPPOSE THE WAR IN IRAQ.

This woman, of course, lost her son in the war. Casey Sheehan joined the military, re-enlisted and then volunteered to take part in a specific military action when as a mechanic he was not required to do so. His actions were selfless and heroic.

The question is whether his mother's actions are similarly so. Opponents of the war have no doubts and have given her an iconic status, transforming Sheehan into a living testimony to the futility and error of President's Bush's policies.

The right have reacted, using what are sometimes thuggish personal attacks and accusing her of being a stooge and a fool who has allowed herself to be used by dangerous groups and individuals.

The truth, as so often, is somewhere in the middle. Cindy Sheehan seemed not to have any politics for the longest time, met with the President after her son's death and praised George W. Bush's warmth. Then the change occurred.

Suddenly the Bush regime was conducting "an evil war", the United States government was "a morally repugnant system" and "the biggest terrorist is George W. Bush." She compared Lynne Stewart, a lawyer convicted of providing material support to terrorism, with the greatest of civil rights campaigners.

She made numerous inflated statements, demanded that the President meet with her again and marched with Marxist revolutionaries who are far more concerned with the violent overthrow of democracy than with the well-being of the Iraqi people.

All of which she has a perfect right to do. And all of which may well be provoked by guilt and shame and sorrow. The guilt that she was unable to prevent her son from going to war, the shame that as a mother she could not protect her boy, the sorrow at unimaginable loss.

Of course it was not her fault and of course she should not blame herself. But of course she may well do so and you and I may do the same in such a hellish circumstance.

The tragedy is that even moderates on this issue now see an exploitation of Casey Sheehan's death and resent his mother and her friends for it. Those moderates include her husband of 28 years, who has filed for divorce.

Also Casey Sheehan's paternal grandparents, who have stated that, "We do not agree with the political motivations and publicity tactics of Cindy Sheehan. She now appears to be promoting her own personal agenda and notoriety at the expense of her son's good name and reputation. The Sheehan family lost our beloved Casey in the Iraq War and we have been silently, respectfully grieving. The rest of the Sheehan family supports the troops, our country and our president, silently, with prayer and respect."

I find it impossible to take an absolute stand on this case, partly because I oppose the war myself but also because I am not sure how I would react if, God forbid, such a fate ever befell me.

I would, however, respectfully advise Cindy Sheehan to ask her comrades certain questions.

Why did they not march against Saddam Hussein when he was murdering hundreds of thousands of people?

Why are they so angry with their own government but so quiet about the routine torture and incarceration of political and religious dissidents in, for example, Cuba?

Why are they not demanding an end to the murderous regimes of Syria and Iran and why are they so selective in condemning flawed democracies but ignoring or even supporting brutal dictatorships?

The answers will tell us if they are enlightened opponents of an unjust war or hateful extremists with a poisonous agenda. Demand answers Cindy, for your sake and for the sake of your son.

MC

Heather Mallick

HEATHER MALLICK MUST BE LOVING IT. THE LARGELY ANONYMOUS JOURNALIST, A LEGEND IN HER OWN LUNCHTIME, IS NOW THE SUBJECT OF CONTROVERSY BECAUSE SHE CALLED AMERICAN REPUBLICANS "WHITE TRASH", SAID SARAH PALIN LOOKED LIKE A PORN ACTRESS AND MADE REPUGNANT PERSONAL COMMENTS ABOUT THE GOVERNOR OF ALASKA'S FAMILY. SHE DID ALL THIS ON THE CBC WEBSITE, PAID FOR BY PUBLIC DOLLARS. THE CONTENT OF THE DIATRIBE IS LESS OSCAR WILDE THAN OSCAR THE GROUCH BUT IT'S BECOME MAJOR NEWS IN THE UNITED STATES.

This is not a woman whose career has exactly blossomed and the consequent anger and bitterness is obvious, as is her evident jealousy of Sarah Palin's physical attractiveness. None of this matters very much; what does matter is that once again the Canadian public is obliged to fund this nonsense. Beyond the abuse of public money, however, is hypocrisy.

Mallick's defence is one of freedom of speech. Yet last year I was approached by the editor of a newspaper called *The Women's Post* and asked if I would write a column for her, providing what publisher Sarah Thomson called "a conservative voice." She explained that she already had plenty of liberal writers but wanted some balance.

One of those left-wing writers employed by *The Women's Post* was Heather Mallick. When she heard about me being offered a column she became extraordinarily angry and threatened to resign. The good people at *The Women's Post* called the enraged journalist's bluff and it was goodbye to our control freak comrade. So when Mallick's defenders cry about unfettered expression and the right to offend they ought to know of whom they speak.

Which brings us nicely to radio presenter Michael Enright, who on CBC this Sunday said that he had been fortunate in his life to avoid such unpleasant things as "Michael Coren and the Ebola Virus." Proving that genuine wit and humour require more than pomposity and a silly bow tie. Much as I'm delighted by the attack, twice in two weeks now CBC types have used child-like insults to pursue their own leftist agenda.

Enright was the man who some years ago said that the Roman Catholic Church was the largest criminal organisation in the world outside of the mafia. Enright or anyone else has a perfect right to express an opinion, even one as suburban and daft as this. Such ignorance and extremism does, however, bring the man's ability and objectivity into severe doubt. Has he been informed and balanced in his interviews over the years or is he merely a conduit for the clichéd Toronto leftism?

I assume that before long Bollinger Bolshevik journalists will simply be throwing bricks through people's windows if they disagree with them. So much easier than writing anything down or picking up a microphone. There is something exciting and vibrant about the meaty exchange of ideas and ideals, and from such a clash of ideologies Canada becomes a more interesting place. Instead we have dreary and predictable abuse from Enright, Mallick and their dowdy friends.

Time and change are against the corporation. Simply put, the CBC as it stands now has no future. For the time being people who somehow think they're clever will apparently argue with you by the equivalent of calling you smelly or putting a "kick me" sign on your back. How sad. And these dunderheads say Americans are dumb!

MC

Royal Pain

Sometimes I have an overwhelming desire to shake the collective heads of the media and make them see sense. So much ink and tape about 17-year-old Prince Harry and his spoilt, indulged antics with alcohol, women and drugs and so much sudden understanding, empathy and forgiveness. In the words of the philosopher, give me a break.

Yes of course every teenager has to be given a second chance and yes of course there are many worse things than going off the rails a little. But thousands of young people face arrest for even a portion of the same sort of antics performed by Mr. Windsor. And seldom is a note of compassion heard from anyone.

In fact journalists have known for some time that Harry is a troubled young man who has regularly gotten drunk, fallen into confrontations, smoked cannabis and was more than friendly with the local girls. The story wasn't reported because of royal clout, and because of sympathy with a teenager who lost his mother when he was a mere lad. Quite right too. The loss must have been devastating.

But similar restraint is not shown for the legions of youngsters from other single-parent families who are routinely incarcerated for alcohol and substance abuse. To put it bluntly, Harry should be very grateful indeed that he isn't poor or black. The results could have been very, very different.

The prince was taken by his father to see a rehabilitation centre, where he was treated with the greatest concern and respect that money can buy. No thought of the police giving him a thump or two - you know it happens – or scaring the living daylights out of him. On the contrary, it seems that the worse Harry behaved the more he was cared for. A good thing, but quite the reverse of what usually happens in such circumstances.

Prince Charles has also been almost universally praised by reporters for his handling of his son's problems. Now this genuinely astounds me. He may have taken action now, but the man not only betrayed

Harry's mother during their engagement as well as throughout their marriage, but publicly admitted that he was having sexual intercourse with another woman and probably never loved his wife in the first place.

Which is exactly what a young boy wants to hear as he plays with his toys and wonders where daddy is tonight. Such trauma would confuse or break anybody. Much as we are supposed to laugh at the innocent fun of adultery, in actual fact it wounds, rips and kills. Charles was a dreadful husband who put his perverse desire for an older, dominant woman before the sanctity of marriage and family.

Yet we have again to remember the double standard here. For most children who are the victims of unfaithful parents there are no outbursts of sympathy, only ugly disputes in family law courts and the chilling emptiness of what used to be a home and the warm certainty of mum and dad.

One would have thought that after the death of Diana her boys would at least have been kept close to their father. Not always so. Harry was sent off to Eton. For those unfamiliar with British society and all its class-ridden nonsense, Eton is the quintessence of elitism. Incredibly expensive, and rigidly guarded by the regiments of privilege, it offers a fine academic education but also has a sordid history of buggery and bullying.

Charles has certainly made efforts to be a better father in recent years, but he surely should have been aware that Harry was surrounded by some extremely rich young men who are known to be drug-users and whose parents long ago replaced love with cash. Costly vacations instead of hugs.

Teenagers face tough lives all the time yet triumph over far greater obstacles that those faced by Harry. To forgive someone because they are exotic and famous is not forgiveness at all but mere glamour-worship. As for Charles, he shamed his wife, his children and his office. I pity the man for the pain he must feel at the situation, but perhaps at long last he understands the consequences of his actions. Or does Ms Parker-Bowles need to explain it to him?

MC

Ben Affleck

BEN AFFLECK CHANGED THE WORLD LAST WEEK. NO, OF COURSE I DON'T MEAN THAT A TEDIOUS MOVIE STAR ACTUALLY CHANGED INTERNATIONAL EVENTS. CHANGED DESIGNER JEANS PERHAPS BUT NOT THE WORLD. I MEAN THAT HE PERSONIFIES WHY GEORGE BUSH AND THE REPUBLICANS WON THE ELECTION.

They won because Middle America bit back. Simple as that. Middle America bit back. The abused, the marginalised and the mocked decided that they had had enough. Those taken for granted, those patronised, those treated with disdain voted to no longer play the silent victim.

For months a daft coalition of the extremely willing played their guitars, sang their songs and read their Hollywood statements about Iraq, oil, the evil George Bush and the foolishness of the American people. They would deny, of course, that they accused their fellow Americans of being stupid but this is precisely what they did.

True understanding and enlightenment, it seemed, only came after you'd appeared in a sequel to a super hero movie or seen your last album go platinum. Bruce Springsteen might claim to be a workingman, but workingmen don't have bank accounts the size of Rhode Island.

The assembled pop stars and actors meant no harm when they demanded that Americans vote Democrat but what they were really saying was that only certain people really got it. Michael Moore got it. Rosie O'Donnell got it. Academics at universities got it. Howard Stern got it.

Yes, Howard Stern. America listened to Stern and his giggling sidekick explain why only a "retard" would vote for George Bush. In between fart noises and references to naked lesbians this tired peddler of smut made fun of people who spoke with southern accents and voted on "moral issues."

The clever people at the mainstream television networks, the stylish types in New York and Los Angeles, the icons of glamour and glitz all said that John Kerry was the only choice for a person with any intelligence.

As for those ignorant evangelicals, those stupid church-going Catholics, those family values fools, those dumb redneck hicks, they weren't real Americans in the first place. Then, in the smiling twilight of the new political morning, the unwashed told their betters to shove it.

They realised that their kind were smart and sophisticated enough to storm the beaches of Normandy and wrestle Europe from the Nazis and Asia from the Japanese fascists. They realised that they were suave and urbane enough to work the farms, make the cars, drive the cabs, do the work.

Middle America experienced an epiphany. We are not bigots or yokels just because we believe in the family and in traditional virtues and values. We are not hateful merely because we support our troops and cry when we hear the national anthem.

Working-class Americans began to ask some questions. They wondered why wealthy, white entertainers, artists and, I'm sure, freelance manufacturers of organic yogurt, were announcing that they would leave the United States if George Bush won the election.

Imagine that. If democracy didn't provide the result they wanted, these selfish rich kids would run away to Canada or Britain. Is that patriotism? Middle America didn't remember Republicans threatening to leave when Clinton won a second term as President.

Middle America grew tired of the insults. We're not voting out of fear, they said, we don't accept every word we hear from the government and we're not so easily manipulated. Stop telling us that we don't understand what's going on.

We've raised kids and paid mortgages and we resent listening to lectures, especially when delivered by an actress with a vacant smile and a copy of Socialism For Beginners. Middle America shouted its impatience. It wasn't that it so liked George Bush, more that it was so tired of George Bush's critics.

Middle America remembered a time when actors, singers and writers reflected the nation. These performers no longer aspired to reflect but to reshape. In their own narcissistic image. John Kerry was too close to that clan, too much part of the culture of smug assumption.

It wasn't George Bush who was the victor last week but men and women who stood up and announced to the self-defined elites that "the people" is not a concept but a flesh and blood reality. And one that bites back.

MC

Bob Geldoff

THANKS GOODNESS FOR PARIS HILTON. SHE MAY BE A VACUOUS BIMBO WITH THE INTELLIGENCE OF AN INAMINATE OBJECT BUT SHE KNOWS PRECISELY HOW HOLLYWOOD CELEBRITIES ARE SUPPOSED TO BEHAVE. GET DRUNK, DRIVE FAST, DANCE LONG, CRY IN PUBLIC, BE SLUTTISH AND MAKE ABSOLUTELY NO CONTRIBUTION TO ANYONE OR ANYTHING.

And for all of her witless posing, she does little harm and claims nothing more than what she is. Which is, oddly enough, nothing. No attempt to tell the unwashed how to live, no inflated political statements, no irksome posturing on the international stage.

Which brings us to the glamerous set who have never understood their place. Because they've written a pop song or made a movie they assume that they have not only the right but the duty to instruct the world's elected leaders on any policy that comes into their over-privileged head.

As long, naturally, as it's a left-wing policy. This was made abundantly clear recently by Sir Tom Stoppard, the Oscar-winning screenwriter of *Shakespeare In Love* and one of the finest playwrights in the English language. He said that he kept his conservative politics quiet for fear that such original sin would damage his career.

Serves him right of course. Stoppard is merely considered a genius and a master of his craft. He didn't sing in a band called The Boomtown Rats that was once, very breifly and long ago, relatively well-known. But Bob Geldof did.

Then Bob discovered African poverty and decided to tell the world about it. Including those old twits like the churches who had been working and dying with starving Africans for generations. But Bob has lots of hair and a loud voice and he swears. And his career in the being nice business has lasted a lot longer than his career as a pop star.

So much so that even now he is insulting the Canadian government and telling us that we're all a bunch of nasties. Which leads one to wonder why he wasn't such a disciplinarian with Peaches. Who is she?

Peaches Geldof. Or to name her in full, Peaches Honeyblossom Michelle Charlotte Angel Vanessa Geldoff. Sister of Fifi and Pixie and half-sister of Tiger. Bob's daughter is a regular in the British tabloids, making abusive gestures, falling out of night clubs in a somewhat jolly state, being stopped by store detectives or taking a sniff from a white paper cone which, she says, was just a cigarette.

Raising daughters can, of course, be a challenge. Which is why Peaches and Fifi and Pixie need dad around. Dad, however, is a vey busy man. As is dad's ever so good friend Bono. So busy in fact that he can't find the time to pay taxes in his native Ireland, where public education, public healthcare and immigration and welfare services for the needy cost a great deal of cash.

So instead his band U2 transferred much of its business empire to the same Dutch finance house used by the Rolling Stones because royalties are almost tax-free in Holland. Contrary to what the song says, old Bono did find what he was looking for.

The cause may be grand, the work may be necessary but spare me the preaching and the hypocrisy. Stand for office if you want change. Better still, raise your kids and pay your taxes. Paris, you're needed.

MC

Sean Penn

In an attack that was hysterical and frenzied even for him, actor Sean Penn made a speech last week in which he demanded to know if the daughters of President Bush support the war in Iraq and shouted that they should be in uniform and in the armed forces.

Nobody knows what they think because the Bush girls are, well, the Bush girls. In other words, they're not their father. Not political, not public. They get on with their lives, do what young girls do, and don't ask to be engaged in international affairs by spoilt brats who make movies.

A better question would be to ask why Sean Penn is not in prison. After all, he beat up his former wife, intellectual super star Madonna, he beat up a photographer and, on another occasion, illegal firearms were found in his car. Three strikes and you're out. But not being poor, black or Hispanic he could afford the best lawyers in town and escaped a very long jail term.

There's liberalism and equality for you.

Hollywood is the most dysfunctional community in the world. A stew of crass materialism and nauseating decadence. This, of course, is why we love them so. They're at their best when doing what they're supposed to do. Taking drugs, being promiscuous, crashing their cars, holding enormously silly parties and telling the world they were abused as children.

Penn, however, is one of those left-wing actors who know they need to change the world. So he leaves his fortune in the hands of his accountants and sets off for places like Iran. Where he didn't stand in the middle of Teheran and proclaim that contrary to government propaganda the Holocaust did indeed happen.

Or hand out leaflets calling for full civil rights for homosexuals. Or ask the political leaders whom he met to arrest the thugs who beat to death a Canadian woman photographer and raped her before she died so that she wouldn't get to paradise.

He did none of these things because any one of them would have got him arrested. And in Iran, unlike the United States, being a rich and famous actor won't keep you out of prison.

The man's colossal arrogance and sheer childishness was demonstrated when he insisted on smoking during a hotel press conference at the Toronto Film Festival. Smoking is banned in enclosed places in Ontario, the law being a left-wing initiative and just the sort of thing Penn is supposed to support.

But he is Sean Penn. Meaning that the rules of the common scum do not apply to him. Combine this with the fatuous idea that smoking is somehow radical, dangerous and fashionably European and Hollywood revolutionaries are in their element.

There are celebrities who do genuine good with their wealth. Bruce Springsteen, for example, has been financing inner-city projects for some years. He is certainly critical of President Bush but invariably courteous and constructive.

Or you could be like that silly fool Mother Theresa and spend your life picking maggots out of the rotting flesh of impoverished children on the streets of Indian slums. But that is not fun at all and, anyway, nobody wants to attend a film festival in Calcutta.

So there we have Sean Penn. Not an exponent of a school of thought but a product of a kindergarten of privilege and lunacy.

MC

Elton John

I HAVE VERY FOND MEMORIES OF BRITISH SONG-WRITER AND SINGER ELTON JOHN. THE MOST POIGNANT BEING OF THE HIGHLY COLOURFUL FELLOW PERFORMING ON STAGE WHILE DRESSED AS A VERY LARGE DUCK. I THINK THAT IT WAS AT THIS MOMENT THAT WE ALL KNEW THE FORMER REG DWIGHT HAD TO BE TAKEN VERY SERIOUSLY INDEED.

And if that passing quack wasn't enough we then discovered through a 2000 court case that he was spending $3 million a month on personal items, gifts and, presumably, lots and lots of duck food. Oh, and $600,000 on flowers in eight months.

So should we care what Elton says about anything? Not really. Problem is, he speaks for and represents a growing trend in the western world. In a culture where pop stars and afternoon television presenters shape opinion, good old Elton has a great deal of infuence.

Last week he explained that, "Religion has always tried to turn hatred towards gay people. Religion promotes the hatred and spite against gays ... From my point of view I would ban religion completely." And "The reality is that organised religion doesn't seem to work. It turns people into hateful lemmings and it's not really compassionate."

Frankly, I doubt he really has anything much against religion and probably doesn't even undertand what it is. Nor is he speaking about religion in general but the Christianity he assumes to know and its opposition to same-sex marriage.

What Elton John really means, of course, is that he doesn't like it when people disagree with him. Not a problem usually because so few people have the courage to stand up to the homosexual lobby and its supporters. Serious churches do have the courage and because of this we are now told they should be banned.

Just like in so many parts of the Communist and Islamic world. Where, by the way, homosexuality is illegal and Elton John would last about as long as a candle in the wind.

Thus once again it's all about Elton. Just as it's always about Rosie O'Donnell or Barbara Streisand or Ted Turner. The new ruling class who refuse to respect freedom of speech and call for intolerance in the name of progress as they try to impose their views on small people with small incomes.

It's perhaps the "hateful lemmings" line that is most interesting. Lemmings don't actually have the capacity for hatred but liberal God-haters certainly do. They also have the capacity to act like lemmings, as they illustrate by all delivering the same cliches, dressing in the same clothes and supporting the same causes.

No original thought and no difference of opinion. Unlike the "organised religion" types who Elton so hates. The Vatican, for example, wants the death penalty to be abolished, Third World debt to be forgiven and the arms trade to disappear.

The evangelical church runs some of the largest hostels for the poor and homeless in North America and spends billions of dollars fighting poverty in Africa and Latin America. Almost half of all AIDS patients are cared for by the Christians who Elton so despises.

So if it looks like a duck and sounds like a duck, it must be a champion of the brave new world that is coming to a town near you any moment now. Don't shoot the piano player, he's only the messenger.

MC

Madonna

SHE'S JUST A MATERIAL GIRL IN A MATERIAL WORLD WHO MERELY WANTS A BLACK BABY. NOTHING WRONG WITH THAT. IF BRAD AND ANGELINA CAN HAVE ONE THEN MADONNA SHOULD BE ABLE TO PLAY AS WELL. AFTER ALL, THERE IS NO RISK THAT ONE-YEAR-OLD DAVID BANDA WILL NOW DIE OF STARVATION OR MALARIA.

There is every risk, however, that David's family will die of starvation or malaria. Every risk that hundreds of thousands of Davids will die of all sorts of diseases and deprivations in the third world. Diseases and deprivations that are of no threat to children in North America.

It's very simple. The solution to a child living in poverty in Africa is not to take the child out of Africa but to take the poverty out of Africa. Madonna can't transform a continent but she could easily transform a village. Just a fraction of her fortune would introduce clean water, sustainable crops and a new school into a town and save the lives of hundreds.

This is precisely what is done by charities every day in Africa and much of the money comes from the very Christians who Madonna mocks and abuses in her concerts when she pretends to be Jesus on the Cross or grinds out erotic gyrations by a church altar.

But then this is the woman who told the press that she refuses to let her children watch very much television because it is sometimes pornographic, while still making pots of money from her sexually explicit videos.

The father of little David, Yohane Banda, cannot read or write, lost his wife when she gave birth to their child and lives in a country where men are fortunate if they live to middle age. If this wasn't enough, he is told lies. The person who is adopting your beloved son, he was told, is a "lovely Christian lady."

Another example of the wealthy north once again lying to the poor south. We lied to them when we colonized, enslaved, sold them arms, propped up their warlords, imposed ethnic divisions, destroyed cultures and them blamed them for living under heavily armed warlords and killing each other in tribal wars.

Madonna continues the lie. She stood in front of a line of African children and chose one to be her latest pet. Nothing new. For generations Africans were lined up to be purchased by the wealthy in the United States and Europe. Hey, Madonna will treat David far more nicely than they treated their slaves. Or her nanny will.

So she is selfish and ludicrous and annoying. But she is loved by countless fans, is famous and admired and regarded as an icon of the empowered woman who takes chances. The embodiment of the modern world.

Quite so. The modern world. Money and decadence disguised as progress and freedom. A woman who performs a mock lesbian sexual encounter in front of millions of people on television also exploits the poorest of the poor and doesn't seem to give a damn. Why on earth would we be surprised?

This isn't a contradiction but a continuum. If personal morality is meaningless there is no place for public morality either. If we don't understand that we are a part of the problem and not the solution. Just material fools in a material world.

MC

Pop Star

"Isn't it awesome", said Dave Remington, the Mayor of Napanee, Ontario. And thus inadvertently summed up the vacuous and inflated hype over media creation Avril Lavigne. Because in the world of the teenaged and teen-minded, everything is awesome. 18-year-old Avril is from the good mayor's town, and has just made even more money by being nominated for various Grammy Awards. She is also known as the "Anti-Britney."

Now this is positively funny. Because far from being a counter to Britney Spears, Ms. Lavigne is merely the contrived reverse side of the glittering coin. Consider the proposition. She wears too much make-up, she dances around the place while singing meaningless lyrics, she tries to persuade fans to identify with her alleged struggles and aspirations and she is backed by a multi-million dollar industry.

If one is honest about it, the awful Spears is in many ways more honest than the allegedly ordinary Lavigne. Do we really think that painting chipped short fingernails is any more profound than painting manicured long fingernails?

Well, teenagers have been made to think so by the old guys who run the music business and write the music stories. They have swallowed the whole line about Avril having street credibility and relevance because she wears baggy clothes, makes funny devil's horns signs with her fingers and yells rather than pouts.

I see. So in a world full of poverty, injustice and war this makes her serious. She's been compared to Bob Dylan and some of the protest singers of the 1960s. Okay, let's see what she has to say. From *Nobody's Fool*, the young lady writes:

"Fall Back. Take a look at me. And you'll see I'm for real. I feel what only I feel. And if that don't appeal to you. Let me know. And I'll go. 'Cuz I flow. Better than my colours show. And that's the way that it has to be. Honestly. 'Cuz creativity could never bloom. In my room. I'd throw it all away before I lie. So don't call me with a compromise.

Hang up the phone. I've got a backbone stronger than yours. La la la la la la. La la la la la la. La la la la la la."

Then we have *Things I'll Never Say*. "I'm pulling at my hair. I'm pulling at my clothes. I'm trying to keep it cool. I know it shows. I'm staring at my feet. My cheeks are turning red. I'm searching for the words inside my head."

But there's more to this song, and it becomes much deeper. "If I could say what I want to say. I'd say I wanna blow you … away. Be with you every night. Am I squeezing you too tight." And so on and so on.

Which is not to say that silly words written to a formulaic pop rhythm are such a problem. Most of us have at some time or other believed that our favourite musicians had something to say, and I still think that the New Wave British bands of the late 1970s spoke for a generation of young people.

Because they did. There was a genuine rawness and honesty to their lyrics, which is why they were banned, attacked, barred from entering various countries. There was something dangerous about them. Avril Lavigne is not even dangerous to Britny Spears. The two of them act in symbiosis, fuelling their fans to become ever more partisan and to spend even more money.

"Avril is true and real and speaks for me dude."

"No, she's not. Britney has seen and heard my dreams."

Whatever. Whoever. Whenever. You've got me in a fever. Because you wouldn't leave her. And my thoughts of love are turning. When I feel my deeper yearning. Won't you do some learning. And take me by the hand. Yes take me by the hand. Chorus. And buy my albums and posters and fan magazines. Oh yeah.

The song "Whatever, Whoever" written by Michael Coren, while sitting at his desk and sipping a latte. Just one sip. All it took. Yes sir, I'm the new anti-Avril, and watch me shake my bald head in joy at how awesome it all is.

MC

Business History

Freedom Press has been in operation since 2003. Established initially as a self-publishing venture, Freedom Press quickly recognized the need to serve a specific segment of the Canadian book buying public.

Mission and Vision

Freedom Press is dedicated to producing, promoting and distributing excellent books by Canadian authors who write from a conservative and libertarian perspective. As a niche publisher, Freedom Press features Canadian authors whose message and ideology reflect Freedom Press's core principles: Free Speech and Freedom of Religion; Limited Government; Liberty through Law, Personal Responsibility, the Free Market, and Free Market Charity Initiatives; Individualism and Exceptionalism; and Positive Canadian Patriotism.

Description of Products and Services

A niche publisher since 2003, Freedom Press currently has 6 books in its catalogue. Although our authors range in their ideological commitments, all fall within the general framework of Freedom Press values. Our market strategy is to work with a client author (that is, someone who is a recognized leader/writer/thinker within the conservative and libertarian camp) to showcase his or her work to the best advantage.

Key Features of the Products and Services

As a niche publisher that exclusively promotes conservative, libertarian authors who are Canadian and write for Canadians, Freedom Press has a unique mission and a particular advantage in developing a relatively untapped market. Conservatives and libertarians make up 35% of the voting public and are avid readers and buyers of books.

In evaluating the potential marketability of a client author, Freedom Press focuses on media exposure and an existing network of supporters and followers via web writings, print columns or monthly newsletters. The client author's public relations exposure is vital to the success of all publishing projects, because marketing and promotion will be directed at existing networks of supporters.

Future Products and Services

Freedom Press will continue to expand and diversify its roster of authors. In the next 5 years Freedom Press plans to publish 20 new authors and increase its catalogue to 50 – 70 excellent books. Freedom Press also plans to host yearly book launches that will highlight our writing talent. And Freedom Press will organize several conferences for its client authors and their networks of supporters.

Comparative Advantages in Production

Freedom Press's competitive advantage is simple: It is the only publisher focusing on a particular political market and seeking ways to serve that market's needs.

FREEDOM PRESS
CANADA INC.

Current Catalogue

Jean Chretien: A Legacy of Scandal

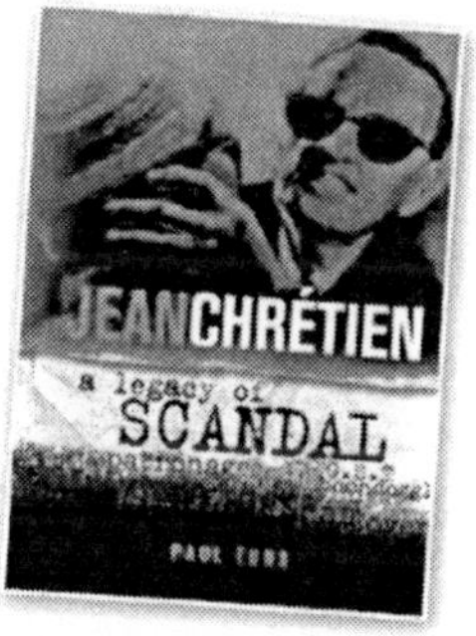

Anyone interested in a serious examination of the Chretien years will benefit from Paul Tuns' *Jean Chretien: A Legacy Of Scandal*. Tuns' outstanding new book gives you the factual story behind the man, the party and the ten years of greed, power, corruption and scandal – from the many broken election promises like the G.S.T. to Shawinigate, APEC, Airbus, and finally Ad Scam, this book is a serious analysis for anyone interested in the hard facts. Paul Tuns truly leaves no stone unturned to get at our recent history.

Paul Tuns

Paul Tuns is a public affairs commentator and political analyst whose articles have appeared in more than 35 publications including the *National Post*, *Globe and Mail*, and the *Toronto Star*. He is the editor-in-chief of *The Interim*, Canada's life and family newspaper, and is a contributor to *Business Report*. He lives in Toronto with his wife and five children

Loyal to the Core: Stephen Harper, Me and the NCC

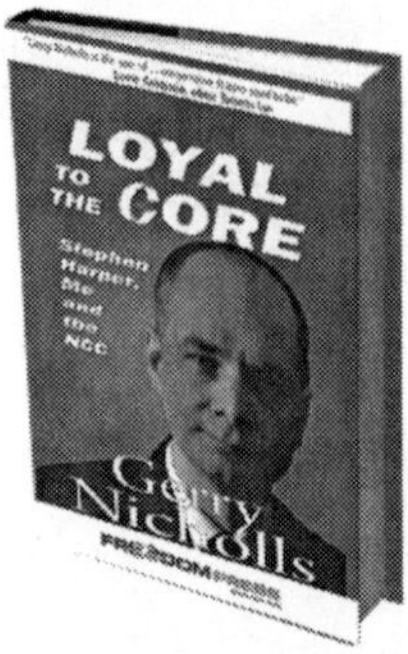

Gerry Nicholls calls himself "one of the top five political minds in the country."

Without question, Nicholls is one of Canada's most outspoken and articulate defenders of conservatism. For more than 20 years, Nicholls served as the political and communications strategist for the conservative organization, the National Citizens Coalition.

For five of those years, he worked closely with the group's president, a man who would go on to become Canada's Prime Minister—Stephen Harper.

Now, in his first book, *Loyal to the Core*, Nicholls reveals the story of how he went from being a friend and close ally of Harper's, to one of his most fierce and unrelenting critics.

Nicholls provides a frank assessment of Stephen Harper the man, and Stephen Harper the leader, tracing his evolution from hardcore conservative ideologue to partisan, pragmatic politician.

It is also a story of secret political meetings, clashing personalities and the lure of power.

In addition to the candid portrait of Harper, Nicholls offers an unauthorized history of the National Citizens Coalition, Canada's largest independent, pro-free market organization. Who created this unique advocacy group and why? How did this organization, using political guerrilla warfare tactics, help change the face of Canada? We learn how the NCC fought to expose government waste and oppose arrogant politicians, how it battled both in the court of law and the court of public opinion to protect our most cherished individual freedoms.

But most of all, *Loyal to the Core* is a cautionary tale for Canada's conservative movement. Principled conservatives must, says Nicholls, "resist the corrosive influence of partisan politics and focus on what matters: winning the war of ideas!"

Environmentalism and the Death of Science: Exposing the Lie of Eco-Religion

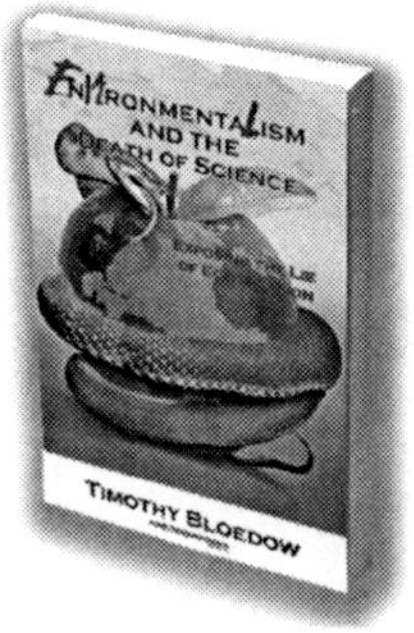

Environmentalism has become the leading religion in Canada and the Western world. It's a globalist ideology that is at war with science and at war with Christianity. This might be the only book published in North America that tackles the key religious components of modern Environmentalism, exposing their errors and demonstrating the incompatibility of orthodox Christianity and Environmentalism. In an era when Christian leaders, including the leadership of the National Association of Evangelicals, has embraced false notions such as cataclysmic climate change theory, this book is a timely antidote to such deception and ignorance.

Tim Bloedow

Timothy Bloedow has worked as a researcher, speech writer and media coordinator for two Members of Parliament in Canada's federal government. He is a writer and a real estate investor. He worked as a researcher and lobbyist for Campaign Life Coalition. Mr. Bloedow has run for office as a member of the Christian Heritage Party of Canada. He co-founded and published The Ottawa Times, a monthly newspaper, in the early 1990s. Mr. Bloedow has a Bachelor of Theology from Tyndale Bible College (then Ontario Bible College). He is married to Lynette and has two children, Ulyn and Daniel. He is motivated by a desire to explain and advance the comprehensive claims of Christ over every area of life.

Standing on Guard for Thee

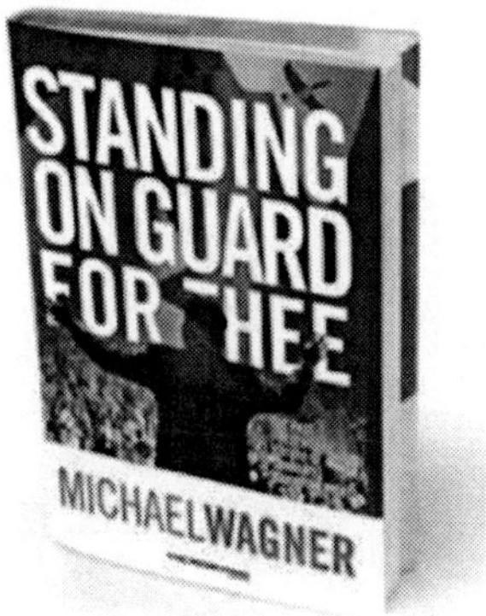

This book is the antidote to those who would portray the Christian Right as a bunch of inarticulate Bible-thumpers, trying to impose their morality on everyone else. Michael Wagner proves, among other things, that Christianity was here first. And that, rather than being an "American import", Canada's Christian Right was a reaction to the secularist drive for influence in society, and an attempt to preserve what is best in Western culture.

Alberta: Separatism Then And Now

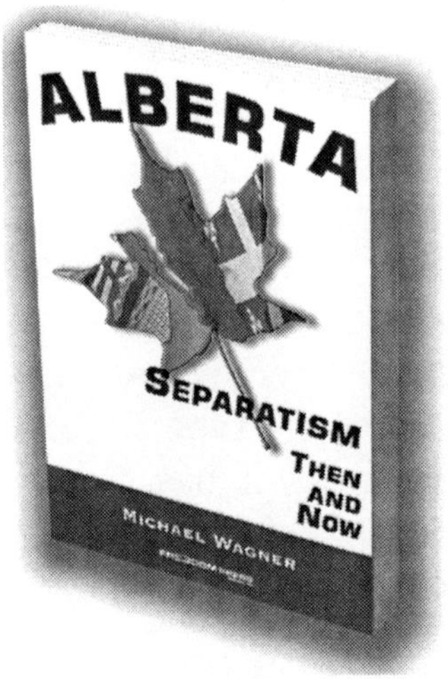

What is Alberta Separatism?

In December, 2008, the NDP and Liberal Party of Canada attempted to form a coalition with the Bloc Quebecois to replace the minority Conservative government of Stephen Harper. There was outrage in Alberta, which had voted solidly Conservative in the recent federal election. Separatism in the province – dormant for years – was reawakened. But what do we really know about Alberta separatism?

The Alberta separatist movement showed strength at times during the 1980s, but the creation of the Reform Party of Canada later redirected separatist sentiment in a federalist direction. The Reform Party is now gone, and as the events of December, 2008, have shown, the potential for a revived Alberta separatist movement is very real.

This book explains the history of the movement and the issues that have led to its occasional appearance since the 1970s.

Michael Wagner
PhD, University of Alberta, Author
Michael is a freelance writer and homeschooling father with a BA (Honours) and MA in Political Science from the University of Calgary, and a PhD in Political Science from the University of Alberta. He makes his home in Edmonton with his wife and nine children.

Experts Are Saying

"Wagner's book is an excellent and balanced history of separatism in Alberta. The very real factor of separatism in Alberta politics has been long overdue for examination."
Cory Morgan,
Former leader of the Alberta Independence Party

"Michael Wagner has performed a patriotic service by reminding Albertan (and Westerners) of what academics call a suppressed discourse. In this case it concerns the great fraud of national unity, which is code for ripping off the west in order to pay off Quebec, and the efforts of Albertans to stop picking up the tab."
Barry Cooper,
PhD, FRSC, Professor of Political Science, University of Calgary

"This is a story well worth the telling, and well told indeed by a qualified and diligent researcher into the past half century of politics in Canada's other 'distinct society'. Apart from its being a tale of intrinsic interest to political junkies of all stripes, it does what Hobbes proclaims all worthwhile political history should do: secretly instruct the reader, conveying practical lessons of lasting importance. Moreover, in tracing out the reasons for the persistent waxings and wanings of separatist sentiment in Alberta, Wagner's account serves as an expose of how (mainly Liberal) Federal government policies have been designed to exploit the West, and Alberta in particular. This is a book that deserves to be read by every citizen concerned to understand this province's peculiar politics, and its place in the Canadian federation."
Dr. Leon Craig,
Professor emeritus of Political Science at the University of Alberta

"I'm glad my friend Michael Wagner has documented the rise and fall of that unusual movement, and analyzed the forces which drove it then, and might in some future circumstance drive it again. Perhaps next time will lead to a different outcome."
Link Byfield,
Chairman, Citizens Centre for Freedom and Democracy

The Great Canadian Comedy: From Laughter To Tears

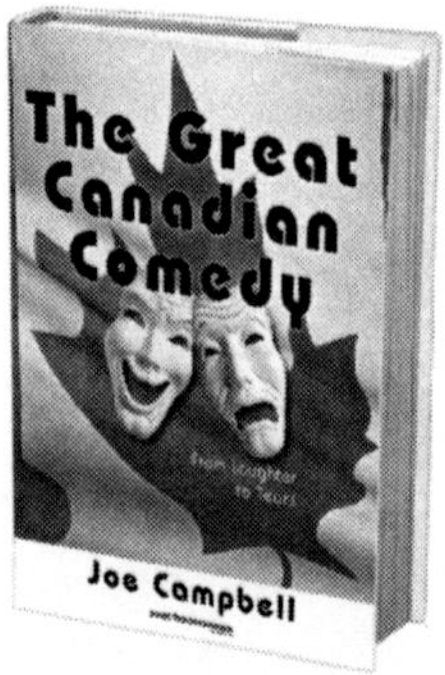

Freedom of spoof and the right to levity are upheld and celebrated in this collection of 50 humour pieces.

Joe Campbell makes fun of doctors, lawyers, educators, literary critics, scientists, politicians, judges, royalty, journalists, comedians and hockey and football players, among others. He also takes aim at the Canadian Constitution, Dan Brown's Da Vinci Code, the uses and abuses of Christmas and Valentines Day, social engineering, gobbledygook and telephone chatter.

His treatment of the last two has given rise to Campbell's laws: 1) The volume of verbose writing varies directly with the ease of producing it; 2) The amount of idle chatter varies inversely with the cost of transmitting it.

Much of the time, though, Joe makes fun of himself, especially when he describes his encounters with writing, music, ballroom dancing, history and grammar, and his trying to learn a second language, being a temporary house husband, and growing old.

The humour ranges from farce to satire. The attitude is that of a somewhat bemused observer trying to make sense of the contradictions and incongruities of the world in which he lives.

Joe writes from the perspective of a small "c" conservative. Consequently, his satirical pieces are, no doubt, seen as politically incorrect and controversial.

Joe Campbell

Joe Campbell began producing humour in high school and published a few pieces after graduating from the University of Saskatchewan in arts and education. But distractions—earning a living, raising a family, leading a jazz band—sobered him up and he pronounced himself cured.

He spent ten years as a radio and television newsman, followed by 28 years as a "tame journalist" with his alma mater, handling media relations and various writing and editing chores.

Alas, after taking early retirement, he suffered a relapse into humour and some 130 of his light or satirical pieces have appeared in newspapers and magazines in Canada and the US.

Fifty of his previously published pieces are included in Take Me Out of the Ball Game, his first book of humour, which was shortlisted for the 2006 Stephen Leacock Memorial Medal for Humour.

Like writing, music has been an abiding interest. Joe took up the trumpet in high school, began playing with various bands and orchestras at age 15, and led the Joe Campbell Sextet in university. In 1967, he co-founded the Bridge City Dixieland Jazz Band, which was featured on radio and TV, on record, at Expo '86 in Vancouver, at the 1990 Chilliwack International Jazz Festival, and regularly at the SaskTel Saskatchewan Jazz Festival in Saskatoon, among a host of other events spanning more than a quarter of a century.

In retirement, he began concentrating on piano, in case his lungs give out before his fingers, and has performed publicly with another musician in what they call The Semi-Dynamic Duo.

Joe and his wife, Rosemary, live in Saskatoon, where they raised their nine children.

Christophobia: The Real Reason Behind Hate Crime Legislation

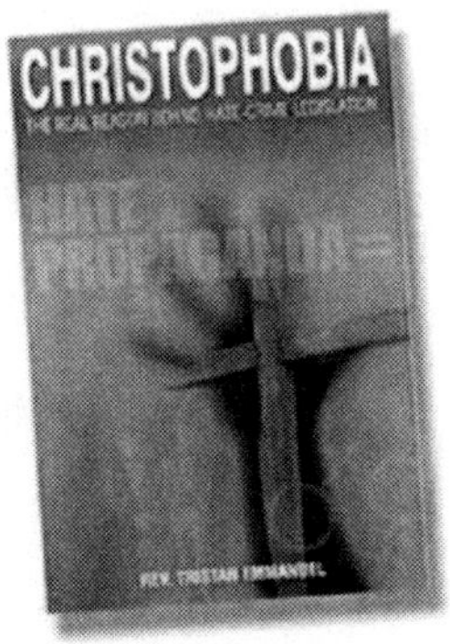

This book is about Bill C-250. Bill C-250 was known as "an Act to amend the Criminal Code of Canada (hate propaganda)." Actually, to be more precise, this book is about legal oppression. Bill C-250 represented the latest legislative initiative to silence moral disapproval of homosexuality. And ultimately, Bill C-250 is an attempt to suppress the Christian Gospel. The Bill was the legal face of a very real problem: Christophobia.

Warned: Canada's Revolution Against Faith, Family and Freedom Threatens America

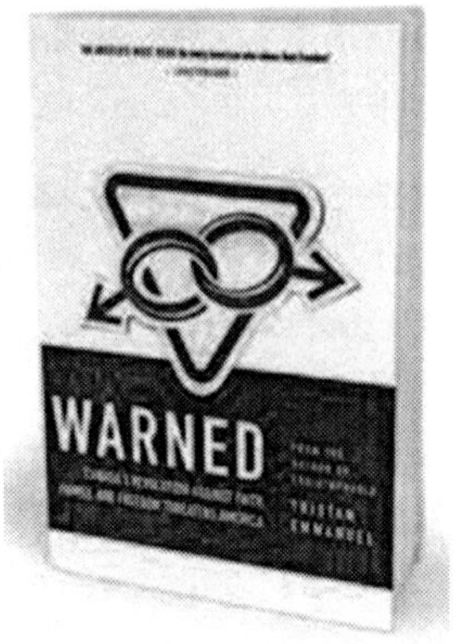

This book is essential reading for both Americans and Canadians even though it is more particularly directed to our American friends. Both countries face a serious challenge to their cultures. This book exposes the radical exploitation of Canada at the hands of extremist activists, leftwing politicians and a plethora of crusading activist judges, who are using their status in Canada to get at America. Their aim is marriage. But the prize is America. They want to use marriage as a weapon to systematically destroy the Judeo-Christian civilization of North America, but to do that they need America to "go gay". Gay "marriage" will open America up to the rest of the demands of the homosexual political movement. Everything from school curriculum to parental rights, adoption, the age of consent and religious freedoms will be up for grabs once gay "marriage" is made legal in America. Unless socons in both countries unite and work to resist these political opponents, we can kiss our continent good-bye.

To order any of these books go to:

www.freedompress.ca

LaVergne, TN USA
09 December 2009

166444LV00001B/34/P

9 780981 276724